THE AUTHORITY
OF EXPERIENCE

Curzon Studies in Asian Philosophy
Series Editors
Brian Carr and Indira Mahalingam

The **Curzon Studies in Asian Philosophy** address various themes in a manner that does not presuppose the specialist linguistic knowledge which has tended to make these traditions closed to the wider philosophical audience. Among the projected volumes, some reflect recent conferences and others are papers specially written for the series. Some have grown out of recent controversies in the Carfax journal **Asian Philosophy.**

Pali Buddhism
Edited by Frank Hoffman and Deegalle Mahinda

Friendship East and West
Philosophical Perspectives
Edited by Oliver Leaman

Morals and Society in Asian Philosophy
Edited by Brian Carr

THE AUTHORITY
OF EXPERIENCE

ESSAYS ON BUDDHISM
AND PSYCHOLOGY

edited by
John Pickering

CURZON

First Published in 1997
by Curzon Press
15 The Quadrant, Richmond
Surrey, TW9 1BP

© 1997 John Pickering

Typeset in Sabon by LaserScript Ltd, Mitcham
Printed and bound in Great Britain by
TJ International, Padstow, Cornwall

British Library Cataloguing in Publication Data
A catalogue record of this book is available from the British Library

Library of Congress Cataloguing in Publication Data
A catalog record for this book has been requested

ISBN 0–7007–0450–7 (cloth)
ISBN 0–7007–0455–8 (paper)

Contents

Foreword   vii

Contributors   xv

Section 1: Making comparisons

1 Transformation of the Wolf Man   3
   Eleanor Rosch

2 Authority in Buddhism and in Western Scientific Psychology   28
   David Fontana

Section 2: Textual fundamentals

3 Buddhist Psychology: Some Basic Concepts and
   Applications   51
   Padmal de Silva

4 Basic Features of Buddhist Psychology   72
   Herbert Guenther

Section 3: Towards therapy

5 Creating a Comtemporary Buddhist Psychotherapy   99
   Joy Manné

6 Exploring the Visiccitudes of Affect and Working with
   Emotions: An Early Buddhist Perspective   123
   Padmasiri de Silva

Section 4: Psychological theory

7 Selfhood is a Process   149
   John Pickering

Contents

8 The Mythology of Anatta: Bridging the East-West Divide   170
    Brian L. Lancaster

Section 5: Knowing and doing

9 The Validation of Knowledge: Private and Public   205
    Elizabeth Valentine

10 Authenticity and the Practice of Zen   219
    John Crook

    Afterword   247
    Index   251

Foreword

'Authority' means both the power to convince and the power to compel. The latter sense takes us towards Hobbes' concerns with law, sanctions and obedience. However it is the former sense that is of interest here. This takes us towards a concern with discourse where words like 'author', 'authoritative' and 'authentic' reflect their Sanskrit origin, meaning 'what is produced by your own actions is yours'. Here we find the more humane sense of authority; as when someone says "I saw it with my own eyes". It is the conviction which arises when something is known through direct experience. It is this that confers authority in the sense of the right to be believed and the informed power to persuade.

This collection of essays addresses two apparently contrasting sources of authority: Western psychology and Buddhism. To compare scientific inquiry with, for example, meditation contrasts what is objective and public with what is subjective and private. Nonetheless, method and experience are central in giving each system the authority to say something about the mind. Science and Buddhism are both founded on what can be made to appear in human experience by the application of a method. The contrast lies in how these experiences are created and in the assumptions that are built in to the methods of each system.

Experience itself is culturally conditioned. During the past five hundred years or so in the West, human experience has been fundamentally reformed by science. From the rediscovery of Greek philosophy, through the scientific revolution to the contemporary explosion of cybernetic technology, our sense of ourselves, our world and our place in it have all been transformed. Science is now a highly authoritative source of knowledge in contemporary culture. It provides most people with their creation myth, with an image of themselves and their relation to the rest of the universe. It has thus acquired some of the cultural roles of religion, whether scientists wish it or not.

But discovery did not begin with science. Human beings make an effort after meaning as naturally as they act and breathe. This effort produces growth and order at levels ranging from the evolution of cultural forms to the development of more natural skills like walking and talking. What makes scientific inquiry unnatural is it's system.[1] Indeed, scientists might just as well be called systematists whose goal is, or was until recently, absolute certainty; another unnatural condition. Science harnesses the human effort after meaning to drive an epistemological system. Its success is patent in the power human beings now have to order things as they wish. This, as much as the depth of its insights into nature, is what gives science its authority. So powerful was the ideal of systematic understanding, prediction and control that it gradually emerged as a political and even spiritual goal. The Enlightenment project was to improve the human condition by progressively disclosing the secrets of nature and using them to conduct society on firm rational principles. This project has transformed world culture from its medieaval to its modern condition during a period of heroic achievement and change.

But the project has failed. There is a growing sense that this modernist image of progress is flawed. Progress has been achieved, but is now being overhauled by a coarsening and commodification of the human condition, by growing inequality and by the loss of biological, cultural and experiential diversity; the condition of alienated experience that Weber called 'disenchantment'. The rational clarity and confidence of the modern period has collapsed into postmodern confusion and uncertainty. The heart of the postmodern predicament is constant choosing, both stylistic and ontological. Realism has not failed, but it has become merely one of many options. In *The Birth and Death of Meaning*, Ernest Becker disclosed the essentially fictional nature of all human world views; the postmodern predicament is learning how to live with the consequences of this disclosure.[2]

For Weber, a major contribution to this condition of disenchantment was the misuse of science. Although this is actually a political and economic matter, it is sometimes attributed to the nature of science itself. Over the past few decades, a number of critiques have blamed science's mechanistic world view and reductive methods for devaluing life and experience. But, in fact, there is nothing in the nature of science itself that devalues anything. It is the search for consistent ways of ordering and understanding phenomena. This search may be based on inappropriate methods or an inadequate image of nature, but so long as science is practiced as a genuinely open system, shortcomings can be recognised and overcome.

However, this seldom happens without turmoil or resistance. Just such a period of contested revision is presently occuring now the limits of reductive mechanism are clearly recognised. An organic view of nature is returning. The notion of a unified theory of all levels of phenomena is treated as a symbolic rather than practical objective of scientific inquiry. While particular levels of phenomena may be more or less completely explained by a particular theory, other levels will not. The order found in nature at higher and lower scales is clearly interconnected but not in ways that necessarily permit prediction. Consistency is sought horizontally and locally, as it were, rather than vertically, implying a genuine plurality in theories and an eclecticism in methods.

This turn to plurality and eclecticism is central to postmodernism. Indeed, the idea that a unified world view will be produced by any department of knowledge or practice has all but disappeared. Postmodernists, although they are analytic in their own way, are anti-systematists whose discursive methods turn rationality inside out. Rhetoric, quotation, irony, deconstruction, relativisation; all these are responses to the failure of the Enlightenment project. The foundations of nature and society have not been disclosed. No indication of how human affairs might rationally be conducted has appeared. Skepticism now greets any totalising system such as Marxism, Capitalism, religious fundamentalism or scientific reductionism. All our 'isms' are now 'wasms', as Charles Jencks has it. There is now an informed mistrust of all-encompassing world views, since none can hold all truths.

Yet, amid this collapse, intellectual and cultural life goes on. As Rorty puts it, we have learned to proceed without foundations, to walk, as it were, without the ground to walk on.[3] The reactions to this vertiginous condition vary. In the humanities and arts, postmodern critiques are seen as relevant, whether they are accepted or not. Scientists by contrast are more likely to claim that to talk of pluralism, eclecticism, relativism and so on is simply irrelevant. Science, they might say, deals in systematic empirical inquiry into nature and so evades any critique of culturally relative styles, practices and beliefs.

But that is precisely what science is, claims to unnatural absolutism notwithstanding. Only over the last few centuries in Europe has the human effort after meaning been channelled and systematised on the basis of materialism and rationality. Science is a cultural practice with demonstrable powers, but it is not an absolute system to replace all others. Moreover, if science is a genuinely open practice, it will constantly reform itself and its world view. There is plenty of evidence to show that the development of science is as much influenced by the postmodern turn as any other department of culture.

This has liberating implications for Western psychology. A major impetus for this collection is the idea that the postmodern turn opens the way for a broadening of psychology's methods and concepts. Psychology has been restricted by an overcommitment to natural science as a model. In particular, since it deals with the human condition, it is more impeded than other disciplines by the mistaken opposition between science and other cultural frameworks, such as religion, for understanding the human mind. This unwelcome historical imposition can now be eased. The postmodern shift is towards dialogue between a multiplicity of perspectives rather than the effort after an exclusive, unified view. This will allow a more realistic and informed interaction between different images of the mind and different methods to investigate it.

This is not only beneficial but timely. Consciousness is now once again the central phenomenon of psychology, following a long exclusion. If psychology is to investigate experience more fully then it will need to find a new balance between phenomenology and the scientific method. Now many Buddhist traditions approach the relationship of subjectivity and objectivity in ways that anticipate recent development in Western thought. What is emerging here is a more equitable balance between rational and intuitive modes of knowing.[4] Interaction with Buddhism may thus complement current psychological methods, and help to bring experience and experiment closer together. It is interesting that the modern sense of 'experiment' only appeared with the rise of science. Prior to this, 'experience' also meant what 'experiment' now means. Engagement with Buddhism thus throws psychological science back to premodern times. But such anachronistic recombination of traditions is precisely what post-modernism is about. With the ending of the authoritarian rhetoric of scientism, theoretical and methodological pluralism makes an informed engagement with Buddhism a timely addition to the agenda of psychology.

But we need to ask of this agenda: what is it for? What goals, beliefs and values are here? This question is important because psychology, more than other sciences, influences what human beings think they are and hence how they behave towards each other. Psychology is presently dominated by cognitive science's computational metaphor. This has been hailed as '... the last metaphor for the mind'[5] and as the 'unified theory' of cognition.[6] It is suggested that the ordinary language used to decribe experiences such as emotion and intentionality will be replaced by a scientific vocabulary to do with cognitive or neurological processes.[7]

Now such rhetoric of reduction, like that of behaviourism before it, leaves psychology at an *impasse*. It is attempting to do for mental phenomena what natural science appears to have done for physical and biological ones. Thus, physics suggested that heat was 'just' motion. Biochemistry suggested that being alive was 'just' to metabolise. Genetics suggested that evolution was 'just' altering the genome .... and so on. Given the status of these sciences, it is no surprise to find psychologists suggesting that experience is 'just' brain mechanisms.

In trying to emulate the natural sciences too slavishly, psychology has impoverished both its theories and its methods. The mechanistic worldview implicit in cogntive science excludes experience, since machines patently have no interiority. It has also left psychology's methodological resources awry, since they deny the significance of individuals and exclude direct inquiry into experience. Students are frequently disappointed to find that psychology virtually ignores experience. After all, an interest in the experience of selfhood was often what brought them to do psychology in the first place. It is, as Adrienne Rich has put it, as if psychology were a mirror in which no reflection of themselves appeared. This disappointment reflects a wider unease over the shortcomings and misue of science. The more psychology employs patently inadequate theories and methods, the more likely is it that its findings will be abused. The result, which is already with us, is a dimished image of the human condition, contributing to the loss of experiential diversity. To repair psychology will require adopting an organic rather than mechanistic world view and a return to phenomenological methods.

But phenomenology is marginalised in Western psychology since the failures of introspection has left an abiding mistrust of subjective reports. This has interacted with the realpolitik of the academy during psychology's long struggle to be accepted as an empirical discipline. In this struggle psychology has grossly overpaid debt its to the ethos of natural science. This has meant the exclusion of experience, the 'decapitation' of science and philosophy, of which Husserl warned in *The Crisis of European Sciences and Transcendental Phenomenology.*

To treat experience as data is difficult and we are not helped by the fact that Western phenomenological traditions tend to be long on words and short on practice. Eastern traditions can help us here, so long as they are taken up in an informed and critical way. Moreover, they help us to recognise and repair the fact/value split that has arisen in Western science. Buddhist psychology, by contrast, cannot be separated from Buddhism as a whole, where ethics and epistemology are blended into a system of practices designed to help human beings understand their own experience.

The experimental methods of psychology are often presented as the means to overcome the supposedly inaccurate, non-repeatable and essentially private nature of experience. Occasionally there are reports of what people actually said about what they were doing. These, however are mere adjuncts to the 'real' results, which are quantitative measurements made during properly controlled experiments. Here, 'proper control' often meaning that subjectivity is objectivised away, as it were, by setting up conditions where a single variable is isolated from the play of influences that attend every moment of real experience. This methodology is modelled on that of the natural sciences where single causes with well defined effects can be found. But it can be quite inappropriate if over extended into disciplines like psychology, where such simplified cause and effects relations may be unrealistic.

This ideal of reduction still drives the discipline. Despite the postmodern turn towards discourse and folk psychology, there is a near-triumphalist confidence that such naive and superficial naturalism has, or soon will have been debunked by cognitive neuroscience. The vigour and relish with which this sugggestion is made betokens just this sense of confidence. It is often claimed that descriptions of mental life in ordinary language can be shown to be unreliable, systematically distorted and just plain wrong. On the other hand, tremendous advances are being made in experimental investigations of the nervous system. So, as the authority of ordinary discourse about experience diminishes, so the authority of scientific discourse about the vehicle for that experience grows. This matches all too well psychology's historical need to ape the natural sciences. It is a scientific status symbol to be able to explain that common-sense experience is 'really' something else.

But while cognitive neuroscience may yield finer and finer descriptions of the spatio-temporal structure of brain activity, what is this going to tell us? This is a description of the vehicle for consciousness, not of the dynamic flow of consciousness itself. It is to miss the emergent causal powers of the larger system in which brain activity is participating.[8] This system does not stop at the boundaries of the body. This means that consciousness is intrinsically attached to situations and embodied in particular forms of life. Events within the brain are one part, and possibly a rather small part, of an enormously extended system. To think that a description of them will provide a complete account for experience with no remainder is a reductive mistake.

It imports into psychological science what Whitehead called 'the fallacy of misplaced concreteness' when speaking of science more generally. Nature is a process. A system in constant creative advance within which consciousness plays a role at all levels of order. The fallacy arises when one particular level is assumed to have explanatory or causal primacy. This fallacy is easier to recognise and to repair with the postmodern turn since, surprisingly perhaps, it has a strongly Whiteheadian character when applied to science.[9] In psychology this will promote a style of inquiry in which process, meaning and feeling are primary.[10] Consciousness and selfhood, now may be treated as process-like and embodied within a form of life rather than thing-like and thus to be isolated and formalised.

New ideas and new methods are needed to carry out this inquiry. As part of the growing interaction between psychological science and phenomenological traditions, we need to integrate qualitative and phenomenological methods with those of cognitive neuroscience.[11] As the essays in this collection suggest, it is here that Buddhism can be of help. There have existed for millennia techniques for systematically investigating experience. With the postmodern shift toward eclecticism and plurality of both theory and methodology these techniques can be adopted as empirical resources in their own right and not as historical curios that science will somehow explain away.

Of course, science and Buddhism cannot just be seamlessly joined to create a new psychological discipline. We need to investigate their similarities and differences in an informed and critical way. Here that the postmodern turn helps us to question cultural assumptions about whether one system of ideas is simply incompatible with another. This in turn helps to create the broader and more inclusive science of experience sought by Whitehead and Husserl. In offering this collection of essays, we hope to have shown that even though Buddhism and psychology may make different claims to authority they can nonetheless be brought closer together within a systematic and realistic inquiry into experience.

NOTES

1 Wolpert, L. (1992) *The Unnatural Nature of Science.* Faber and Faber, London.

2 Becker, E. (1962) *The Birth And Death Of Meaning, A Perspective In Psychiatry And Anthropology.* Free Press, New York.

3 Rorty, R (1980) *Philosophy & the Mirror of Nature.* Blackwell, Oxford. Last section.

4 Pickering. J. (1995) Buddhism and Cognitivism: a postmodern appraisal. *Asian Philosophy.* Vol. 5, number 1, pages 23-38.

5 Johnson-Laird, P. (1989) A computational analysis of consciousness, in *Consciousness in contemporary science*, edited by Marcel, A. and Bisiach, E., Oxford University Press, London. Page 367.

6 Newell, A. (1991) *Unified Theories of Cognition.* Harvard University Press.

7 Churchland, P. S. (1986) *Neurophilosophy: Toward a Unified Science of the Mind-Brain.* MIT Press / Bradford Books, Cambridge.

8 Sperry, R. (1986) The New Mentalist Paradigm and Ultimate Concern. *Perspectives in Biology and Medicine, 29*(3): 413–422.

9 Griffin, D. R. (1988) Introduction, in *The Reenchantment of Science: Postmodern Proposals*, edited by Griffin, D.R., State University of Ney York Press, Albany, NY.

10 Kvale, S. (1992) (Ed.) *Psychology and Postmodernism.* Sage, London.

11 Varela, F. (1996) Neurophenomenology. *Journal of Consciousness Studies.* Vol. 3 (4), pages 330–349.

Contributors

NOTES ON THE CONTRIBUTIONS

The chapters in this book were solicited by the editor. Authors were invited to write on Buddhism and psychology, to discuss experience and to compare the different meanings of authority as used to describe Buddhism and Western psychology. On receiving an initial version of the chapter the editor made various observations and suggestions and the authors then provided a second version. This, without any significant alteration, is the text that has been used.

NOTES ON THE CONTRIBUTORS

John Crook began his career in ethology, studying animal social behaviour at Cambridge. After a year as a Fellow at the Centre for Advanced Study in the Behavioural Sciences at Stanford University he became interested in humanistic psychology and group psychotherapy. He is the author of a major book on consciousness, (*The Evolution of Human Consciousness*, Oxford University Press, 1980) as well as numerous other works. The more recent of these reflects his work on the Buddhist cultures of the Himalayas, especially Ladakh (*Himalayan Buddhist Villages*, edited by Crook, J. & Osmaston, H., Bristol University Press, 1995). He is a teacher or Tibetan and Zen Buddhism and has been instrumental in the setting up of the New Ch'an Forum, a UK group for the teaching and practice of traditional forms of Buddhism.

Padmal de Silva is senior lecturer in psychology at the Institute of Psychiatry, London and consultant clinical pschologist for the Maudsley and Bethlem National Health Service Trust. In his clincal practice and research he has been interested in adult problems, especially obsessive-compulsive disorders, eating disorders, post-traumatic stress and sexual problems. He is the author, with S. Rachman, of *Obsessive-Compulsive Disorder: The Facts* (1992) and *Panic Disorders: The Facts* (1996), both published by Oxford University Press. His many pubications stress that the relevance of Buddhism to psychotherapy should be assessed empirically. His work ranges from the use of meditation as a tension control stragey to the systematic study of early Buddhist texts.

Padmasiri de Silva was formerly Head and Professor of Philosophy and Psychology, Peradeniya University Sri Lanka. More recently he was Senior Teaching Fellow at the National University of Singapore and also Director of the project on 'Environment, Ethics and Education' at the International Research Centre there. He is presently a Research Fellow at Monash University, in the Philosophy Department. His work explores how Buddhism contributes to understanding contemporary patterns of human disorientation in relation to society, nature and personal identity. His works include *Introduction to Buddhist Psychology* (Macmillan, 1979) and *Buddhist and Freudian Psychology* (Third edition, University of Singapore Press, 1992).

David Fontana holds a Professorship at the University of Minho, Portugal and is a Distinguished Visiting Fellow at the University of Wales at Cardiff. His main areas of interest are education and counselling on which he has published over 100 papers in academic journals and written many books that have now been translated into 20 languages. He has taken a long term interest in psycho-spiritual traditions and has carried out research into meditation, humanistic and trans-personal psychology. Recently he has helped to form the Transpersonal psychology section in the British Psychological Society.

Herbert Guenther's background is the Vienna and Munich schools of structural linguistics. From these beginnings he was drawn towards phenomenology, especially the works of Husserl and Heidegger, from whence he arrived in the area on which his international reputation is founded, the psychology and philosophy of Buddhism, especially the Abhidhamma and Tibetan traditions. He has authored numerous books and articles in these topics, including *Philosophy and Psychology in the Abhidhamma* (Shambala, 1976) and *From Reductionism to Creativity* (Shambala, 1989). His most recent book

A World of Light (E.J. Brill, 1996) is on the imagery of ancient Tibetan literature

Brian Lancaster is a Senior Lecturer in Psychology at Liverpool John Moores University, where he teaches an MSc programme in The Psychology of Human Potential. Following research into brain function at Manchester University, he developed a specific interest in consciousness which led him to focus on the psychology/religion interface. In addition to his interest in Buddhism, his work in this field has included rabbinical studies in Jerusalem, and he currently lectures on Jewish mysticism at Yakar Educational Foundation in London. He is author of *Mind, Brain and Human Potential* (Element, 1991), which won an award from the Scientific and Medical Network, and *The Elements of Judaism* (Element, 1993).

Joy Manné began Vipassana meditation in 1965, taught by Dhiravamsa. Her doctoral thesis was based on case histories in the Theravada Buddhist texts in Pali. She was trained in Spiritual Therapy and Rebirthing by Hans Mensink and Tilke Platteel-Deur. She has taught meditation, using various exercises taken straight from these texts. The method of therapy she uses, Conscious Breathing Techniques, is based upon the development of awareness through the breath, as is meditation. Her work as a therapist is profoundly influenced by Buddhist psychology.

John Pickering. After two postdoctoral years at the universities of Rochester and Stanford, John Pickering has worked in the Psychology department at Warwick University. His interests cover cognitive science, consciousness and postmodernism. Since visiting Peradeniya University, Sri Lanka, he has become interested in the overlap between Western psychology and Buddhism. During the early part of 1998 he will be a visiting scholar at the Institute for Higher Tibetan Studies in Sarnath, India. He was involved in the setting up of the Consciousness and Experiential Psychology section in the British Psychological Society. He edited, with Martin Skinner, a collection of readings on consciousness: *From Sentience to Symbols* (Harvester, 1990, reprinted 1994).

Eleanor Rosch started her career in cognitive psychology with many influential studies of how people categorise what they perceive and remember. These studies combined experimental psychology with anthropology and led her on to look at categorisation in broad cross cultural terms. This brought her into contact with Buddhism which now forms an important part of her research interests. She is presently Professor of Psychology at the University of California, Berkeley. Among her many papers and other publications, she is the co-author, with Francisco Varela and Evan Thompson, *of The Embodied Mind* (MIT Press, 1991), a book that has had an important role in promoting contact between Cognitive Science and Buddhism.

Elizabeth Valentine is a reader in psychology at the Royal Holloway College, London University. She has wide interests in psychology covering it's history, philosophy and methodology. She has done research on music, on the teaching of psychology and especially the use of religious literature in his area, on the relation between cognitive psychology and meditative and mystical traditions. Among her publications is *Conceptual Issues In Psychology* (Allen & Unwin, 1982). She has for a number of years helped to run the History and Philosophy section of the British Psychological Society and recently she has been involved in the setting up of the Consciousness and Experiential Psychology section.

Section 1

Making Comparisons

Chapter 1

EDITOR'S PREFACE

Eleanor Rosch begins her chapter with a story. Is this appropriate as the opening to a piece of scientific writing? Stories are expressive and fanciful while science deals in hypotheses and experiments. But in cultures where science does not have the role that it does in the West, stories have a far more substantial role than mere amusement. Across cultures, myth and legends are important vehicles for fundamental beliefs about the nature of the world and it's origins, the place of human beings in it and, perhaps most importantly, lessons for how we might act for the best. In any case, what a story can convey depends a great deal on whether those who hear it have the capacity to recognise what it offers. C S Lewis objected to Christian images of the afterlife being derided as childish. He suggested that the childishness lay in hearers who, if they couldn't understand stories for adults, should avoid them.

In something of the same way, Rosch here shows how the tale of Shalipa offers a number of insights into Buddhist practices for investigating mental life. In these practices we find nothing like the historical method of psychoanalysis, the functional metaphors of cognitive science or the anatomical descriptions of neuropsychology. Instead there is the direct investigation of experience. The investigation portrayed in the story is ordered, progressive and based on a model of mental processing. Thus we observe a systematic, empirical psychology with an explicit methodology. The result is not a body of scientific knowledge. Rather it is a gradual change in the scientist. This is towards a more satisfactory condition that provides insight and the means to help others.

Eleanor Rosch compares the image of the mind offered by the story with that provided by cognitive science. Cognitive science too systematically investigates the mind though comparatively little attention is paid to what the present moment offers. Introspective methods have proven limited and unreliable. Objective and operationalised approaches have predominated and the image of mind that emerges is that of the executive, the functional level of rational processing that controls the actual physical actions of brain and body.

This, as Rosch points out, has a great deal in common with the self-interested consumer of economic theory, the rational actor of social exchange and the logician of problem solving. The roots of this image of mind reach back to thinkers such as Leibnitz and Hobbes. In *Leviathan*, the conflict and suffering intrinsic to the human condition is controlled by common assent to external rules to order human affairs. These rules, produced by the exercise of reason, regulate the relationships between individuals and between individuals and the state. In thus designing the modern state, Hobbes took an understanding of human psychology as a pre-requisite. Indeed, the first third of *Leviathan* is devoted to a psychological theory which is remarkably modern. In particular, it prefigures the proposal that mental life can be treated as if it were an internal form of rule following. The essence of mental life, concluded Hobbes, is reasoning and 'reasoning is naught but reckoning'. It is in this sense that cognitivism and the computer metaphor are descendants of the European Enlightenment. The rational principle at the core of human mental life is utterly other than the material vehicle that supports it. This promises, on the one hand, to make psychology as formalised, explicit and thus productive as any other science. On the other, it generates an image of the mind that is disconnected and alienated from the rest of the natural order.

The range of psychological theories reviewed by Rosch shows that it is not just cognitive science that adopts this rational, rule-following image of mental life. One way or another, the notion that the flow of experience is subject to implicit rules is a fundamental, though often implicit, aspect of Western psychological and social science. The conundrum then arises: who or what follows the rules? To claim that the follower of the rules is something different from the rules themselves appears to take us back to pre-scientific, soul like homunculi that inhabit the body and make it go. Advocates of cognitive science offer as one of its many strengths that it provides an explicit way to dispose of such primitive notions.

At a quite fundamental level, Buddhism offers a similar view, though for very difference reasons. The doctrines of *anatta* and of conditioned arising (*paticca samupadda*) state explicitly that nothing other than the ceaseless arising and of physical and mental conditions underlies our sense of self. The basis for these doctrines is not hypothetico-deductive but experiential. In sharp and critical distinction to the reductive, analytic approach of Western science, the methods dealt with in this chapter investigate mental life as it unfolds within the mind and body as they interact with the conditions that surround them. The failure of Western attempts at analytic introspection will naturally make psychologists wary of claims that anything reliable and public can be found by such methods. Getting close enough to experience to observe it properly is very difficult and requires a great deal of training.

Rosch's view, which is echoed by many others who know both Western and Buddhist traditions, is that nevertheless such training can and has been undertaken and that a great deal of reliable knowledge has been the result. This knowledge is primarily experiential and the purpose in acquiring it is not to add to some depersonalised canon of facts, but to lead a more satisfactory life. The object of knowledge in these traditions is the knower, not the known. Rosch lists ten aspects of the mind that are discovered through meditative investigation. In comparing them with Western psychology many significant differences are immediately apparent. These range from claims about the limits on mental capacity to metaphysical statements about the nature of mental life and how it may be known and described.

The interesting thing about these differences, however, is that the direction in which contemporary psychology is moving tends to reduce them. Moreover, they act as trails or pointers that will help to fashion the techniques and objectives of postmodern psychology. In making this comparison, long neglected aspects of mental life are re-introduced into Western psychology. In complementary ways, many Buddhist practices and beliefs may be subject to more refined investigation and development. Together, this interchange participates in the return of consciousness and subjectivity to Western science. It sets an agenda, as Varela points out, that will see the resources of science amplified and broadened by the integration of experimental techniques with the practices of phenomenological traditions. The result will be a more balanced and inclusive discipline.

★ ★ ★

Transformation of the Wolf Man[1]

Eleanor Rosch

From the Tibetan Buddhist tradition comes the following story:

Shalipa was a low caste woodcutter who lived near the charnel ground of Bighapur. Packs of wolves came by night to eat the corpses (in a charnel ground, corpses are simply deposited on the ground to decay or be eaten by wild animals). The wolves howled all night long, and Shalipa became more and more afraid of them until he could neither eat by day nor sleep by night for fear of the howling of wolves. One evening a wandering yogin stopped by his cottage asking for food. Shalipa gave him food and drink, and, well pleased, the yogin repaid him with a discourse on the virtues of fearing samsara (conditioned existence) and practicing the dharma. Shalipa thanked him but said, 'Everyone fears samsara. But I have a specific fear. Wolves come to the charnel ground and howl all night, and I am so afraid of them that I can neither eat nor sleep nor practice the dharma. Please can't you give me a spell so that I can stop the howling of the wolves?' The yogin laughed and said, 'Foolish man. What good will it do you to eat the food of greed when you do not know what food is? What good will it do you to sleep the corpse-like sleep of ignorance when you do not know what rest is? What good will it do you to destroy the howling of the wolves with the spells or anger when you do not know what hearing or any other sense is? If you will follow my instructions, I will teach you to destroy all fear.' Shalipa accepted the yogin as his teacher, gave him all that he had, and begged him for instruction. After giving him initiation, the yogin told him to move into the charnel ground with the wolves and to mediate ceaselessly upon all sound as identical to the howling of wolves.

Shalipa obeyed him. Gradually he came to understand the nature of all sound and of all reality. He meditated for nine years, overcame all obscurations of his mind and body, lost all fear, and attained great realization. Thereafter, he wore a wolf skin around his shoulders and was know as Shalipa (the wolf yogin). He taught his disciples many different practices about the nature of appearances and reality. He taught the unity of appearance, emptiness, wisdom, and skillful means. Finally, in that very body, he went to the realm of the Heroes.[2]

If ever there was an ancient portrait of the alienated modern (or post-modern) man, it is Shalipa as we first see him. He has societal problems, being poor, low caste and powerless; environmental problems, being forced to live beside a charnel ground in which wolves roam and howl; medical problems since he can neither eat nor sleep properly; psychological problems, a rampantly spreading wolf phobia; and spiritual problems, for he says he is too upset to practice the dharma. We can readily understand and empathize with him when we first meet him, shivering in his hut and complaining to his visitor.

But then the story shifts, becoming less readily available to the modern sensibility. Shalipa's mentor does not advise him to move away, to sue the owners of the charnel ground, to delve into the meaning of wolf howls in his personal history, or to endure his fate as a means of religious salvation. Rather he is instructed to use his own experience in meditation to undergo a radical transformation in how he senses, knows, and feels. He emerges with freedom from his problems and the power to act on and for others. What is this transformation in knowing, feeling, acting, and relating and how it is achieved? What might this story have to tell us about how we view the world in our present psychology and how it may be alternatively viewed through the eyes of the meditative traditions?

In this chapter, I will first delineate our present understanding or portrait of a human as it appears in the cognitive sciences and in folk psychology, arguing that this portrait precisely fits Shalipa's initial status and condition. Second, I will attempt to show that this portrait is not a modern anomaly but matches the description of *samsara* in ancient Buddhism (and other meditative traditions) and that it has a universal experiential basis which is discovered by self observing beginning meditators. (The material on mediators is based on observations, participations, conversations, and interviews with meditators from various groups.) Finally, I will seek to show how continued experiential examination in the meditative traditions reveals an alternative mode of knowing, feeling, acting, and being which offers a radically different human portrait. Might this latter mode of knowing provide a possible basis for a future (post post modern perhaps) science of psychology?

I. PORTRAIT OF THE MIND IN THE COGNITIVE SCIENCES

What is a human being? What is the human mind? When we hear such questions, what do we think? What images come to mind? Cultures, religions, and the various sciences offer differing portraits of the human being; these are crucially important to the ways in which we may then seek to study, help, instruct, regulate (or perhaps enjoy) those humans. What portrait of the human do we have that leads the scientist to feel that experience is not a proper approach to the study of minds, that the mind must be treated as though it is an external object to be examined objectively according to the canons of natural science? What portrait of the human do we have that led to modernism and to it's present breakdown as described elsewhere in this volume? The information processing view of the mind held by present experimental psychology (and the cognitive sciences as a whole) may be our most concise formulation, a pinpointing, of the principles underlying such a portrait.

Let us begin, therefore, with the model of the mind provided by the modern cognitive sciences. The mind is seen as an information processing system.[3] Outside of the mind is an objective world, such as is studied by physics. Information from that world enters the mind through the sense organs where it proceeds through various stages of short term memory and is finally stored in long term memory. In this process the information is transformed into cognitive representations (re-representations) of the external world and of one's self in that world. One also develops causal theories about the world and one's self and habits of actions based on these. Information from the representations and theories in long term storage also go back to the sense organs so that one knows how to interpret and appraise (in accordance with one's expectations and goals) incoming stimuli, and it goes out along the motor pathways so that one can act.

Now let's look at the implications of this portrait of the mind for the issues raised by the Shalipa story. For the sake of organization we can divide these implications into the three classical divisions of

8

knowing (cognition), feeling (conation), and action, and add to it a four category, implications for relationships with other people.

In terms of *knowing* the information processor is inside of the information processing system and is separate from its objects. This separated knower constructs its cognitive representations out of bits of information that come its way, and it sees everything in terms of these representations. As to the *feeling, appetitive, wanting* part of the person: just as objects of knowledge are outside of the system, so are objects of desire, while the independent, separated wanter of objects is inside of the system. Perhaps the most clear cut rendition of this separated wanter appears in classical utility theory in economics.[4] Inside the information processing system is a rational wanter who computes the utilities and probabilities possessed by external objects of desire and then acts rationally on the world to try to obtain these objects ... and then more objects and more objects. And what is action in the cognitive science mode of thinking? It is based on rules. How can someone catch a baseball? We can work out a rather elaborate set of rules of motion based on vectors and trajectories from physics and then attempt to program a robot to catch a baseball based on those rules. How can a person make a moral decision? Now we need an explicit set of moral rules and a program for weighting and combining them to make moral judgements.

Finally how does the information processor so described relate to other people? In a certain sense, (s)he never does. Isolated inside the information processing system, all (s)he ever sees or knows or wants or can act from is his/her cognitive representations which are related only indirectly (perhaps in the long run only by evolution) to anything or anyone in the autonomous outside world. Popular psychiatry says we have intimacy problems with other people. Of course! From this point of view, I do not actually see this hand which is in front of my eyes or feel this table I am touching, so we have intimacy problems with everything – sensations, perceptions, thoughts, emotions, actions, much less with anything as global and awesome as another person.

This model of the human mind is not confined to the single discipline of academic psychology. A major theme of modern philosophy since Brentano and then Husserl has been how it is possible for mental states to be always *about* something other than and separate from themselves (see, for example, Dreyfus[5]), an issue misleadingly called the problem of *intentionality*. In linguistics, it has generally been assumed since antiquity that language can only get its meaning by means of *reference* to independent objects and states of

9

the world[6]. Psychoanalysis, one might think, is sufficiently intimate and internal to be an exception to the model, but if we actually look at Freud, his system is a perfect portrait of cognitivism[7]. The mind is made of mental representations which are *about* something external, even in the unconscious. Objects of desire are always outside: the id wants to grab them right away; the superego generates rules that say *no*; and the best that the beleaguered ego can do is make some compromises, while the person remains ever unsatisfied. On the more societal level[8], the popular social exchange theory in sociology, anthropology, social psychology, and economics views the psychological motives behind social interaction as the attempt of each individual to bring as many good things as possible within his/her boundaries while paying out as little as possible of his/her scarce resources. It isn't just professionals who think in these ways; as surveys how, the (wo)man in the street largely agrees.

Such an alienated portrait of the human has not gone unnoticed by thinkers in our culture, and it is popular to attribute it to some aspect or fault in modern civilization. In fact you may be saying to yourself right now, 'Ah-hah! That's Cartesianism! That's our modern western dualistic portrait of the mind, and that should be contrasted with all the rest of the world which doesn't see things that way.' Or you might think that such a model is the product of post-industrial-revolution alienation which is now spreading around the world but that it does not apply to peoples in pre-industrial or ancient times. Or that it is the result of secularization, patriarchy, or any number of particular causes without which it did not or would not operate.

But what about Shalipa as we originally meet him? Here is a pre-Cartesian, pre-industrial revolution, pre-secularization, nonwestern man as alienated from his world and his feelings as ever you might wish. We have no trouble at all understanding and identifying with his state of mind as he sits huddled in his hut, terrified of the howling wolves; our difficulties or questions have to do with what happens to him after that when his understanding and experience start to change.

I wish to argue that the dualistic and alienated understanding of a human being which prevails today in the social and cognitive sciences is not a historical or social accident; rather, it is a representation of a deep and universal aspect of folk psychology, an aspect which in the Buddhist (and to some extent Hindu) traditions is called *samsara*. Samsara is where humans will, it is said, discover themselves to be as, though training in meditation, they become mindful, instead of mindless, of their mental processes and actions in everyday life.

So let us turn now to the issue of meditation, of experience, and of experimental method. Western scientific psychology explicitly seeks to study mind from the outside as though it were an object of the natural sciences. The meditative traditions provide an alternative route, methodologies for learning about the mind/consciousness/living being from the inside, paths for gaining knowledge about the living being as that being itself.

II. PORTRAITS OF THE MIND FROM THE MEDITATIVE TRADITIONS

A. Meditation as a Means to Knowledge

It is common for western experimental psychologists to equate any use of the mind for self investigation with introspection, a mode of inquiry to which we are understandably allergic. Introspectionism as a school of psychology, made popular by the nineteenth-century psychologist Wilhelm Wundt, failed definitively to provide a basis for experimental psychology. The reader has probably discovered the problem with what we call introspection for him or herself many times. When one simply tries to introspect, to look inward, about a problem for example, the chances are that one finds one's thoughts going round and round, and the best one can hope for is to think some additional, hopefully satisfying, thought about one's thoughts. Without a proper method we are caught in our conceptual systems. It is precisely to cut through such introspection that various meditative techniques were discovered.

A second misleading picture of meditation held by westerners involves dissociation of mind and body: trance, hypnotism, 'mystical' experiences, and altered states of consciousness. While such states must be included in any psychology of the whole of human capacity, they are no more central to what the meditative traditions have to tell us about knowing than any other human state or activity.

Perhaps the simplest contrast to both introspection and dissociation is the meditative methods called mindfulness. *Mindfulness* is a term used in some of the Buddhist traditions, particularly Theravada, some Zen, and by some Tibetan teachers[9]. Mindfulness is described as experiencing what mind and body are doing as they are doing it, being present with one's mind, body, and energy in their ordinary states of occurrence. A related concept from the more bodily oriented practices, such as the martial arts, is *integration* in which body, energy, mind, intention, awareness, and action come to form one nonfragmented, integrated whole[10]. Whatever the terminology or school of meditation, in my observations, meditative techniques of concentration, calming, alert observation, and integration render people more viable instruments of self observation. What then is the portrait of the human that emerges from the meditative traditions? I will trace the evolution of this portrait and what it has to tell us about modes of knowing though several stages of development.

B. Discoveries of the Beginning Mediator

Attention. Beginning meditators are usually shocked. Their first and immediate discovery is often about the nature of attention. Mental contents change rapidly and continuously: thoughts, sensations, feelings, worries, daydreams, inner conversations, sleepiness, fantasies, plans, memories, theories, emotions, self instructions about the techniques, judgements about thoughts and feelings, judgements about judgements. All meditators who sit still and use a mental technique, regardless of their tradition, purpose, or technique report these kinds of experiences. This is a point easily discoverable also by the nonmeditating reader; simply notice what the mind is doing as one tries to keep attention on some simple mental, or even physical, task.

Even more pointed than noticing the constant shifting of attention is the discovery that attention is, for the most part, indirect. That is, the mind is not sharply present with its experiences as they are happening but rather drifts about not noticing that it has left its assigned object or task until the meditator or task oriented person 'comes back' with a 'jerk' to the present. Then the meditator realizes, not only that he had been 'away', but that while he was wandering, he was not really aware of what he was thinking or feeling; he now only remembers what had been going on in his mind through a haze of summarizing concepts and judgements. This is not merely the case for unpleasant experiences from which one might expect a person to want to dissociate. Even the simplest or most pleasurable of daily activities – eating, walking, talking with a friend – tend to pass rapidly in a blur of commentary as one hastens to the next mental occupation. (Just notice what your mind does at the next meal).

In the cognitive science portrait of the mind, knowing was indirect. Now we see one experiential basis for modelling it in this way. However, meditators (or anyone else) can only discover the indirectness of attention by contrast, that is, by experiencing moments of being present which are less indirect than the moments of wandering. Thus an alternative experience, one of directness, has its birth at the same time as the experiental discovery of indirectness.

The self. When meditators begin to notice themselves, even if they are being explicitly taught about nonself in the Buddhist tradition, what they tend to report is amazement at the power and ubiquitousness of their self concern. Thoughts, memories, plans, goals, hopes, fears, judgements, etc., all are about oneself or others important to oneself. The constantly shifting emotive tone of experience centres on judgements of whether events are good, bad, or irrelevant to oneself.

And who or what is this self? Leaving theories aside, let us contemplate a given moment of experience. We ordinarily take experience to be composed of at least two aspects: subject and object, perceiver and thing perceived. And, as the discovery of self referencing has shown, the object of perception is normally seen as either desirable or threatening or boring to the perceiver who then has impulses to get the desirable and avoid or destroy the undesirable. This is a relatively simple point (William James[11], for example, noticed it), which can be readily verified by the reader. Just look at something, say the wall in front of you. Isn't there some sense of a looker, perhaps located in the head behind the eyes, looking at an object spatially located outside yourself? Now try looking at an emotionally relevant object such as your relationship, favorite food, enemy, or an irritating appliance.

Thus in the ordinary experience of the self, we see the basis for the separated knower and wanter of cognitive science models. However, any meditator who gets close enough to experience to begin seeing this knower and wanter in action also begins to feel a kind of vertigo of the knower and curiosity about the wanter. Who is it who is seeing that see-er who is looking at the wall – a second see-er? Beginning mindfulness meditators may try to become such a second looker, a stance which is quite awkward. But if I am *not* such a second separate and temporally continuous knower, then who is it about whose fate I am so emotionally concerned? What is knowing and wanting? Again, as with attention, the very discovery in experience of the cognitive sciences' separated knower and wanter brings with it a sense of the limitations of this approach to understanding.

The body and emotions. Experience of the body and experience of emotions are aspects of the knowing and feeling self so pointedly confusing to beginning meditators that these areas deserve special comment. Is my body a part of myself as subject or is it an *other*, a separated object of experience? Where is the mind when I am 'spaced out' and not 'in' the body? Isn't it odd that I can feel alienated from something as much part of me as my own body? What do all of the mind/body issues of philosophy actually mean experientially?

Even more puzzling is the relation of a person to his or her emotions. At the same time that people identify themselves with an emotion they may also be seeing that emotion as an *other*, as something outside of themselves of whose 'attack' they can be afraid. Both the body and emotions are boundary areas where the model of the separated knower and wanter is still in operation but is strained. Such issues become matters of living contemplation for meditators, especially Buddhist meditators whose tradition may point them toward these conundrums.

Goal directedness and action. The mind becomes acutely uncomfortable without goals, without something toward which the cognitive and emotional system is aiming. That is why satisfied desires no longer please, and new desires constantly spring up. Meditators discover this as, sooner or later, their peace providing meditation technique becomes irritating or boring and the mind reaches out, over and over again, for something else, some goal, something to do.

This constant activity of mind appears directly related to action. In fact, some Theravada Buddhist mindfulness techniques direct the meditator to slow all actions to a crawl and carefully observe the impulses and intentions preceding the smallest movement. Thus observed, action in general begins to show up as a complex matter engendered by self referring goals, intentions, plans, evaluations, reasoning, strategies, doubts, and efforts. Is this not the very picture of the cognitive scientist's models of action? 'Yet is all this *required* for actions?' the meditator may begin to wonder? Does the popping up of a thought in the mind require preceding plans and efforts to think that thought? Does one get out of bed in the morning by means of thinking about it? Thus, as with the knower and the wanter, the beginning meditator both discovers and comes to question the cognitive scientist's rule based view of action.

Interpersonal relationships. Self referentiality applies to interpersonal relationships. Other people, like any other object of the external world, are the objects of desires, aversions and indifference depending on whether they are seen as good, bad, or irrelevant to the self's goals. How saddening it is for decent meditators who had thought themselves as altruistic as anyone else to begin to notice the subtle and devious ways in which self referentiality may manifest. For a mind in its egocentric mode there is no way out of this cocoon of self reference.

This then is the portrait of the alienated information processor assumed by the cognitive sciences, decried by the humanities, and discovered in experience by the beginning meditator. It is where we first meet Shalipa, cowering in his hut wishing to sleep the sleep of ignorance, eat the food of greed, and terrified of the threatening wolves. It is the mode of knowing, feeling, and acting called *samsara* in Buddhist terminology, the wheel of existence to which sentient beings are bound by their habits unless they do something to break those habits. Other meditative traditions bear similar descriptions. Most Hindu schools speak of gross or lower levels of consciousness which replicate this picture. The beginning Taoist meditator discovers his Monkey who lives 'alone in the branches of his small tree world ... his environment a blur of the frantic activity created by unchecked desire.'[12] And western religions speak of sin or distance from God.

As indicated previously, what all this suggests is that the cognitivist model of modern psychology actually has its roots in our basic folk psychology, a psychology which is not a product of the modern (or postmodern) world, nor of contemporary philosophy, nor of social changes, nor of particular customs or cultural values. Does that mean that humans are in a hopeless situation with respect to these matters? To be sure, the cognitivist and folk psychological models stop here with the isolated information processor. However, the meditative traditions do not stop here. What is to come is the portrait of the *full* human being which is uncovered by pursuing the further discoveries of meditation. Our beginning meditator may have discovered the alientated samsaric information processor experientially, but (s)he did so in a context in which that disconnected and needy self did not make complete experiential sense. Indeed, each time the meditator finds himself as the dualistic information processor, (s)he does so against a background of intuition that there might be an entirely different way of knowing and being. Must not we suppose something like this to have happened to Shalipa if we are to make sense of his perseverance and eventual realizations? Let us look at these further developments in the meditative traditions.

C. Further Meditative Discoveries: The Process View

Attention can be trained. The ceaseless ungrounded activity of the mind can be pacified and the mind can be taught to hold an object of attention. All meditation traditions acknowledge and sometimes use this. Almost any object of attention can be used: a sight, a mental image, the breath, a mantra, sensations, the body in motion, space. The technique is usually to return again and again to the object of meditation. The mind can be taught not only to cease wandering away from its object, at least temporarily, but also to remain alert while holding it. But then attention has to be further trained, or perhaps untrained, to let go. Holding a particular mental content is not the goal of any meditative tradition, and some traditions teach letting go in other ways. The goal is to develop (discover, click into) a different mode of knowing and being which is available to humans. The attentional aspect of this mode is that the mind appears to have the natural ability to be present with the flux of experience, the knowing *and* the not knowing aspects of experience, in a relaxed and natural way. From the vantage point of this kind of attention, the self and the other aspects of experience which we have discussed, begin to take on a rather different appearance.

The self is unreflectively assumed to be a *thing* which abides through time, is independent of other things, and needs to be nurtured and protected by the person who has it. As meditators become more in touch with the reality of their experience, a view of the world in terms of unitary things and events tends to shift to an experience of ongoing processes. For example, experiences that were once assumed unitary wholes (e.g. 'I was angry all morning' or 'I spent the whole night afraid of the howling of the wolves') are seen to be a sequence of particular, ever-changing sensations and concepts. Traits once seen as part of an independent self are noticed to arise interdependently with circumstances, and those circumstances to arise interdependently with increasingly more extensive arenas of world events.

Such shifts in view are very useful but are not quite the essence of the shift into a new mode of knowing. Who is it that is perceiving these interdependent processes? As previously stated, we ordinarily take experience to be composed of at least two aspects: subject and object, knower and known, perceiver and thing perceived. Initial forms of meditation instruction and of meditation may sound as though they are intended to exaggerate the sense of a constant perceiver, a homunculus who watches and comments on the passing flux of experience. Buddhist instructions often stress watchfulness, and some forms of Hinduism teach a *witness consciousness*. In order to counteract self identification with passing experiences or with the personality, meditators might be taught to say to themselves: 'I am not my thoughts,' 'I am not my emotions,' etc. But this sense of an exaggerated separate perceiver is limited, temporary, and somewhat artificial. Eventually meditators come to see, suspect, or at least have a glimmering that the subject or perceiver is only the subject side of a momentary experience, an aspect of the perception or thought itself.

This is an extremely important point in the meditation process. None of the traditions teach that meditation is a means of separating oneself from one's experience – a contradiction in terms at best. Each tradition, at some point, directs the meditator to be *in* experience but with the broader sense of knowing engendered by the training and then relaxation of attention. A panoply of techniques exist in all the traditions for challenging or pacifying the sense of separateness and for an intelligent destruction of the artificial sense of an observer. The meditator may be told to *be* the object of meditation (the image, breath, howling of wolves, etc.), or perhaps to try hard to 'catch' the watcher, or perhaps to relax and trust completely, or perhaps to perform daily work tasks very very rapidly – the possibilities are limitless. This is a point where, when such teachings are explicit, meditators are likely to feel pushed. An analytic approach to no self can be interesting, but the precise experiencing of the lack of a separate observer is something from which the mind recoils like putting a finger on a hot stove. With perseverance, however, new possibilities for knowing, feeling, and relating can open from this way of experiencing.

The body. In western psychology, physiology, medicine, theology, and common sense, body and mind are generally considered separate things. The body is seen as undebatably material and solid while the mind is a something else, a something whose nature and relationship to the body has long been the subject of much speculative debate. There are several ways in which meditative experiences challenge our notions of the body and of the body/mind experience.

1. The body can be experienced as patterns of energy and space rather than solely as solid matter. To get a sense of this vision the reader might try the following contemplation[13]: imagine your body as a giant and your mind as a tiny traveler inside the body. Progressively increase the size of the body so that the traveler is exploring at increasingly micro levels of structure; then turn the contemplation onto the traveller who is doing the exploring.
2. Body and mind can be experienced in a meaningful way as actually not separate. In that case, the body is described as a part

of knowing, as self-knowing, rather than as an inert thing that can be known only from the outside.

3. Bodily energy is experienced as moving in certain channels (as in acupuncture meridians in Chinese medicine). These are experientially quite real, and manipulating them has notable effects (as you may have experienced if you have ever undergone an acupuncture treatment). These channels do not correspond to western neurological maps. When observer and observed are experienced as not separate, the energy flows can be self manipulated without medical assistance[14].

4. There are certain energy centres within the body (the chakras) which have particular characteristics. Most of the meditative traditions acknowledge the existence of these, but by no means all techniques or all meditators work with them. For those who do, the centres can be of central importance. When perceived or approached with our usual restricted, dualistic mode of knowing, the centres themselves appear constricted or closed, and each centre appears to form the nexus of its own type of neurotic energy. When approached with a nondualistic openness, each centre can be experienced as the seat of its corresponding broader knowing or wisdom. For example, the head centre, normally the basis of intellectualization and criticism, is said to open to a pure mirror-like seeing, and the heart centre, in which feelings of sadness and grief are often experienced, is said to give rise to the experiences of inclusive, accepting, timeless space and of connectedness to the world.

Emotions. As was previously pointed out, for a mind in its egocentric mode of knowing, emotions are the monitoring of duality, of how the subject is doing in relation to its objects, to its desires and goals, to others, to its world. The slightest threat to the self's territory (a cut finger, a disobedient child) arouses fear or anger. The slightest hope of self enhancement (money, praise, pleasure) arouses excitement, desire or greed. The first hint that a situation may be irrelevant to the self (waiting in line, meditating) produces boredom. In Buddhism, these three motivational factors, aggression, passion, and ignorance, are what keep samsara operating. They are said to be what keep humans, such as Shalipa, bound to the habitual mode of knowing and feeling.

But in many of the meditative schools, emotions, like other phenomena, are Janus faced. When they are experienced in a nondualistic, open mode of knowing, they can be seen, it is said, not as problems but as the basic energies of the universe. Some meditative traditions talk of coming to see, tuning into, riding on, being with, or becoming one with the energy level of the emotion and thereby achieving wisdom. Taoism talks of seeing the energy of the different emotions as the very elements out of which nature is composed (how could it be otherwise?) and thereby achieving harmony. For example, anger might be recognized as the element fire which can be used appropriately. In Tibetan Buddhism, basic emotions, when seen in their totality, are the very stuff of the basic wisdoms. For example, the energy of pride is (transmutable into) the wisdom of equanimity. In short, emotions can function as egocentric obstacles or as potent catalysts for wisdom.

Goal directedness and action. The constant discontent of habitual desires and goal orientation obscures the broader, more open sense of knowing of which we have been speaking. Meditation techniques abound to relax, outwit, stun, or perhaps utilize the energy of desire and goal directness of the apparently separated knower and wanter. We ordinarily think of freedom as being able to do what we want to do following our desires and goals. But meditators being to see that their goals and sense of choice are determined by habits, conditioning, and circumstances and are anything but free. With great delight people report an occasional experience of what feels like real freedom – precisely when they have done what they describe as letting go of desires, goal directedness and choice.

But without desires and goals, how can there by action? Would one lie in bed unable to get up, even for growing physical necessities? Would one randomly and affectlessly murder respectable people? These are our fantasies about freedom. What meditators, artists (and many ordinary people) say is that it is precisely when they are, even very briefly, without the usual sense of goal directedness that they can act spontaneously in ways appropriate to the situation at hand. For example, it is well documented that people who act heroically in times of emergency (plunge into icy water to save a drowning child and so on) often report that they did not think, decide, or choose but simply did it. Furthermore, such actions may involve skills which the rescuer says he did not know he possessed. Action is not necessarily what we assume it is.

Interpersonal relations. From the point of view of the limited, dualistic, samsaric information processor, relating with other people is a dismal business, which, just like relations with the rest of nature, can only consist (with varying degrees of refinement) of separation,

19

ignorance, aggression, and greed. Meditators say that meditation affects their view of interpersonal relationships. Glimpses of a state in which there is neither separation of the knower nor desire for future goals also reveals the possibility of an open and receptive relationship to people beyond the manipulative streetfighter mentality. I have never spoken with a meditator who was pleased with his progress (an important caveat) who did not mention something about feeling more at ease, more understanding, or more kindness towards other people. Many, including the dissatisfied, have experienced glimpses described as non-separateness, open heartedness, or compassion. A few individuals appear to undergo a marked change in their orientation to people.

D. A New Mode of Knowing and Being

Some meditators in all traditions find or glimpse a truly new mode of knowing and being. They variously attribute their ability to do this to factors such as perseverance, relaxation, or special attunement to realized teachers (or deities). The glimpse is generally described, not as a new experience, but as a finding, or tapping into, a mode of knowing and being which was there all along within ordinary experience but which they had hitherto ignored.[15] These glimpses, they often say, are what keep them going. Various characteristics (or noncharacteristics) are ascribed to this mode of knowing and being:

1. It is not a subject/object form of knowing, not located in a knowing subject who knows objects. There is just the knowing; experiences are 'self known.'
2. There is no desire in it, no reaching beyond the experience itself. It is contented, relaxed, adequate, doesn't care about the concerns of passion and aggression.
3. It has a spacelike or spacious aspect. This experience can be evoked by experiences of ordinary space. (Perhaps that is why humans are so enamored of views and sweeping vistas.)
4. It is nontemporal, not located in time, not localizable in the past, future, or even present, timeless. (For this nontemporality, *some* traditions use the word *permanent*.)
5. It has no limits or boundaries. It is not a limited capacity system; capacity is not a relevant descriptive dimension.
6. It is not graspable, describable, conceptualizable, formulatable or modelable; it is a nonconceptual knowing. It is said to be beyond

words, beyond concepts, and not an object of the conceptual mind. It is violated somewhat by any description of it including all that is said here.

(It should be noted that the Buddhist term *emptiness* can be, and has been, used with respect to any or all of these first six aspects.)

7. It accommodates/includes/accepts everything, all content, unconditionally.

8. It is of supreme value, worth everything. When meditators speak of their actual experience, this is the most important aspect, the *sine qua non*, the reason why anyone would want to bother with boring meditations, arcane retreats, humbling mindfulness, frustrating spiritual groups, or cantankerous gurus in the first place. Our culture and our psychology separate the knowing dimension from the value/emotive dimension[16] as I have been doing hitherto in this chapter. But the experience here is that at the very basis of experience, the two are not separate.

9. Knowledge of the ordinary subject/object, space/time limited world can be from this broader, unlimited, accommodating, unconditionally valued perspective. The more limited known world is seen as not separate from the broader view. This can be expressed as a new epistemological vision of the origin of experience – that relative experience is born afresh each instant out of the ground of this nonconceptual, primordial knowing. Or it can be expressed as an ontological statement – that nothing is ever born or separated from that ground when viewed from the perspective of the broader experience of totality. But perhaps foremost it is a very personal, transformative, deeply therapeutic vision of the inherent value of the world and of experience.

10. When actions 'come from' this mode of knowing and being, they happen with felt spontaneity, and turn out to be situationally appropriate, of benefit to others, and sometimes shockingly skillful. This is perhaps the state which is called *nonaction*.

E. Integration and Wholeness

In the final vision, all of the aspects of experience which we have treated as separate are seen to form an integrated whole. Cognition is not separate from emotion. Mind and body are not separate. The perceiver is not separate from the perception. Action is not separate from knowing in its broadest sense. Time is not separate from the timeless, desires, from the desireless, nor emotions from the sense of unconditional accommodation. The self is not separate from the rest of the world, from others, or from inherent value. Fundamental value is not separate from knowing, from emotion, from anything. And this very vision of integration is not separate from the fragmented world which does not see but does need it.

This is finally the vision of Shalipa who came to see all sound as not separate from the howling of wolves, the hearer and fearer of the howling of wolves as not separate from the sound, and the sounds and their fearer as not separate from the limitless, timeless, spacious, ungraspable, unconditionally valued mode of knowing and being which the meditative traditions claim is the heritage of all people.

III.   IMPLICATIONS FOR PSYCHOLOGY

There are two kinds of implications for psychology. For psychology as it is presently constituted, a few specific suggestions come to mind which might affect various content areas. The more general implication, however, concerns the building of a new psychology from the point of view of the meditative mode of knowing and being. Let us begin with the specific suggestions.

Attention. What is even more remarkable than that the contents of mind are continually shifting is how little interest researchers in attention have shown in this phenomenon. William James[17] speculated about the stream of consciousness at the turn of the century, and the portrayal of stream of consciousness has had various literary vogues, but experimental psychology has remained mute on this point, the very building block of phenomenological awareness.

Psychology has been likewise mute about the training of attention – other than to classify some extreme problems as attention deficit disorders for which drugs are prescribed. Meditators who have actually succeeded in some form of attention training and stabilization report benefits in other aspects of their lives such as work and school. It is interesting that we have no methods for training attention and do not teach such matters in school despite the great prevalence of attention problems among students at all levels.

The indirect or *post hoc* quality of attention has not gone totally unnoticed by western psychology. A classical debate exists between the bottom up and top down approaches to processing models with top down models emphasizing the role that concepts, memory, theories, goals, and intentions play in determining attention and perception. In the present era of computer modeling, top down theorizing has gained ascendancy, and it is often asserted that perception is inherently abstract and theory laden. What both approaches miss is the distinction between the usual indirect, conceptualized state of mind and a mind directly present with its perceptions and thoughts.

Finally, while the relaxation industry has some awareness that changes in attention can lead to relaxation, there is little popular exploration of the idea that the training and then letting go of attention can lead to wisdom.

Emotion. Since the Greeks, western psychology has treated affect and cognition as separate faculties, states, or processes, and through history cognition has been valued more positively than affect. Emotion tends to be seen as irrational and reason as affectless. The meditation traditions offer a direct challenge to this model. In the first place affect and cognition are not separate. It takes only a little mindfulness to realize that emotive tone, a feeling quality, is universal in experience.

Emotion is an area in which interesting congruences exist between reports of meditators and some laboratory experimental work. Contrary to folk psychology, both meditators and laboratory studies show that emotions occur in momentary bursts rather than in continuous sequences[18] and that actual affect is quickly replaced in memory by conceptual summaries[19]. A number of other interesting parallels are outlined by Pickering[20]. The meditator's discovery that for the samsaric mind, emotions are the monitoring of how well the self is doing in relation to its desires and goals in the world is strongly reminiscent of a number of self monitoring and appraisal accounts of emotion[21]. What the psychological paradigms lack, however, and could well use, is the account contributed by the meditative traditions of how people can go beyond the self monitoring and appraisal mode of feeling and acting to tap into their more integrated 'wisdom' mode.

The body. The body could be a fertile ground for interaction between meditative and scientific approaches. Practical interest in the relationship between body and mind is growing in the west – as witnessed by numerous new body oriented psychotherapies[22], by programs in somatic psychology which are appearing on college campuses, and by private and government funding of research on eastern medical systems. At this time, actual research tends to be still largely oriented toward proving whether particular nonwestern treatments cure particular diseases. At some point, researchers will need to address a potential revolution in our understanding of the body: what new view of psychology and physiology might we need that can encompass phenomena such as space, energy, channels, chi, and chakras as well as the phenomena of western medicine?

The self. Many aspects of the analysis of the self in the meditative traditions could provide grist for western psychology[23]. Researchers on the self might well notice that their subjects think, feel, and act as though they, personally, are dealing with a real and supremely important self and not merely with a hierarchy of concepts. The interdependence of the so-called self with the rest of the world is addressed most explicitly in psychology by the use of dynamical systems theory modeling[24], but this global system is not of use for most issues and needs to be augmented.

In regard to the self's relation to *other people*, given the current interest in altruism research in psychology, not to mention the state of the world, any leads which the meditative traditions can provide concerning the transformation of an attitude of passion, aggression, and ignoring into an attitude of compassion are surely not to be neglected. Likewise, the world is certainly in need of spontaneous, surprisingly skillful *actions*, and research on spontaneous actions (as in 'impossibly' well handled emergencies) is surely to be supported.

In our culture, societal problems are dealt with by governments, medical problems by doctors, psychological problems by clinicians, and questions about perception, bodily processes, and emotions by the burgeoning technical experimental literature modeled after the physical sciences. The Shalipa story shows how, from the point of view of one meditative tradition, all of these issues are dealt with in an integrated fashion based on experience. Virtually any aspect of the meditative path by which the separated and needy information processor is transformed into the integrated knower with which we ended our account should be of great interest to clinical psychology. Such work is beginning[25] but rather tentatively, with the tendency to keep western clinical models relatively intact (but see Henderson[26]; Pransky & Mills[27])[28]. It should be obvious that from the point of view of the meditative traditions in their original context, (from the point of view, let us say, of Shalipa after he attained realization), what passes for clinical practice in the west is little more than rearranging the deck chairs on the Titanic. Which is to say that the contact between our clinical theories and the meditative traditions has far reaching, as yet undeveloped, potential.

All this said, what psychology may really need is a major paradigm shift to take into account the broader portrait of what a human being is and can do provided by the meditative traditions. The only way to do this is to rely on the authority of individual experience; quibbling about established usages and the so-called canons of science at this point is simply blindness. Perhaps such a shift requires a body of psychologists who have personal experience themselves of that broader mode of knowing and being; perhaps it is such a community which will eventually rewrite psychology.

Actually coming to see and realize any of the aspects of that new mode of knowing and being is immensely transformative to individuals personally. Hopefully, it can likewise be transformative to our science.

NOTES

1 Portions of this chapter have been previously published in Rosch, E. (in press a). Mindfulness meditation and the private(?) self. In U. Neisser & D. Jopling (Eds.) *Culture, experience, and the conceptual self.* Cambridge, Eng.: Cambridge University Press; and Rosch, E. (in press b). Portraits of the mind in cognitive science and meditation. In S.S. Bahulkar & N. Samten (Eds.) *The doctrine of universal responsibility: A festshrift for H.H. the Dalai Lama.* Varanasi, India: Inst. of Higher Tibetan Studies.

2 This version of the Shalipa story is from an oral account by the late Jamgon Kongtrul. Variant written version can be found in Dowman, K. (1985). *Masters of mahamudra.* Albany, N.Y.: State University of New York Press; and Robinson, J.B. (1979). *Buddha's lions: The lives of the eighty-four siddhas.* Berkeley, CA: Dharma Publishing

3 Anderson, J.R. (1980). *Cognitive psychology and its implications.* San Franciso: W.H. Freeman & Co.
Lindsay, P.H. & Norman, D.A. (1977). *Human information processing: An introduction to psychology (2nd ed.).* New York: Academic Press.
Matlin, M. (1994). *Cognition* (3rd Edition). Fort Worth: Harcourt Brace.

4 Fishurn, P. (1970). *Utility theory for decision making.* New York: Wiley
Sen, A. (1987). *On ethics and economics.* Oxford: Basil Blackwell

5 Dreyfus, H.L. (Ed.) (1982). *Husserl: Intentionality and cognitive science.* Cambridge, Mass.: MIT Press/Bradford Books.

6 Rosch, E. (1987). Wittgenstein and categorization research in cognitive psychology. In M. Chapman & R. Dixon (Eds.) *Meaning and the growth of understanding: Wittgenstein's significance for developmental psychology.* Hillsdale, N.J.: Erlbaum.

7 Turkle, S. (1988). Artificial intelligence and psychoanalysis: A new alliance. *Daedalus* (Winter): 241–268.

8 Hardin, G. (1968). The tragedy of the commons. *Science*, **162**, 1243–1248.

9 For examples see: Goldstein, J. & Kornfield, J. (1987). *Seeking the heart of wisdom*. Boston: Shambhala; Kabat-Zinn, J. (1990). *Full catastrophe living: Using the wisdom of your body and mind to face stress*. New York: Delacorte; Nhat Hahn, T. (1975). *Miracle of mindfulness: A manual on meditation*. Boston: Beacon Press; Trungpa, C. (1976). *Myth of freedom*. Boston: Shambhala.

10 See for example Ralston, P. (1989). *Cheng hsin: The principles of effortless power*. Berkeley, CA.: North Atlantic Books.

11 James, W. (1890 reprinted 1950). *Principles of psychology*. New York: Dover

12 Belyea, C. & Tainer, S. (1991). *Dragon's play*. Berkeley, CA.: Great Circle Books, p.11.

13 Tulku, T. (1977). *Time, space, and knowledge*. Berkeley, CA.: Dharma Publishing

14 See for example Chia, M. & Chia, M. (1993). *Awaken healing light of the tao*. Huntington, N.Y.: Healing Tao Books.

15 Note how different this description is from from the model of meditative 'achievement' as an advanced developmental stage, as suggested, for example, in Wilber, K., Engler, J. and Brown, D. (1987) *Transformations of Consciousness: Conventional and Contemplative Perspectives on Development*. New Science Library.

16 For a review see Donaldson, M. (1992). *Human minds: An exploration*. New York: The Penguin Press.

17 op.cit James, 1890.

18 Ekman, P., Levenson, R.W., & Friesen, W.V. (1983). Autonomic nervous system activity distinguishes among emotions. *Science*, 221, 1208–1210.

19 Fredrickson, B.L. & Kahneman, D. (1993). Duration neglect in retrospective evaluations of affective episodes. *Journal of Personality and Social Psychology* 65,45–55.

20 Pickering, J. (1995). Buddhism and cognitivism: A postmodern appraisal. *Asian Philosophy*, 5, 23–38.

21 Frijda, N.H. (1986). *The emotions*. Camblidge, Eng: Cambridge University Press; Lazarus, R.S. (1991). *Emotion and adaptation*. New York: Oxford University Press; Scherer, K.R. & Ekman, P. (Eds.) (1984). *Approaches to emotion*. Hillsdale, N.J.: Erlbaum

22 For example Mindell, A. (1982). *Dreambody: The body's role in revealing the self*. Santa Monica, CA.: Sigo Press.

23 See for example Varela, F., Thompson, E. & Rosch, E. (1991). *The embodied mind: Cognitive science and human experience*. Cambridge, MA: MIT Press.

24 See Thelen, E. & Smith, L.B. (Eds.) (1993). *A dynamic systems approach to development: Applications*. Cambridge, MA: MIT Press/Bradford Books; Thelen, E. & Smith, L.B. (1994). *A dynamic systems approach to the development of cognition and action*. Cambridge, MA: MIT Press/Bradford Books.

25 See for example Epstein, M. (1995). *Thoughts without a thinker*. New York: Basic Books; Kabat-Zinn, J. (1990). *Full catastrophe living: Using the wisdom of your body and mind to face stress*. New York: Delacorte; Kornfield, J. (1993). *A path with heart*. New York: Bantam Books.

26 Henderson, J. (1986). *The lover within*. Barrytown, N.Y.: Station Hill Press.

27 Pransky, G.S. & Mills, R.C. (1995). *Psychology of mind: The basis for health realization: The founders' monograph*. La Conner, WA: The Psychology of Mind Training Institute.

28 Henderson (1986) offers an energy based account of psychological functioning. Pransky & Mill (1995) trace the development of a remarkable new indigenous western clinical psychology called Psychology of Mind (POM). Based on the insights of its founders concerning the psychology of well functioning people, it (at least appears) to replicate many of the insights offered by the meditative traditions outlined in this chaper.

Chapter 2

EDITOR'S PREFACE

A distinction is often made by those wanting to keep science and religion apart. This is that religions hold to timeless, transcendental views of the world while science, by sharp and important contrast, is open to fundamental change as new observations and theories arise. Here, David Fontana evades this distinction completely. He opens his chapter by pointing out that at the heart of Buddhist teachings and practice lies *annicca*, impermanence. This applies to the objects and events of the world, to states of mind, to selfhood and to Buddhism itself. Whatever has persisted from the time of the original Buddha figure to the present, it is not a uniform, self-identical set of teachings, practices or views. How then has this body of human practice managed to survive and to have such influence in human affairs?

David Fontana's answer, going directly to the central issue of this book, is that Buddhism has endured, and hence acquired its authority, because its teachings rest on common human experience rather than on intellectualised and arcane knowledge. In Western accounts of Buddhism, there is often an exaggeration of mystical and transcendental states. The more practical meaning of such states is as goals or ideals of knowledge. These encourage us to attend to our minds and how they work, as an empirical psychological project. The experience of exceptional states of consciousness may be very rare, but their significance is that they have led people down the ages to make the effort to investigate their own minds and hence to manage them more skilfully.

This effort is personal, and the responsibility for making it lies with the individual. Buddhist teachings emphasise the observation of what actually happens in the mind rather than reading books or listening to teachers. David Fontana points out that as exploration begins, unexpected discoveries can be made. For example, the claim that 'normal thought is out of control' sounds very odd to most Westerners. We imagine the individual as a centre of rational agency and responsibility. In fact, this discovery is one of the most immediate, disturbing but in the end productive results of meditative practice. It is a result of the sensory barrage that intrudes into our minds from the very earliest stages of human existence. Words, images, sounds and myriad sensations drive the mind this way and that. More than at any previous times, political and economic forces shape our sensory surroundings expressly to create desires and intentions. This makes it difficult for human beings to discover a state of quiet autonomy in which they can discover feelings and goals which are truly their own.

This discovery is the empirical project of Buddhism. David Fontana presents the methods of Buddhism as a way to quieten the confusion and tumult of the mind. This after all, is not the mind's nature. The ever-flowing stream of thoughts, feelings and intentions are an acquisition. The mind's essence though formless and empty, is nonetheless sensitive. It is the discovery of this sensitivity, known as Buddha-nature in many traditions, to which many meditative practices are directed. The goal being to go beyond forms and movements that have been impressed on the mind. It is thus a psychological project to disclose the capacity for non-discriminative awareness that forms the core of our mental life. This is hidden under layer upon layer of structures and processes that naturally gather to the sensitive core as we live and experience the complex and intrusive conditions of collective living.

There is a productive complementarity here with Western psychology. Cognitive science, for example, also claims as its project the discovery of hidden structure in the mind. Theories of memory, perception and language are often framed as mechanisms. These cannot be directly seen, as one might expose the workings of clock for example, but are assumed to be functionally 'there' in the brain. Experiments and computer models are then designed to compare theories and to gradually reveal the hidden structure of the mind.

Buddhism too is concerned with structure, and seeks to reveal what is hidden. However, the structure is what does the hiding. What is hidden is the sensitive core whose nature can be known through experience. This experience has a direct effect on the behaviour of those who achieve it. Satori is the name given in Zen traditions to the direct encounter with the core of mental life.

David Fontana discusses here two aspects of authenticity that arise from satori. One is the experience itself which is recognised by the individual. The other is the change that this produces in the individual. This is recognised by others. The authority of teachers lies in the encounter with them. Individuals who, as a result of their practice, live more skillfully and insightfully are thereby authoritative. This authority lies in their capacity to help, which often arises naturally in any encounter they have with others. The authority of someone who knows a great deal is rather different. What they know may be extremely powerful and tell us a great deal about the external conditions of the mind. However, it may or may not be of use to others. This is part of the difference between knowledge and wisdom traditions.

David Fontana finishes his chapter with a discussion of therapy, to which the notion of helping is central. The question might be asked of scientific psychology, although it seldom is: 'what help is it?' One answer might be that it is not intended to help with anything but to investigate how the mind works, as a natural object. If reliable, this understanding will be helpful in much the same way that, for instance, biological knowledge has proved helpful. Therapy, by contrast, is specifically directed at helping and is therefore a different practice.

There is less of a contrast here than may appear at first sight. The essence of Buddhist practices is indeed said to be that they are helpful. But the help also comes from investigating the mind as a natural object. To discover how it works and how it can be made to work more effectively is the point. Hence, now that consciousness itself has returned as an objective of scientific psychology, the integration of scientific psychology and Buddhist practices may no longer be the contradiction in terms that it might have appeared a few decades ago. Accordingly, those teaching and learning the discipline may now seek to bring together both knowledge and wisdom traditions. David Fontana's chapter not only helps to create a discipline that addresses the facts of mental life but also points to the use that may be made of it in living more skilfully and effectively.

★　★　★

Authority in Buddhism and in Western Scientific Psychology

David Fontana

AUTHORITY IN BUDDHISM

One of the central tenets of Buddhism is that all created things are impermanent. Thus Buddhism, being a set of created teachings, is by its own definition impermanent (as opposed to the Buddha mind itself, discussed more fully later in the chapter, which is beyond such restrictions). Thus authenticity in Buddhism cannot be represented by a static tradition, taken over ready-made from others, and applied as a doctrine or dogma. Indeed, the Buddha's dying words referred to the necessity for each person to work on his or her own salvation. There is, in effect, no authenticity for the individual in Buddhism unless it has been verified in the light of personal experience.

This aspect of Buddhism is at once intensely liberating – take nothing on trust, subject everything to the illumination of personal experience – and intensely unsettling. If there is no undying set of rules (whether of conduct or of material science), no tablets of stone, where does one look for authority, for the voice of the master who, like someone who has already read the script, knows the ending of the drama in which we are the struggling and suffering players? As in Krishnamurti's austere teachings[1], it may seem to many that in Buddhism truth is a pathless land, in which each of us must ultimately find our own way.

In part, the Buddha's teaching was aimed at highlighting the inadequacy of language. There are certain things that cannot be said but that must be experienced because, in a very real sense, their nature *is* experience (a conclusion reached, albeit from a rather different route, by Wittgenstein). To accept the dogma of others on trust is like believing one knows the wind without feeling it on one's face. In the *Prajnaparamita*[2], one of the highest expressions of Buddhist philosophy,

31

it is stated that 'one cannot apprehend perfect wisdom', and that when one practises the six perfections (i.e. when one works at apprehending the intrinsic emptiness of data yielded by the five senses and by consciousness – of which more later) one 'should not take anything as a basis'.

The extraordinary thing, however, is that in spite of the clarity of this teaching, the Buddhist canon extends to a vast array of sutras, many times more extensive than the Christian bible, and many of them (apart from the original Pali Canon) still available only in Chinese or Tibetan. Much of this literature lays down very detailed rules of conduct, and expounds specific psycho-philosophical inter-pretations of existence, consciousness, karma, re-birth, and spiritual principles. Even Soto Zen, one of the most iconoclastic of the great Buddhist traditions, lists no less than 62 precise rules which monks should observe when in the presence of their seniors.

These rules are in part a reflection of those Asian cultures that regard the master-pupil relationship as containing a special sacredness in that the master, out of his compassion, becomes responsible for the karma of the pupil, and in return is accorded absolute obedience. An understanding of the cultural-embeddedness of the master-pupil relationship, as of so many other aspects of the teachings, is essential before we can even begin to grasp the meaning of authority within the Buddhist context.

There may be a certain parallel here with the master-pupil relationship at postgraduate level in Western scientific psychology, in that the postgraduate works with a supervisor who in a sense takes on his academic karma (i.e. responsibility for the consequences arising from his work). In return, the student is expected to follow the rules of thought laid down by the supervisor. However, the parallel is a superficial one. In Buddhism, the emphasis is upon furthering the pupil's own development; in Western psychology it is upon furthering the development of psychology as a scientific discipline. In Buddhism, the master is a master by virtue of what he is. In Western psychology, the supervisor is a supervisor by virtue of what he knows.

THE APPARENT PARADOX OF BUDDHISM

Without a deep understanding of the master-pupil relationship, Buddhism presents to the Westerner the paradox of a system that eschews absolute authority, yet which behaves with authority, that rejects dogma yet is replete with dogma. *With* such an understanding, we recognize that unlike the Western psychology student, the Buddhist is taught an activity of mind which allows him, at a certain point in his development, to test the teachings of the master against his own inner experience. The mind of the master and of the pupil are in essence one and the same. What the pupil finds within himself is neither more nor less than what the master found within his own mind at the same stage of the journey.

An early feature of this activity of mind is that it allows the student to see beyond the rigid 'either-or' categorisation that is such a feature of Western thinking, and to recognise a more flexible (and mystical) 'both-and'. This 'both-and' arises from an appreciation that there are in fact no ultimate opposites (and therefore no such thing as ultimate independent existence) in nature. Definition and function are meaningless when taken in isolation. An example often given in Buddhism is the cup. A cup combines form (the outside) and space or emptiness (the inside). Without both form and emptiness there would be no cup. Further, without form we would have no concept of emptiness, and without emptiness, we would have no concept of form. Form and emptiness therefore have no practical or conceptual existence apart from each other.

As with so many features of Buddhist authority, one does not have to take this on trust. The truth of the matter becomes self-evident as soon as one looks in the right direction. In the light of this ultimate absence of independent existence, the pupil is urged to meditate upon *sunyatta*, the infinite, attribute-free potential from which all created things emerge, and to which all created things return. Again, *sunyatta* does not have to be taken on trust. The method of meditation is described to the pupil, and he is then able to look into the matter for himself, reflecting upon and observing the arising and passing away of phenomena, ideas and emotions in a constant flow of inter-connected states of being.

As an aside, it is worth saying that if the present concern was with Buddhism and physics rather than with Buddhism and psychology, we could at this point pursue the analogy between the concept of *sunyatta* and some of the contentions of quantum theory. In view of the methodological differences between Buddhism and modern physics it would be unwise to press this analogy too far, but it has been explored at some length in popular books by Capra[3] and Zukav[4], and is implicit in certain conclusions to be drawn from more serious studies such as those associated with Bohm's theory of the implicate and the explicate order[5].

David Fontana

THE 'ABSENCE OF BASIS'

The illusory nature of opposites is stressed in the *Prajnaparamita*, which tells us to practise the six perfections with an *absence of basis*. 'Where there is duality' (i.e. the opposites) 'there is a basis, where there is non-duality there is lack of basis'. Dualistic thinking splinters reality into mutually opposing fragments, a habit of thinking which prevents us from recognising not only that phenomena, but the mind itself which registers these phenomena and is therefore in a sense their creator, are also non-dual. Recognition of this non-duality prevents us from playing the same trick with our inner experience as we do with our perceptions of the outer world, and becoming caught in the illusory opposites of attachment to the things we find pleasant, and aversion towards the things we dislike. Attachment and aversion (or in stronger terms greed and hatred) are the main bulwarks of that other illusion, that the 'self' exists independently of the rest of creation.

This recognition of our embededness in creation is in marked contrast to the individuality which is such a feature not just of Western psychology but of Western thinking and social action in general. It brings with it a range of important consequences, from selflessness and a concern for the environment and other living creatures to a deeper understanding of our own essential nature.

The recognition by Buddhism of an absence of opposites means that in its theory and practice there is an absence of the oppositional thinking that marks the differences between the various schools of Western psychology (and Western religion). In consequence, no Buddhist school claims its authority is absolute over that of any other school (or indeed necessarily over any other spiritual tradition), or that it provides the only path to enlightenment. The authority of each school lies not in its claim to a monopoly of the truth, but in its recognition of the fact that if you wish to follow any particular Buddhist path, then success depends upon your doing so in the most effective way.

This necessarily means the way developed over the centuries by the masters and patriarchs who have preceded you on that path. Thus although the pupil submits voluntarily to the path, while he or she is on it they are expected to obey strictly its rules. Should they find the rules too arduous, they are free to leave the path in favour of another. The differences between the path are dictated more by the varying needs and propensities manifested by people *when they begin their practice* than by doctrinal dissimilarities particular to the paths themselves. Thus those who are drawn towards devotion and what appears at first sight to be 'other power' may wish to practise Pure Land Buddhism and dedicate themselves to meditating upon Amitabha and repeating his mantra, while those drawn towards what appears at first sight to be 'self power' may be attracted to Zen Buddhism and the use of koan or silent illumination meditation.

When the practitioner sees beyond the opposites, there is of course no difference between 'other power' and 'self power', and the same teacher (as in the case of many Chinese Ch-an – Chinese Zen – masters) may happily teach both Pure Land and Zen, dependent upon the temperament of his pupils. Can one readily imagine the Western psychology professor teaching both psychodynamics and behaviourism, dependent upon the temperament of his students? Similarly, the Buddhist teacher may advise his pupil to seek a master within another Buddhist tradition whose teaching may be more in tune with his present needs. Again the contrast with Western psychology is all too apparent. Ultimately, in Buddhism everything is done in the service of the pupil and of his journey towards enlightenment, rather than in the service of the subject or some outside authority who has to be pleased and placated.

RECONCILING BUDDHISM AND WESTERN PSYCHOLOGY

It is not easy to see how the authority of Buddhism's 'lack of basis' can be reconciled with the authority of Western psychology's supposedly objective science. The latter authority is culturally grounded in a belief-system that there are certain absolute 'laws' which govern reality, and which are in some sense 'out there', replete and self-contained, and awaiting discovery like lost coins in a muddy street. As an extension to this belief-system, there is the notion, claimed by Armstrong[6] to be 'steadily gaining ground', that 'we can give a complete account of man in *purely physico-chemical terms*'. This means that each mental event is seen as 'identical to, not merely correlated with, some physical state'[7], and is therefore as ultimately lawful and explicable as are all other materialistic processes.

The personalised nature of the process in which the pupil, under the guidance of the Buddhist master, is engaged also contrasts importantly with the modernist, reductionist methodology with which the Western psychology student has characteristically to work. Such a methodology, which can be traced through Comte, Mach, Helmholtz and others, strives to be objective, detached, and abstract (and often manipulative and adversarial in consequence). Typically it holds reality to be aloof from socio-cultural constructs, and separates the researcher and the researched in a way that flies in the face of actual human experience.

The postmodernist approach, which is skeptical towards universal claims regarding existence, and which finds space for plurality and the play of differences[8], is closer to Buddhism, but lacks both its universal goal-directedness (enlightenment, Nirvana, the discovery of one's own true nature), and the subtle authority that arises from the pupil's conviction that the master has had direct experience of the vicissitudes with which he or she is faced. Even in its postmodern thinking, there is an absence in Western psychology of that balance we find in Buddhism between inner and outer. The Buddhist looks inwards in order to look outwards, in contrast to Western psychology which looks outwards to look – if at all – inwards.

As that peerless interpreter of Buddhism for the Western mind D. T. Suzuki points out[9], the reason Western science loses the balance between inner and outer is that it regards the former (which Suzuki refers to as 'the world of spirit') as less real than the latter ('the world of the sense-intellect'). In fact, as Suzuki makes clear, we should recognise that the former world is directly revealed to the mind, whereas the latter world is a reconstruction by the mind. 'The two worlds ... are ... two phases of one world ... and it is only by not understanding the fact of one world that ... (we) ... foolishly believe there are two'. Both phases derive their reality 'only in connection with a greater reality' that lies behind them, and neither should be accorded more status than the other.

Indeed, both are representations arising from the action of our skandhas (senses). And unlike Western science, Buddhism regards mental cognition (consciousness) as a skandha like any other, and no higher in value than the five recognised senses of seeing, hearing, smelling, tasting and touching. All six skandas are simply mechanisms for presenting stimuli to the human mind, and allowing it to form representations of phenomena. In fact consciousness, for all its importance, can often come between us and a more immediate representation of outer reality by virtue of our ingrained tendency to attach concepts to all sense experience. In seeing, Buddhism tells us, there should be only the seeing, in hearing only the hearing, and so on. Like a child, we should engage directly with the data yielded by our senses (as perhaps we do when hearing great music or viewing great art), instead of losing ourselves in interpretation, definition, and categorisation,

It is this tendency towards interpretation, definition and categorisation that leads Western science to impose an artificial fragmentation upon experience, instead of allowing it to speak for itself. There is nothing anti-intellectual in allowing it to speak for itself. For just as we should be focused and concentrated upon the experiences that arise through the five recognised sense, so should we be upon the sixth, thinking. Normally thought is out of control, and we live within a clouded consciousness that not only prevents us from seeing what is going on within our own minds, but which is grossly inefficient in its operation. Just as in the seeing there should be only the seeing, so in the thinking there should be only the thinking.

THE BUDDHIST MODEL OF MIND

An understanding of this last point is essential if we are to grasp anything of the Buddhist model of the mind. For although Buddhism, like Western scientific psychology, is concerned with the mental representations of sense data, it differs from Western psychology in that it recognizes a state beyond these representations and the six skandhas upon which they are based. We are urged constantly to 'look into' this state. Referred to as the Buddha mind, it is sometimes characterised as pure awareness, as *mind-as-such*, as *no-mind*, and as *primordial mind*. It is the mind that is prior to both the subject or the object of experience, and prior to the arising of thought. It is the mind that cannot be comprehended by mundane concepts as it has no location within space or within the lexicon of thinking. Like the perfect wisdom of which it is an expression, the Buddha mind cannot be reduced to language. The Buddha spoke of it in the Lankavatara Sutra as 'unborn, unqualified, and devoid of will-effort', and stressed he only spoke of it at all in order 'to make the ignorant cast aside their fear when they listen to the teaching of egolessness, and have them realise the state of non-discrimination and imagelessness'[10].

Faced with the difficulty of defining the Buddha mind, Buddhist teachers sometimes resort to analogy. Zen Buddhism refers to it as the circle whose centre is nowhere, and whose circumference is everywhere. The analogy of a mirror is also sometimes used. A mirror reflects whatever is placed in front of it, yet does not contain the images thus formed, still less *is it* these images. In the case of the Buddha mind, sense data and thoughts are analogous to the images, and the mind itself analogous to the mirror. Sense impressions and thoughts make their impressions upon the mind as images do in the mirror, but the mind is no more these impressions than the mirror is its reflections.

The aim of Buddhist practise is to prevent the Buddha mind from being obscured by the transitory images and impressions that pass constantly in and out of awareness. Only in this way can the Buddha mind be experienced in its 'unborn, unqualified' essence.

BUDDHISM AND BEHAVIOUR

And yet there are certain dangers in over-emphasising the differences between authority in Buddhism and authority in Western scientific psychology. To do so would be to fall into the very dualistic error against which Buddhism so comprehensively warns. For in the final analysis both Buddhism and Western psychology are products of the human mind, and thus both are expressions of the effort after meaning and explanation which is such a feature of mental functioning. The one is the result of the mind turning inwards, the other the result of its turning outwards, but as Buddhism again stresses, there is ultimately no difference between inner and outer, as both arise from Sunyatta, the underlying emptiness. Buddhism teaches that even Nirvana (ultimate reality) and Samsara (relative reality) are not opposites but two aspects of the same thing, and therefore in essence one.

Is there any way in which Western psychology can engage with such an apparently abstract concept as the Buddha mind – or grapple with the collapse of the distinction between inner and outer reality? The most obvious approach is to observe what effect certain states of mind appear to have upon action. Specifically, we can make comparisons not only between the serious Buddhist practitioner and the non-Buddhist practitioner, but between the Buddhist practitioner before and after particular inner experiences such as the mind state known as satori.

The experience of satori, if it can usefully be spoken about at all, lies beyond discrimination and differentiation. It is a state in which the individual experiences (as opposed simply to knowing about) non-duality, and the ultimate unity which underlies and includes all things. In satori, reality is experienced through the unsullied Buddha mind. Satori may vary in quality and duration from the merest glimpse to a long and seemingly timeless interlude. Although basically incommunicable, it is a state that is unmistakable both to the individual him or herself, and to the teacher, who it is said (in Zen Buddhism in particular) can authenticate it simply by observing the changes that come about in the individual concerned.

Such experiences (and indeed those that take place at a much less exalted level of Buddhist theory and practice) have in fact a profound effect upon how men and women live their lives. Impressive examples exist throughout the literature (as they do in the literature of the other great spiritual traditions), but the most notable is probably that of the Buddha himself, who left a young wife and child and a princely life, who subjected himself over a long period to the most self-punitive austerities, and who, after the achievement of enlightenment, trod the dusty roads of Asia for over 40 years in order to lead others out of the path of suffering. Our admiration for the Buddha and for those great teachers and practitioners who have come after him may in part be based upon value judgments of what it means to be a whole or a self-transcendent or an enlightened (whatever term we choose to use) individual, but there is no denying the transformation in behaviour wrought by the inner experiences these men and women have undergone.

The example could be extended to cover whole cultures. Before the Tibetans adopted Buddhism fully between AD 650 and 900, the country was feudal, and riven by incessant internal quarreling and conflicts. Buddhism brought a completely new dimension into the social structure, the art and the philosophy of the country, inaugurating an unprecedented period of peace and harmony which was only brought to an end by the Chinese invasion of 1950, and the excesses of the so-called cultural revolution during the years 1966-1976.

There may have been other factors behind the extraordinary cultural metamorphoses that took place in Tibet after the coming of Buddhism, but the depth and intensity with which Buddhism entered into the Tibetan psyche, penetrating every aspect of life for a thousand years, leaves us in little doubt that it provided by far the most important element. Whether its wide-ranging socio-cultural effects were the result of a critical percentage of highly developed spiritual men and women at work in the community, or whether they came about because of less exalted but more ubiquitous levels of development within the population as a whole is unclear.

Once these effects upon behaviour are recognised, two questions arise, firstly what stimuli or intervening cognitive processes produce transformations of this kind? And secondly, how can a scientific appraisal of these transformations be attempted without acknowledging the presence of inner as well as outer precipitating factors, particularly when the latter – even if identifiable – carry nothing like the potency necessary to produce the effects concerned? And how can we explain the persistence of these effects throughout the years of the Buddha's solitary practices in the forest, or throughout one thousand years of Tibetan history?

If Western psychology is really concerned with (among other things) a science of behaviour and experience, then it must identify the precise precipitating processes that lead to the profound transformations that take place, not just in the Buddha – it would be difficult to dig back through the intervening 2,500 years – but in others who experience satori. If one wanted to press the matter further, one would have to ask whether (in theory at least), post-satori behaviour can be induced through the manipulation of laboratory variables or not? We must remind ourselves of the statement by Armstrong[11], quoted above, to the effect that 'we can give a complete account of man in *purely physico-chemical terms*', and that in consequence each mental event is seen as 'identical to, not merely correlated with, some physical state'[12], and thus as ultimately as lawful and as explicable as are all other materialistic processes.

NON-REFERENTIAL AWARENESS

If Armstrong and Boyd and others of similar mind are correct, Western scientific psychology can therefore hardly be excused from explaining – or better still mimicking – satori-like experiences through behavioural or other models. At the very least, the challenge is one that should excite and stimulate Western science. It would of course be insufficient for Western psychology to claim that the antecedent circumstances of satori are inaccessible because they have to do with *non-referential awareness*, i.e. with levels of mind below the threshold of scientific accessibility. No science worthy of the name feebly abdicates in the face of data that fit uneasily within its current methodological framework (one cannot, for example, see such a thing happening in physics).

Some advanced Buddhist practitioners, on realising satori for the first time, have resorted to poetry in an attempt, not to describe it, but to awaken in the reader something of its inner lived experience. The 16th Century Chinese Buddhist master Han Shan put it that:

In clear space and the limpid sea the moon shines
   on the snow
Wiping out all traces of the saintly and the worldly.
When the Eye of Diamond opens, all the flowers in
   the sky
Vanish, while the great earth returns to stillness
   and extinction.

Like all artistic creations, it is no good trying to reduce Han Shan's poem to the level of conventional description. You either see it, or you don't. There is of course no Eye of Diamond, no flowers in the sky, and the great Earth certainly does not return to stillness and extinction. Yet every word of the poem carries the truth of inner experience. It is the work of a man trying to convey the essence of something for which language has no appropriate symbols. If the reader has tasted something of satori for him or herself (no matter how faintly), then the poem makes immediate sense. If the reader has not, then it remains at the level of the utterances of Edward Lear or of Lewis Carroll (though one must be careful here – there are hints of satori in some of Carroll's work).

Usually at this point I incline to the view that inner experience of the kind reported by Han Shan is by its very nature (if we are for a moment to use the categorisations prevalent in Western thinking) poetic rather than scientific. That is, that it obeys the logic of metaphor and symbol, rather than of logic and rationality. However, a number of the most profound discoveries in science appear also to owe more to intuition and insight, to the workings of the (for want of a better word) unconscious, than to the inductive or deductive methodology of conscious thinking. And such discoveries are certainly capable of expression in non-poetic language.

For example Freidrich Kekulé's discovery of the benzene ring, which revolutionised modern molecular chemistry, Neils Bohr's model of the atom which figured crucially in the genesis of atomic physics, and Dmitri Mendeleev's computation of the periodic table so vital to modern science, were all apparently influenced by insights obtained from the unconscious during dreaming[13]. Science, like the arts, therefore appears to depend for progress in part upon a non-referential awareness that may not be that different in origin from the insights of a Buddha.

We may risk falling into the error of duality if we see poetry and science, both profound activities of the human mind, as arising from different levels of inner perception. And we may risk falling into equal error if we assume that the descriptions and explanations of inner perception given by Buddhism, and based upon many centuries of acute observation by men and women of the workings of their own mind, fail to contain the empirical validity demanded by science.

BUDDHISM AND PSYCHOTHERAPY

If we turn now from Western scientific psychology to that of Western psychotherapy (with its eclectic and experiential approach), we find that authority takes a rather different form, being grounded in clinical efficacy rather than in experimental methodology. If the psychotherapeutic technique works, then it carries authority, with theory often following practice rather than the other way around. The client feels better after the psychotherapeutic encounter, the improvement is recognised by those in social contact with him or her, and the psychotherapist in consequence gains authority.

The similarities between authority of this nature and the authority of Buddhism are not hard to seek. The Buddha was often described during his lifetime as the great physician, a title we can best understand by looking at the four noble truths which he entrusted to his followers. These were:

There is suffering
The cause of suffering is attachment
There is a cure for suffering
The cure is the noble eightfold path.

These four truths reflected the procedures of physicians during the Buddha's lifetime, whose methods consisted firstly of confirming the presence of illness ('there is suffering'), secondly of diagnosing the cause of that illness ('attachment'), thirdly of pronouncing on the possibility or otherwise of a cure ('there is a cure for suffering'), and fourthly of prescribing the nature of that cure ('the noble eightfold path').

The Buddha therefore was in many ways a physician of the mind. There is nothing anomalous about the use of the word 'physician' here, for at the time of the Buddha (and still today in the great Eastern spiritual traditions), there is no ultimate distinction between body, mind and spirit (how could there be in a scheme of thought that recognises non-duality?).

The efficacy of one of the strands of the noble eightfold path, namely meditation, in positively influencing psychological outcomes is apparent from Western research[14]. The value of another of the strands, mindfulness (focusing awareness upon present experience rather than upon the distractions of inner mental chatter) have been explored at some length by a number of different authorities[15].

We can summarise these two aspects of the Buddha's 'medicine' for the ending of suffering as continuous intro- and extrospective awareness; continuous physical and mental self-control; and continuous self-appraisal. The endless stream of information fed into awareness by the skandhas is watched unflinchingly, with a tranquil still mind, so that their essential emptiness (lack of intrinsic self-existence) can be recognised, and their illusory power over the mental and emotional life thus brought to an end.

PSYCHOTHERAPY AND BUDDHIST PRACTICE

For Westerners this may seem a difficult medicine to take, simply because we are so bombarded with external distractions, variously recognised as important, entertaining, disturbing and threatening and so on, that we have so little control over what goes on inside our own heads. This is easily demonstrated if we try to stop the flow of thoughts emerging into consciousness. My own experience with meditation workshops suggests few people before training can do this for even 30 seconds.

The whole concept of mind training, of gaining control over the chaotic processes of our thinking and feeling, is alien to the Westerner. Yet mind training lies at the heart of any psychotherapeutic process intended to be more than a temporary palliative. We catch glimpses of it in Beck's cognitive therapy designed to help people identify the thoughts that precipitate undesirable emotional states[16], and in self-management strategies aimed at helping the client take more responsibility for his own appraisals[17]. We notice it as well in Berne's transactional analysis which monitors and re-appraises what happens in social relationships[18], in existential-humanistic therapies designed to enable the individual to maximise innate potential[19], and in Ellis' rational-emotive therapy aimed at preventing the suffering caused by unnecessary emotional reactions[20]. And it is identifiable again in psychodynamic therapies designed to carry self-examination to deep levels of the psyche[21].

Surveys such as that by Bruno[22] confirm that the above therapies speak at least some of the same language as Buddhism, and head towards something of the same goal, namely self-insight, mental clarity, and personal growth. But the similarities between Western and Eastern psychotherapeutic approaches become even more evident when we look at transpersonal psychotherapy, a healing endeavour which Vaughan[23] describes as aimed at the 'integration of physical, emotional, mental and spiritual aspects of wellbeing'. Wittine[24] goes further, and sees transpersonal psychotherapy as pointing clients towards 'their rootedness in the nontemporal, formless, depth dimension of being'. The Buddha himself could hardly have put it better.

The methods used by transpersonal psychotherapy approximate closely to those of Buddhism, and include meditation, self-observation, altered states of awareness, dis-identification with the illusory and the impermanent, and a recognition of a level of being beyond that accessible to mundane consciousness. Along with psychosynthesis they also employ imaginative visualisation[25]. In Buddhism these visualizations can be unbelievably complex, requiring long periods of initial practice, but the basic intention is to visualise in meditation the Buddha (or one of the bodhisattvas) replete with all the qualities one wishes to develop in oneself. At the completion stage of meditation, the visualisation is absorbed into the meditator him or herself, thus arousing the latent potential for these qualities already present within the meditator's own being.

It is sometimes argued that all the authority behind the above psychotherapeutic methods – indeed the whole of psychotherapeutic theory and practice – rests upon an unscientific basis[26], due primarily to the lack of a reliable measure for assessing the effectiveness of outcomes, and to the vagueness of some of the terminology used. The counter-argument is that this demonstrates the inevitable limitations of a scientific model which had its genesis in the study of non-living systems rather than in human beings.

The extension of this counter-argument is that Western science should in fact broaden its methodology by adopting some of the approaches used for centuries by Buddhism, offering to individuals not only techniques for self-observation and self-understanding, but categories and levels of attainment which can be used to mark inner progress in something approaching the meticulous way in which such categories and levels are identified in Buddhism. The weakness of this is that it involves self-assessment, with all the difficulties in observation and interpretation that self-assessment implies. However, these difficulties loom no larger in this context than they do in the psychometric assessment of affective states currently so popular in the

West; and in the light of the evidence of centuries one would assume that practitioners of Buddhist mind training have greater insight into their inner states than do the majority of Westerners who have been subjected to this psychometric assessment.

WHICH BUDDHIST TRADITION?

Throughout the chapter, I have talked in general terms about Buddhism, but there are a number of different Buddhist schools in existence, grouped under the three major movements of the Hinayana, the Mahayana, and the Vajrayana. Is any one of these schools better able to engage in dialogue with Western psychology than the others? The answer is that in spite of numerous superficial differences, the Buddhist schools, as indicated earlier, differ much less from each other in any fundamental sense than do (for example) the various Christian denominations. This is one reason why Buddhism has never witnessed the internecine strife that has characterised Christianity and other theist religions. The thread that unites all Buddhist schools is the noble eightfold path of the Buddha, and in particular the right view, right action, and right meditation aspects of that path.

Right view implies an understanding of the impermanent, illusory nature of the contents of consciousness, and by extension of the phenomenal world itself. Right action resides in non-violence and compassion towards all sentient beings. And right meditation refers to the techniques already fully discussed above. These three practices, together with the right motivation, right speech, right thought, right livelihood and right mindfulness that make up the noble eightfold path, are a recipe not just for moral action (although they are certainly that), or for peace and social harmony (although they are certainly that as well), but a grand design for inner transformation leading ultimately to a full understanding of the nature of existence itself. As such, they have served men and women well for two and a half thousand years. If it is to become a complete psychology of mind, behaviour and experience, Western science can no longer afford to ignore such a treasure-house of psychological wisdom.

CONCLUSION

This is not to suggest that Buddhism and Western psychology are potentially two ways of doing exactly the same thing. Buddhism has no experience of (and shows little interest in) the nomothetic approach which characterises part of Western psychology, or in psychometrics, or in the Western experimental method, or in much of the work carried out in the psychology laboratory. On the other hand, Western psychology still shows only marginal interest in consciousness and in spirituality.

However, the unequivocal fact is that, as a model of the mind, as a set of practices for self-exploration and for influencing behaviour, and as an array of psychotherapeutic techniques, Buddhism carries an authority lacking from the various models and practices available in Western psychology. Moreover, Buddhist authority rests upon practice and experience, the very empirical methodology indeed to which Western science professes allegiance. In accepting the contribution that Buddhism can make to human understanding, Western psychology therefore does not have to assume prior acceptance of its metaphysical dimension. This dimension is something that reveals itself (or does not reveal itself) to the practitioner in the course of his or her practice. All that is required from Western science is a recognition that Buddhist techniques for mind exploration and mind control, developed over the centuries by men and women who looked inwards instead of outwards, can supplement and go beyond in a number of vitally important ways the outward-looking discoveries of Western science.

NOTES

1 E.g. Krishnamurti, J. (1952) *The First and Last Freedom*. London: Gollancz; Krishnamurti, J. (1992) *On Living and Dying*. London: Gollancz.
2 See e.g. Conze, E. (1978) *Selected Sayings from the Perfection of Wisdom*. Boulder, Colarado: Praja Press.
3 Capra, F. (1975) *The Tao of Physics*. London: Wildwood House.
4 Zukav, G (1979) *The Dancing Wu Li Masters*. London: Hutchinson.
5 E.g. Bohm, D. (1980) *Wholeness and the Implicate Order*. London and New York: Routledge.
6 Armstrong, D. M. (1980) The nature of mind. In Block, N. (ed) *Readings in Philosophy of Psychology, Vol. 1*. London: Methuen.
7 Boyd, R. (1980) Materialism without reductionism: what physicalism does not entail. In Block, N. (ed) *Readings in Philosophy of Psychology, Vol. 1*. London: Methuen.
8 E.g. White, R. (1996) Exceptional human experiences: the generic connection. *The Psi Researcher 20*, 3–6.
9 Suzuki, D. T. (1969) *The Zen Doctrine of No Mind*. London: Rider, 2nd edn. Suzuki, D. T. (1950) *Manual of Zen Buddhism*, London: Rider.

10 See e.g. Goddard, D. (1983) *Self-Realization of Noble Wisdom: TheLankavatara Sutra.* Clearlake, Cal.: The Dawn Horse Press.

11 *op.cit* Armstrong (1980)

12 *op.cit* Boyd (1980)

13 See e.g. Fontana, D. (1995) *The Secret Power of Dreams.* Shaftesbury UK and Rockport MA USA: Element Books.

14 See e.g. West, M. (ed) (1987) *The Psychology of Meditation.* Oxford: The Clarendon Press; Murphy, M. and Donovan, S. (1989) *The Physical and Psychological Effects of Meditation.* San Rafael Calif.: Esalen Institute; Fontana, D. (1992) *The Meditator's Handbook.* Shaftesbury: Element Books.

15 E.g. Tart, C. (1994) *Living the Mindful Life: A Handbook for Living in the Present Moment.* Boston and London: Shambhala; Ngakpa Chgyam (1988) *Journey into Vastness: A Handbook of Tibetan Meditation Techniques.* Shaftesbury: Element Books; da Silva, P. (1986) Buddhism and behaviour change: implications for therapy. In G. Claxton *Beyond Therapy.* London: Wisdom Books; Fontana, D. (1990) Self and mind in psychological counseling. In J. Crook and D. Fontana (eds) *Space in Mind.* Shaftesbury: Element Books.

16 E.g. Beck, A. T. (1976) *Cognitive Therapy.* New York: The New American Library.

17 E.g. Kanfer, F. H. and Gaelick, L. (1986) Self-management methods. In F. H. Kanfer and A. P. Goldstein *Helping People Change: A Textbook of Methods.* New York and Oxford: Pergamon Press. 3rd edn.

18 E.g. Berne, E. (1972) *What Do You Say After You Say Hello?.* New York: Grove Press.

19 E.g. Maslow, A. H. (1962) *Towards a Psychology of Being.* Princeton NJ.: Van Nostrand; Rogers, C. (1980) *A Way of Being.* Boston: Houghton Mifflin.

20 Ellis, A. (1973) *Humanistic Psychotherapy: The Rational-Emotive Approach.* New York: Julian Press.

21 See particularly Jung, e.g. Jung, C. (1968) *Analytical Psychology: Its Theory and Practice.* London and New York: Routledge (re-issued by Ark Paperbacks in 1986).

22 Bruno, F. (1983) *Adjustment and Personal Growth: Seven Pathways.* New York and Chichester: Wiley. 2nd edn.

23 Vaughan, F. (1993) Healing and wholeness: transpersonal psychotherapy. In R. Walsh and F. Vaughan *Paths Beyond Ego: The Transpersonal Vision.* Los Angeles: Jeremy Tarcher.

24 Wittine, B. (1993) Assumptions of transpersonal psychotherapy. In R. Walsh and F. Vaughan *Paths Beyond Ego: The Transpersonal Vision.* Los Angeles: Jeremy Tarcher.

25 See e.g. Assagioli, R. (1975) *Psychosynthesis.* Wellingborough Northants.: Turnstone Press; Ferrucci, P. (1982) *What We May Be: The Visions and Techniques of Psychosynthesis.* Wellingborough Northants.: Turnstone Press.

26 Eysenck, H. J. (1966) *The Effects of Psychotherapy.* New York: International Science.

Section 2

Textual Fundamentals

Chapter 3

EDITOR'S PREFACE

The textual foundation of early Buddhism, known as the Pali Canon, is some ten times the length of the bible. Pali was the language of ritual and scholarship used in Sri Lanka where the most authentic version of the Canon was assembled some centuries after the Buddha's death. Before this the teachings were transmitted orally, developing into various local and doctrinal variants.

With the appearance of Buddhist writings, their commentaries and interpretations appeared. Many of these will have been attributed to the original teacher as a means of adding authority to them. The fundamental form of the Pali Canon, however, is what is known as the Tripitaka which literally translated means something like the 'three groups'. The oldest and most authentic part is the *Vinaya*, the rules for ordained life. Next are the *Suttas* or sayings attributed to the Buddha, and lastly is a later metaphysical commentary known as the *Abhidhamma*, or higher teaching.

The Pali Canon has attracted an enormous amount of scholastic work and exegesis over the two and a half thousand years of its existence. The resulting corpus is now so large as to be beyond the capacity of a single person to know. When to this are added the doctrinal writings of the various schools and systems into which original Buddhism has diversified, the resulting intellectual system is monstrous and in some way inhumane.

This contrasts ironically with the human scale of the original teachings. These owe very little to scholasticism or metaphysical debate. Personal practice, ordinary human concerns and ethical principles that could be understood by anyone were the foundations of the original system. Since then, a gigantic cultural edifice has been built on top of them. Hence, it is now a virtually unsolvable hermeneutical problem to decide what the original teachings were and what they may have been like as an experience for the people who heard them.

Even so, we can do the best we can, and in this chapter Padmal de Silva reminds us as a preliminary that careful tanslation and constant reference to the original text is a fundamental requirement. His clear and informed summary of the original teachings is organised around a practice that Padmal de Silva knows well, that of therapy. The point he makes is that if there is one thing that is certain about the foundations of Buddhism it is that they were directed at the relief of suffering, a fundamental therapeutic project.

The development of Buddhism can be seen in this light. For example, the metaphysical and psychological concerns of the *Abhidhamma* are not mere sophistry or disinterested inquiry. They are part of a search for a unified system of practice and theory that would help people to understand the nature of human experience and hence to live more skillfully. In Western terms this unified system may at first appear to blend ideas and concerns that need to be kept apart. The unified project of original Buddhism is relatively flexible about conventionally observed Western distinctions between, for example, the mundane and the transcendental as well as the moral and the physical. It does not recognise the problematic gap described by Kant when towards the end of his life he described his work as a project to bring together the physical law without and the moral law within. For original Buddhism, these were never separated. The project was to present an accessible account of the human condition based on common experience. The later metaphysical additions, such as the *Abhidhamma*, are interpretations of the original teaching. The teachings themselves aimed at the relief of human suffering through insight and the direct investigation of experience.

Padmal de Silva reveals shows how modern Pali scholarship reveals a depth and subtlety in the original texts. The psychological content is remarkable, having resemblances to contemporary cognitive and therapeutic systems in the West. Just how far these resemblances can be taken is a open question. Jung for example was wary of facile comparisons and overgeneralisation. In particular he was concerned about the danger of projecting on to systems of Eastern thought things which were not there. The cultural dynamics of the West, especially the over-rationalisation that has followed the scientific revolution of the past four hundred years or so, has meant the loss of transcendental and mystical traditions. This leads Westerners to distort the content of Eastern systems to match their lost complement to rationality. The often superficial adoption of Eastern thought and practices during the 1960's is a good example of this.

Now the systematic and informed investigation of early Buddhist writings is an excellent anditode to this sort of mis-appropriation. Padmal de Silva's work does exactly this. It also may suggest what the experience of these teachings may have been like. In encountering Pali terms such as *papanca* it would be a limiting mistake to stop at the apparently confliciting and diverse translations as a sign that the original meanings has been lost. Instead, by careful investigation of parallel texts and terms, we may be able to come to a more reliable understanding of what it may have meant as something experienced in a culture of oral transmission. The various meanings to do with 'spreading', 'congflagration', 'diffusion' and 'delusion' give us a clue that this term will have pointed people's attention toward the universal tendency of the mind to wander and to add to our experiences things that were not in the original situation.

Here the links to contemporary psychological theory and to therapeutic practice are clear. In cognitive theories of attention, like that of Norman and Shallice for example, we find stages at which incoming information is rapidly interpreted in a very wide range of ways which may conflict or in some sense contest for subsequent processing resources. Likewise in Cognitive Behavioural Therapy, the therapist is constantly trying to get the client to pay attention to what is 'really' in the external situation, and what has been added to it by the client's habitual and emotially charged ways of thought.

Such resemblances suggest that the comparability of original Buddhist teachings and contemporary psychology is far greater than might at first appear. Just how far this comparison will lead to the discovery of common ideas and aims is presently unclear. Indeed, Padmal de Silva's conclusion is that some state of total integration is neither possible nor desirable. Even so, the detailed analysis he presents, along with the informed comparisons he makes with Western psychotherapy, are very useful and productive. They show that the original teachings dealt with common psychological experience and had therapeutic, rather than mystical or metaphysical, objectives.

★   ★   ★

Buddhist Psychology: Some Basic Concepts and Applications

Padmal de Silva

SUMMARY

This chapter gives an account of some of the major aspects of Buddhist psychology. The survey is based on the texts of Early, or Theravada, Buddhism – that is, the canonical texts and their early Pali commentaries and related expository texts. The importance of psychological concepts in the philosophy and practice of Buddhism is highlighted. The problems inherent in the study of Buddhist psychology are discussed, including the problem of translation and interpretation. The paper then describes and analyzes several key Early Buddhist psychological notions including: basic drives that motivate behaviour, perception and cognition, consciousness, personal development and enlightenment, meditation, and behaviour change. Finally, comments are made on the possible interaction between Buddhist and modern psychology, with special reference to therapy and clinical practice.

INTRODUCTION

This chapter aims to provide a descriptive and analytical account of Buddhist psychology. It does not attempt a comprehensive review of the subject; the literature, and the issues that arise in the examination of this literature, are too vast to permit a comprehensive review in a single chapter. What is presented here is essentially a selective account of the psychological notions found in Buddhism. Only some of the major concepts are discussed. Some practical aspects of Buddhist psychology are also briefly reviewed.

The chapter is selective in another way. It is confined to Theravada Buddhism, also referred to as Early Buddhism, and does not deal in

54

detail with later developments, including Zen.[1,2] It is based on the literature of Early Buddhism, which is in the Pali language, consisting of: (1) the original Buddhist canon which was put together soon after the Buddha's death and committed to writing in the first century B.C.; (2) the early Pali commentaries on the cannon that were in their present form by the end of the fifth century A.D.; and (3) other Pali texts of the same period which are best described as expository and interpretive works.

A full account of the Pali canon is given in Webb[3]. The early Pali commentaries include major texts such as *Sumangalvilāsinī, Manorathapūraṇī, Papañcasūdanī, and Dhammapadaṭṭhakathā,* which are commentaries on specific parts of the canon. The early expository and interpretive texts include, among others, *Visuddhimagga, Milindapanha* and *Nettippakarana.*

Problems of Translation

The entire canon, and the majority of the commentaries and expository works, have been translated into English and published by the Pali Text Society, which was founded in London by T. W. Rhys Davids in 1881. However, the English versions are often beset with problems of translation and interpretation. Perhaps it is worth illustrating this problem with examples. A major example if the term *dukkha* (Sanskrit *duhkha*), translated by many as 'suffering'. This has led to Buddhism being described as, essentially, a pessimistic religion, as 'suffering' is stated as characterizing all existence. Some authors have offered alternative translations such as 'unsatisfactoriness', 'disharmony', 'dis-ease' and 'painfulness'. None of these offers a precise rendering of the original term, and some writers leave the term untranslated[4]. Another example is the very challenging term *papañca* (Sanskrit *prapañca*; derived from *pra* + *pañc*, to spread out). In his book, *The Principles of Buddhist Psychology*, David Kalupahana consistently translates this as 'obsession'[5]. This is clearly misleading, although the official *Pali-English Dictionary* of the Pali Text Society does offer 'obsession' as one rendering of this word[6]. This is a key term in Buddhist psychology, and has been variously translated as 'impediment', 'conceptual proliferation', 'manifoldness', 'diffusion', 'delusion', 'complex' and 'imagination', among others. This will be returned to in a later paragraph.

It would be clear from these examples that the problem of translation is a major obstacle to one's understanding of Early

Buddhism, or indeed any other ancient system of thought. For this reason, the material in this paper is drawn from the original Pali texts.

The Buddha and Buddhism

Before focusing on Buddhist psychology, it is necessary to make a few introductory comments on Buddha and Buddhism.

The Buddha (the word, derived from the root *budh*, 'to know', 'to comprehend', literally means 'the enlightened one') lived in the foot-hills of the Himalayan range of mountains in Northern India from 563 to 483 B.C.[7]

The main teachings of the Buddha are contained in the Four Noble Truths. These are: (i) that life is characterized by 'suffering' and is unsatisfactory (*dukkha*); (ii) that the cause (*samudaya*) of the suffering is craving or desire (*tanhā*); (iii) that this suffering can be ended (*nirodha*), *via* the cessation of craving or desire – this is the state of *Nibbāna*; and (iv) that there is a way (*magga*) to achieve this cessation, which is called the Noble Eightfold Path[8].

The Noble Eightfold Path is also called the Middle Path, as it avoids the extremes of a sensuous and luxurious life on the one hand, and a life of rigorous self-mortification on the other. The eight aspects of the Path are: right understanding; right thought; right speech; right action; right livelihood; right effort; right mindfulness; and right concentration. The person who undertakes a life based on this path, renouncing worldly attachments, hopes eventually to attain the *arahant* state, which may be described as a state of perfection; the word *arahant* literally means 'the worthy one'. This state marks the attainment of *Nibbāna*.

The other teachings of the Buddha include the negation of a permanent and unchanging soul (*anatta*), and the notion of the impermanence or transience of things (*anicca*). Buddhism also excludes the notion of a God. There is no creator or a supreme being who rules, purveys and controls the universe. Thus there is no absolutism in Buddhism either in the form of an external God, or an unchanging universe, or an unchanging soul[9].

For the laity, the vast majority of people who did not renounce worldly life to devote themselves to the immediate quest for *Nibbāna*, the Buddha provided a sound and pragmatic social ethic. They were expected to lead a life characterized by restraint and moderation, respecting the rights of others and being dutiful to those around them. Such a restrained and dutiful life was considered not only to be a necessary prerequisite for one's ultimate religious aim; it was also valued as an end in itself. For example, the Buddha advised his lay followers to abstain from alcoholic beverages because alcohol indulgence could lead to demonstrable ill-effects such as loss of wealth, proneness to socially embarrassing behaviour, unnecessary quarrels, disrepute, ill-health and eventually mental derangement[10]. This empirical and pragmatic approach is a prominent feature of the ethical stance of Buddhism[11].

Later Traditions

A brief note is in order at this point about later traditions. Buddhist theory and practice grew in diverse ways, both in India and elsehwere. The main developments include the Mahāyāna tradition, leading to Tantra and, in the Far East, Zen (from *Ch'an*, derived from *dhyāna*). It is Zen Buddhism that first came to the attention of Western thinkers and psychologists as a possible source of ideas for contemporary psychology and psychological therapy. Jung, for example, wrote a foreword to Suzuki's *Introduction to Zen Buddhism*. Much has been written about Zen and modern life, including the influential volume *Zen Buddhism and Psychoanalysis* by Suzuki, Fromm and De Martino. Interest in Early Buddhism, from this perspective, came later[12].

THE PSYCHOLOGY OF BUDDHISM

The considerable interest shown by modern students in Buddhist psychology becomes entirely understandable when it is realised that there is a great deal of psychological content in Buddhism. Some parts of the canonical texts, as well as later writings, are examples of explicit psychological theorizing, while many of the others present psychological assumptions and much material of psychological relevance. For example, the *Abhidhamma Piṭaka* contains a highly systematized psychological account of human behaviour and mind, and the translation of one of the *Abhidhamma* books, the *Dhammasangaṇī*, was given the title *A Buddhist Manual of Psychological Ethics* by its translator, Caroline Rhys Davids, when it was first published in 1900. The practice of Buddhism, as a religion and a way of life, involves much in terms of psychological change. The ultimate religious goal of the *arahant* state both reflects and requires major psychological changes. The path towards the achievement of this goal, the Noble Eightfold Path, involves steps which can only be described as psychological (e.g., right thought, right understanding). As the goal is attainable essentially through one's own efforts, it is not surprising that Buddhism has much to say about one's thinking and behavior. As noted above, there is no God one can turn to for one's salvation. Nor did the Buddha claim to be able to ensure any of his followers the attainment of the goal. On the contrary, the Buddha explicitly stated that he was only a teacher who could show the way, and that the actual task of achieving the goal was up to each individual's efforts. As a much-quoted passage in the *Dhammapada* (which is part of the *Khuddaka Nikāya*) says: 'The task has to be accomplished by yourselves. The Enlightened Ones only teach the way'.

Some Basic Notions

In the following sections, some of the main psychological aspects of Buddhism will be discussed.

Motivation

Perhaps the most logical starting point is the theory of motivation. What drives people in their behaviours? What motivates human action? The unenlightened person's behaviour, it is said, is governed and driven by *tanhā,* or craving, which, as noted in a previous paragraph, is given as the cause of 'suffering' or 'unsatisfactoriness' in the Second Noble Truth. *Tanhā* is classified into three basic forms: *kāma tanhā* (craving for sensory gratification); *bhava tanhā* (craving for survival or continued existence); and *vibhava tanhā* (craving for annihilation).

It is interesting that these three primary drives in Buddhism have been compared, by some authors, to the Freudian notions of *libido, ego,* and *thanatos* respectively[13]. Like Freudian theory, this theory of motivation may be seen as a primarily reductionist one: all actions have as their source a small number of drives. While craving is seen as the source of 'suffering', the term *tanhā* is not exclusively used in a negative sense. There are several instances in the literature where it is acknowledged that one can also develop a *tanhā* for the cessation of 'suffering'. Thus *tanhā* can take the form of, or can be turned into, a desirable force. For example, the expository text *Nettippakarana* says: 'Here, craving is of two kinds, wholesome and unwholesome. While the unwholesome kind goes with the unsatisfactory worldly existence, the wholesome kind leads to the abandonment of craving'[14].

In a further analysis of motivation, Buddhism identifies three factors that lead to unwholesome, or undesirable, behaviors. These are: *rāga* (passion or lust); *dosa* (hatred or malice); and *moha* (delusion, or false belief)[15]. All unwholesome action is seen as deriving from a set of fundamental roots. In fact, the texts explicitly refer to these as 'roots' (*mūla*). They are called *akusalamūlas* – unwholesome or unprofitable roots. It is not made explicit whether these always operate at a conscious level. On the other hand, certain clearly non-conscious factors also have a part to play in determing behavior. One such group of factors mentioned is *anusaya*, translated as 'latent tendency', 'latent bias', 'predisposition' and 'latent disposition'. The Pali Text Society Dictionary adds that these meanings are 'always in bad sense'. The term itself (from *anu* + *si*, 'to lie dormant'), indicates that these are non-conscious factors. These dispositional factors are part and parcel of one's personality, acquired through past experience, and they play a major role in influencing one's behavior and contribute to the perpetuation of the cycle of suffering. Seven types of *anusaya* are often mentioned. The list given in *Samyutta Nikāya, V*, 1884-1898), is as follows: tendency to want pleasure; tendency to anger or disgust; tendency to speculation; tendency to doubt; tendency to conceit; tendency to want continuous existence or growth; and tendency to ignorance.

Another group of factors which are non-conscious and which influence one's behavior are the *āsavas* (Sanskrit *āsrava*, from the root *sru*, 'to flow', or 'ooze'). This term has been variously translated as 'influxes' and 'cankers'. These are factors that affect the mind so that it cannot rise higher. It is said that they 'intoxicate' and 'bemuddle' the mind. They colour one's attitudes, and thwart one's insight. In one's endeavour for self-development, one has to excise them, and this is done through wisdom. The influxes are described as arising from different factors: sensuality, aggression, cruelty, body, and individuality are given in one account. Other lists include, among others, gain, loss, fame, disrepute and evil intentions. Motives for good, or wholesome, action are usually expressed in negative terms. The most consistent account is the one which gives *arāga* (non-passion, or absence of passion), *adosa* (non-hatred or absence of hatred) and *amoha* (non-delusion, or absence of delusion) as the roots of good action – the opposites of the roots of unwholesome behaviours. Occasionally, they are described in clearly positive terms – as *cāga* (renunciation), *mettā* (loving kindness) and *paññā* (wisdom, understanding). It is stated that one must strive to develop these in order to combat their opposites[16].

Perception and cognition

Perception is based on twelve gateways or modalities (*āyatana*), six of these being the five sense organs plus the mind, or 'inner sense', and the other six being the objects of each of these. The status of mind (*mano*) is special. It has the ability to reflect on the objects of the other senses, so in this way it is linked to the activity of all the senses. Each combination of sense organ and its objects leads to a particular consciousness (*viññāna*) – for example, visual consciousness arises because of the eye and material shapes, and auditory consciousness arises because of the ear and sounds. When consciousness is added to each of the pairs of modalities, one gets eighteen factors of cognition, referred to as *dhātus*, or elements. These are presented in Table 1.

It is said:

> The meeting of the three (i.e., eye, material shape and visual consciousness) is contact; because of this contact arises feelings; what one feels, one perceives.

This is a fairly straightforward account of how perception takes place. However, the Buddhist exposition goes beyond this. The account continues:

> What one perceives, one reasons about. What one reasons about, 'one turns into *papañca*'. What one turns into *papañca*, becuase of that factor, assails him in regard to materail shapes recognizable by the eye belonging to the past, the future and the present ...[17].

Table 1 The Eighteen Factors of Cognition

Sense Organ	Objects	Consciousness
eye	material shapes	visual consciousness
ear	sounds	auditory consciousness
nose	smells	olfactory consciousness
tongue	tastes	gustatory consciousness
body	tangibles	tactile consciousness
mind	mental objects	mental consciousness

It will be recalled that the term *papañca* was cited in an earlier section of this chapter as an expample of a word posing particular difficulties for the translator. In this passage the verbal form '*papañceti*' is used. Thus, the final stage of the process of sense-cognition is *papañca*. An examination of the use of the term in various contexts related to cognition shows that it refers to the grosser conceptual aspects of the process, as it is consequent to *vitakka* (reasoning). Once an object is perceived, there is the initial application of thought to it, followed by *papañca* – which in this context is best taken to mean a tendency to proliferation of ideas. As a result, the person is no longer the perceiver who is in control, but one who is assailed by concepts generated by this prolific tendency. He is overwhelmed by concepts and linguistic conventions. One's perception is, in this way, open to distortion and elaboration due to the spontaneous proliferation of thoughts. This proliferation is said to be linked to *tanhā* (craving), *māna* (conceit) and *diṭṭhi* (dogma, or rigidly held views). They are all bound up with the notions of 'I' and 'mine'. This marks the intrusion of the ego into the field of sense perception. In Buddhist psychology, there is no self (*attā* ; Sanskrit *ātman*), but the delusion of self affects all one's behaviours[18].

One of the aims of personal development is to enable oneself to see reality as it is, without the essential distortions arising from the various factors that characterize the unenlightened person's functioning. A major aspect of reaching the state of *arahant* is indeed the freeing of one's perceptions from these distorting influences. When one reaches a state of perfection, one's perceptions become free of such distortions, and allow a direct appraisal of the objects.

The arahant state

It is perhaps the appropriate place now to consier the *arahant* state and its attainment. The religious goal of a Buddhist is to attain this stage, which marks the end of the cycle of 'suffering'. This requires a process of personal development, involving disciplined living (*sīla*), serious meditative efforts marked by concentration (*samādhi*), and wisdom (*paññā*) which is attained through such efforts. But what does it mean to say that someone is an *arahant*? There are numerous descriptions of an *arahant* in the texts. For example:

> The *arahant* has destroyed the cankers, lived the life, done what's needed to be done, set down the burden, achieved well-being,

shattered life's fetters, and is freed by perfect knowledge. He has applied himself to six things: to dispassion, to detachment, to harmlessness, to the descruction of craving, to the destruction of rasping, and to non-delusion[19].

In psychological terms, the *arahant's* actions no longer emanate from the common basic motives of passion, hatred and delusion. He is, however, capable of joy or positive sentiment. He has loving kindness (*mettā*) to all, and compassion (*karunā*). He indulges in nothing, and is restrained in his behaviour. Nine standards of behaviour are listed which an *arahant* cannot and does not transgress: taking life, stealing, sexual contact, uttering falsehoods, enjoying the comforts of wealth, and going astray through desire, through hate, through delusion, and through fear. They contribute to society by being teachers and advisers, and are no burden on their fellow beings.

The state of the *arahaut* is an altered, and higher, state. This notion of attaing a higher state, or self-actualization, is of course found in the writings of several western psychologists, including Carl Rogers among others. Maslow's concept of the self-actualized person also provides an interesting parallel. This person, according to Maslow, has a clear perception of reality, spontaneity, detachment, compassion, and independence from flattery and criticism. Like the *arahant*, it is an ideal end point in the quest for personal development. This state can be seen as an 'ideal type of healthy personality'[20].

Practical Aspects of Buddhist Psychology

Meditation

It was noted above that the attainment of the *arahant* state requires personal development based on both restrained and disciplined conduct and meditative efforts. This explains why meditation is given a central place in Buddhist texts. In addition to numerious canonical discussions, large sections of Buddhaghosa's *Visuddhimagga* are devoted to a consideration of this subject in great detail. It is significant that the Pali word for meditation, *bhāvanā*, etymologically means 'development' or 'cultivation'. As there is a large and still growing amount of literature on this subject in English, only a few brief comments will be made here[22].

Two forms of meditation are prescribed: the first is called *samatha* (tranquility), and the other, *vipassanā* (insight). While further forms of meditation have been developed in later forms of Buddhism, and these include various Tibetan and Zen techniques, these two represent the earliest Buddhist techniques, dating back 2,500 years. It is worth noting that meditation of the *samatha* type is also found in some other ancient Indian systems, while *vipassanā* is a uniquely Buddhist development.

The word *samatha* means 'tranquility' or 'serenity'. *Samatha* meditation is aimed at reaching states of consciousness characterized by progressively greater levels of tranquility and stillness. It has two aspects: (a) the achievement of the highest possible degree of concentration; and (b) the progressive calming of all mental processes. This is done through increasingly concentrated focusing of attention; the mind withdraws progressively from all external and internal stimuli. In the end, states of pure and undistracted consciousness can be achieved. The *samatha* meditation procedure starts with efforts at concentrating the mind on specific objects, and progresses systematically through a series of states of what are called *jhānas*, or mental absorption.

Vipassanā, or insight meditation, also starts with concentration exercises using appropriate objects on which one focuses. In this procedure, however, once a certain level of concentration is achieved so that undistracted focusing can be maintained, one goes on to examine with steady, careful attention and in great detail all sensory and mental processes. Through this contemplation, one becomes a detached observer of one's own activity. The objects of this contemplation are classified as fourfold: body, sensations, mental states, and 'mental objects' – for example, various moral and intellectual subjects. The aim is to achieve total and immediate awareness, or mindfulness, of all phenomena. This leads, it is claimed, eventually to the full and clear perception of the impermanence of all things and beings.

It is held that *samatha* meditation by itself cannot lead of enlightenment or perfection; *vipassanā* meditation is needed to attain this goal. While the former leads to temporarily altered states of consciousness, it is the latter which leads to enduring and thoroughgoing changes in the person and paves the way to achieving the *arahant* state[23].

The practical implications of the claims made in Buddhism for meditation are quite clear. The meditative experiences of both types, when properly carried out and developed, are claimed to lead to greater ability to concentrate, greater freedom from distraction, greater tolerance of change and turmoil around oneself, and sharper awareness and greater alertness about one's own responses, both physical and mental. They would also lead, more generally, to greater calmness or tranquility. While the ultimate goal of perfection will require a long series of regular training periods of systematic meditation coupled with major restraint in one's conduct, the more mundane benefits of meditation should be available to all serious and persisting practitioners.

Other strategies of behaviour change

In addition, the literature of Early Buddhism also contains a wide range of behaviour change strategies other than meditation, used and recommended by the Buddha and his disciples, which can only be described as 'behavioural'. This aspects of Buddhism had been neglected by modern researchers until very recently. It is only in the last fifteen years that these behavioural strategies have been highlighted and discussed. These strategies are remarkably similar to several of the established techniques of modern behaviour therapy. Thus, if Buddhist psychology is akin to modern humanistic, transpersonal and existential psychologies in view of its emphasis on the individual, his problems and anxieties, his predicament, and his development through personal effort, it also has a clear affinity to present-day behavioural psychology in view of these behavioural techniques. The ways in which the overall approach of behaviour modification and that of Buddhism may be seen as broadly similar have been discussed by William Mikulas in 1981. Some areas of similarity high-lighted by Mikulas are: the rejection of the notion of an unchanging self or soul; focus on observable phenomena; emphasis on testability; stress on techniques for awareness of certain bodily responses; emphasizing the 'here and now'; and dissemination of teachings and techniques widely and publicly. Given this broad similarity, and the general empiricist/experientialist attitude of Buddhism as exemplified by the Kālāma Sutta of the *Anguttara Nikāya* in which the Buddha advises a group of inquirers not to accept anything on hearsay, authority or pure argument, but to accept only what is empirically and experientially verifiable, it is not surprising that specific behaviour change techniques were used and recommended in Early Buddhism. It is also entirely consistent with the social ethic of Buddhism, which recognized the importance of behaviours conducive to one's own and others' well-being as a goal in its own right. When and where specific behaviour changes were required, both in oneself and others, these were to be affected through the use of specific techniques[24].

The range of behavioural strategies found in the literature of Early Buddhism is wide. When these are described using modern terminology and listed together, they look like the contents page of a modern behavioural therapy manual! It is beyond the scope of this chapter to discuss these in detail. They have been analysed in detail, and those relevant to present day psychology noted, elsewhere[25].

In addition to these, some of the Buddhist techniques also have remarkable parallels with two other modern theraputic approaches. One is Rational Emotive Therapy (RET) of Ellis[26]. Cognitive therapy, which has developed as an distinctive approach in the last two decades or so mainly through the work of Beck, is the other[27]. In both of these, cognitions are identified as among the key variables involved in psychopathology, and attempts are made to elicit and modify them in a healthy direction. In cognitive therapy, this is done through a variety of cognitive techniques including challenging maladaptive thoughts, and where necessary through behavioural tasks. In RET, these and other techniques, such as dramatization, are used. In RET, it is held that strong irrational beliefs, neurotic feelings and dysfunctional behaviour may need forceful and dramatic interventions if they are to change. There are numerous instances in Early Buddhist texts of the use of such techniques for achieving change. The most impressive examples are perhaps in helping those with morbid grief actions to overcome them. Some of these have been highlighted elsewhere[28]. To illustrate the point, the following Jātaka story may be cited.

Once in the city of Benares, the father of a wealthy land-owner died. The man was unable to overcome his grief and, taking the dead man's bones from the place of cremation, erected a mound in his garden and lamented there every day. He neither bathed nor ate, nor did he attend to his work. His own son, Sujata, was worried about this and thought of a plan to deliver him from his unending sorrow. So, finding a dead ox lying outside the city, he brought grass and water and placed them before it, and implored the dead ox to eat and drink. Passers-by failed to persuade him to stop his seemingly irrational behaviour, so they went to his father and said, 'Your son has gone off his senses. He is giving grass and water to a dead ox'. On hearing this, the land-owner hurriedly went to his son and said: 'My dear son, are you insane? Why do you offer grass and water to the carcass of an ox? No food can raise to life a dead ox. Your words are idle and futile'. Then the son, Sujata, said: 'I think this ox will come to life again. At least his legs and head are still here. But my grandfather's head and limbs are all gone. Yet you weep over his grave every day'. Hearing this, the land-owner realized the futility of his grieving and was consoled, and returned to normal activities[29].

BUDDHISM AND MODERN WESTERN PSYCHOLOGY

Issues of integration

A few comments are in order at this point on the relationship between modern Western psychology on the one hand, and Buddhist psychology on the other. The relationship between the scientific psychology of the West and indigenous sytems of psychology can take many forms, ranging from totally independent existence to complete integration. Buddhist psychology, like other indigenous psychologies, is prescientific, but it is so only in the narrow sense that it developed prior to, and outside the context of, modern Western science. It offers clearly testable hypotheses and therefore can be brought within the realm of scientific inquiry. Further, as noted above, the overall stance of Buddhism is an eminently empiricist one and the process of evaluating the notions and practices of its psychology is something that will be consistent with this stance. Such testing will not be alien to the spirit of Buddhism, which encourages enquiry and discourages dogmatic acceptance of theories and claims[30]. Thus, Buddhist psychology can potentially make a contribution to modern scientific psychology without compromising its basic stance or that of the latter.

What are the chances of the successful integration of the two? In the present writer's view, total integration or fusion between two independently developed systems of psychology, each quite sophisticated, does not seem to be either feasible or desirable. On the other hand, one can legitimately consider the development of a new, combined psychology which brings together ideas, data, and methodologies from different psychologies that come from different traditions. Mikulas, in discussing the issues of integration between Eastern and Western psychologies, has made the point that it is not a matter of whether the Eastern or the Western approach is 'better'[31]. There are, he stresses, strengths and weaknesses in both; and the combinations of the two can be very powerful. Mikulas has discussed the interrelated domains of (a) biological, (b) behavioural, (c) personal and (d) transpersonal, and argues that any integrative or conjunctive psychology must include all four levels. It is clear that different pre-scientific or indigenous psychologies have different degrees of contribution to make to these domains. The same applies to modern Western psychology. The psychology of Buddhism can certainly contribute significantly to the development of a conjunctive psychology as envisaged by Mikulas. Of the four domains enumerated above, the potential contribution of Buddhist psychology is perhaps limited in the biological domain. By contrast, with regard to the other three domains, Buddhist psychology has a great deal to offer. The relevance of Early Buddhist notions of behaviour and behaviour change to present day theory and practice has already been commented on (see above). Much, however, remains to be done in the area, and it is the present writer's view that the Buddhist contribution to this area, broadly defined to include cognitive aspects of behaviour as well as overt behaviours, will turn out to be a major one. Buddhist notions of *sati* (mindfulness) and *samādhi* (concentration) appear to offer particularly valuable ways of enhancing this aspect of psychology. In the personal domain, again Buddhist psychology offers much of relevance and value. The Buddhist analysis of the changing and transient notion of the 'self', and the emphasis on personal development, are of particular relevance. In the transpersonal domain, Mikulas states that Eastern psychologies have an enormous amount to contribute, as these psychologies have traditionally placed much emphasis on consciousness, peak experiences and spiritual insights. This is certainly very true of Buddhist psychology; as noted in earlier sections of this chapter, Buddhist psychology has much to say about consciousness. Of equal significance, in this domain, is the emphasis on self-actualization – i.e., attainment of more developed states. In these three domains, Buddhism has already been recognized as a potentially rich source of ideas, strategies *etc* for the furtherment of psychology. If a superordinate conjunctive psychology, as envisaged by Mikulas, is developed, the Buddhist contribution to these domains will, almost certainly, be a very major one. Even if such a conjunctive psychology does not develop, it is the present writer's contention that in all of these areas Buddhism will continue to provide modern Western psychology with concepts, strategies and hypotheses that will contribute to its further development and expansion. The fact that Buddhism encourages testing, verification and evaluation of its notions and strategies will make this process a relatively smooth one.

Relevance to therapy

Finally, a few words on the role of Buddhist psychology in present day mental health practice. In this realm, there has been an increasing use of ideas and strategies from Early Buddhism (and indeed other forms of Buddhism). These are bieng used as part of the repertoire of tools of the clinician, and applied in the same empirically-based way as others in the repertoire. Recent work has shown the undoubted value of some of these, and this has led to these Buddhist ideas and techniques being seen not as just interesting curiosities at the fringe of psychology and psychiatry, but as acceptable options for legitimate practice. There is an impressive literature on the use of Buddhist meditational techniques for a variety of clinical problems. Jon Kabat-Zinn and his colleagues have shown the efficacy of mindfulness meditation for the control of pain, in the treatment of psoriasis and the alleviation of anxiety[32]. The most exciting new development is the work, currently being carried out by John Teasdale and colleagues, on the use of mindfulness as a way of preventing relapse in those who have been successfully treated for clinical depression. Teasdale makes the point that mindfulness training, as found in Early Buddhist practice, is particularly useful for this task, for several reasons[33]. Firstly, it is a generic skill which can be practised in many situations and on many aspects, on a wide range of thoughts, feelings and experiences. Secondly, mindfulness training should help those patients to recognize the early signs of relapse in their derpession. Thus, the person is able to 'turn towards' potential difficulties, rather than 'look away' or ignore them. This would enable early remedial action. Thirdly, as mindfulness is characterized by direct experience of current reality 'in the moment', it could reduce the tendency of those prone to depressive relapse to become locked into ruminitive cognitive cycles which are known to be a major factor in relapse.

These new applications of Buddhist techniques in current clinical practice reflect the willingness of present day psychology and psychiatry to broaden their horizons. These are no longer seen as fringe interventions, or just intresting subjective claims, but as legitimate options for use and evaluation. The work cited here on mindfulness meditation has been, and is being, evaluated rigorously, as all clinical procedures are. Indeed, this is the only way in which orthodox psychiatry and clinical psychology accept procedures which are new to them, whatever their original source. Buddhist techniques have begun to achieve acceptance by virtue of their passing this test of evaluation. This has been possible due to their essential testability, and is very much in keeping with the overall stance of Buddhism which promotes and values enquiry.

NOTES

1 For an account of Theravada Buddhism, see: Gombrich, R. (1988). *Theravada Buddhism*, London: Routledge & Kegan Paul.
2 For a discussion of the different schools of Buddhism, see: Kalupahana, D. J. (1976). *Buddhist philosophy: A historical analysis*. Honolulu: University of Hawaii Press.
3 Webb, R. (1975). *An analysis of the Pali canon*. Kandy: Buddhist Publication Society.
4 For different translations of *dukkha*, see: Gunaratna, V. F. (1968). *The significance of the Four Noble Truths*. Kandy: Buddhist Publication Society; Matthews, B. (1983). *Craving and salvation: A study of Buddhist soteriology*. Waterloo, Ontario: Wilfrid Laurier University Press; and Rahula, W. (1967). *What the Buddha taught*. London: Gordon Fraser.
5 Kalupahana, D. J. (1987). *The principles of Buddhist psychology*. Albany, NY: State University of New York Press.
6 Rhys Davids, T. W. & Stede, W. (Eds.) (1921–1925). *The Pali Text Society's Pali-English dictionary*. London: Pali Text Society.
7 Excellent accounts of the Buddha's life are available in, among others: Kalupahana, D. J., & Kalupahana, I. (1982). *The way of Siddhartha*, Boulder, Co: Shambhala; Schumann, H. W. (1989). *The historical Buddha*. London: Arkana Books; and Carrithers, M. (1983). *The Buddha*, Oxford: Oxford University Press.
8 For a fuller discussion of the main tenets of Buddhism, see: Rahula, W. (1967 *op. cit* (Note 4).
9 These tenets are found, in detailed form, in the original Canon – *e.g.* *Majjhima Nikāya*, Vols. I–III. (Edited by V. Treckner & R. Chalmers, 1888–1902). London: Pali Text Society; and *Samyutta Nikāya*, Vols I–V. (Edited by L. Feer, 1884–1898). London: Pali Text Society.
10 This account is found in the Sigalovada Sutta of the *Dīgha Nikāya*, Vols I–III. (Edited by T. W. Rhys Davids & J. E. Carpenter, 1889–1910). London: Pali Text Society.
11 Two recent publications provide excellent discussions of Buddhist ethics: Kalupahana, D. J. (1995). *Ethics in Early Buddhism*. Honolulu: University of Hawaii Press; and Premasiri, P. D. (1991). *Ethics. (Encyclopaedia of Buddhism*, Offprint No. 1). Colombo: Department of Buddhist Affairs.
12 See: Suzuki, D. T. (1957). *An introduction to Zen Buddhism*. London: Rider; Suzuki, D. T., Fromm, E. & de Martino, R. *Zen Buddhism and Psychoanalysis*. London: Souvenir Press; and Mikulas, W. L. (1981). Buddhism and behavior modification. *Psychological Record*, 31, 331–342.
13 See M. W. P. de Silva's discussion of this in: De Silva, M. W. P. (1973). *Buddhist and Freudian psychology*, Colombo: Lake House Publishers.

14 *Nettippakarana*. (Edited by E. Hardy, 1902). London: Pali Text Society.
15 See Vols 1 and 2 of *Anguttara Nikāya*, Vols I–V, (1922–1938). (Edited by R. Morris & E. Hardy). London: Pali Text Society.
16 These are discussed in various discourses in the *Dīgha Nikāya (op. cit.* (Note 10), and *Anguttara Nikāya*, *op. cit.* (Note 15).
17 *Majjhima Nikāya*, *op. cit.* (Note 9).
18 These aspects are considered in: *Mahā Niddesa*, Vols. I–II. (Edited by L. de la vallee Poussin & E. J. Thomas, 1916–1917). London: Pali Text Society; and *Sutta Nipāta*. (Edited by D. Anderson & H. Smith, 1913). London: The Pali Text Society.
19 *Anguttara Nikāya, op. cit.* (Note 15).
20 See, on this point: Rogers, C. (1961). *On becoming a person*. Boston: Houghton Mifflin; Maslow, A. H. (1964). *Religions, values and peak experiences*. New York: Harper & Row; and Maslow, A. H. (1970). *The farther reaches of human nature*. New York: Viking. The quote is from Goleman, D. (1988) *The Meditative Mind*. Los Angeles: Tarcher.
21 Detailed discussions of Buddhist meditation are available in several sources, including: Claxton, G. (1987). Meditation in Buddhist psychology. In M. A. West (Ed.). *The psychology of meditation*, Oxford: Clarendon Press; Kwee, M. G. T. (Ed.) (1990). *Psychotherapy, meditation and health*. London: East-West Publications; Pradhan, A. P. (1986). *The Buddha's system of meditation*, Vols. I–III. London: Oriental University Press; Solé-Leris, A. (1986). *Tranquillity and insight*. London: Rider; and Vajiranana, P. (1978). *Buddhist meditation in theory and practice* (2nd ed.). Kuala Lampur: Buddhist Missionary Society.
22 See Rahula, W. *op. cit.* (Note 4).
23 Accounts of meditation are found in many canonical texts and, in much detail, in Buddhaghosa's *Visuddhimagga*, Vols. I–II. (Edited by C. A. F. Rhys Davids, 1920–1921). London: Pali Text Society.
24 See: De Silva, P. (1984). Buddhism and behaviour modification. *Behaviour Research and Therapy*, **22**, 661–278; and de Silva, P. (1986). Buddhism and behaviour change: Implications for therapy. In G. Claxton (Ed.), *Beyond Therapy*, London: Wisdom Publications; also Mikulas, W. L. (1981). Buddhism and behavior modification. *Psychological Record*, **31**, 331–342.
25 See Note 24.
26 Ellis, A. (1974) *Humanistic psychotherapy: The Rational-Emotive approach*, New York: McGraw-Hill; also see Dryden, D. (1984) *Rational-Emotive Therapy: Fundamentals and innovations*. London: Croom Helm.
27 Beck, A. T. (1976). *Cognitive therapy and the emotional disorders*, New York: International Universities Press.
28 De Silva, P. (1984) *op. cit.* (Note 24).
29 This is from Vol. III of: *Jātaka*, Vols. I–VI. (Edited by V. Fausboll, 1887–1896). London: Pali Text Society.
30 For a discussion of the Early Buddhist attitude to enquiry, evidence and dogma, see: Jayatilleke, K. N. (1963). *Early Buddhist theory of knowledge*. London: Allen & Unwin.

31 Reports of the work of Jon Kabat-Zinn and his team are found in: Bernhard, J. D., Kristeller, J. & Kabat-Zinn, J. (1988). Effectiveness of relaxation and visualization techniques as an adjunct to psychotherapy and photochemotherapy of psoriasis. *Journal of the American Academy of Dermatology*, **19**, 572–573; Kabat-Zinn, J., Lipworth, L., Burney, R., & Sellers, W. (1986). Four-year follow-up of a meditation-based program for the self-regulation of chronic pain: Treatment outcomes and compliance. *Clinical Journal of Pain*, **2**, 159–173; and Kabat-Zinn, J., Massion, A. O., Kristeller, J. et al. (1992). Effectiveness of a meditation-based stress reduction program in the treatment of anxiety disorders. *American Journal of Psychiatry*, **149**, 936–943.
33 John Teasdale's ideas and work on the usefulness of mindfulness meditation in clinical practice are found in several places. One of the clearest expositions is found in: Teasdale, J. D., Segal, Z. and Williams, J. M. G. (1995). How does cognitive therapy prevent depressive relapse and why should attentional control (mindfulness) help? *Behaviour Research and Therapy*, **33**, 25–39.

Chapter 4

EDITOR'S PREFACE

The allied enemies of insight are ignorance and prejudice. These, available in plentiful supply, have contributed to the misrepresentation and misappropriation of Buddhism in the West. A good antidote here is an informed and evenhanded presentation of the original teachings. This is what has made the work of Herbert Guenther so well respected among scholars of Buddhism throughout the world. His books show the subtlety, depth and richness of Buddhist teachings, especially of Tibetan traditions. His hermeneutic style places these teachings within their the cultural context. Rather than making them estoeric and inaccesible, this is a neccessary preliminary to exploring how these teachings may be relevant to contemporary Western thought.

Here, in setting out some psychological ideas found in those sources, professor Guenther reveals some suggestive points of comparison with Western traditions. While comparison does not necessarily imply correspondance, these points concern selfhood, the relationship between rationality and emotion and the ontological distinction between process and materiality. Where Western thought has in general tended to essentialise and to formalise the world as thing-like, Buddhist traditions have tended to approach reality, including the human phenomenological condition as being essentially process-like.

Of course, if an inquiry is sufficiently superficial, resemblances are easily found. However, professor Guenther's deep understand of both Buddhist and Western traditions, renders these resemblances reliable and rich. In particular, it is clear that Buddhist teachings overlap with Western process thinkers such as Spinoza, Bergson and Whitehead. Structure at all levels of order, whether material and phenomenological, is the result of dynamic, rather than static factors. It is the outcome of a process, not an inherent property of enduring world-stuff, like particles or substances. Likewise, selfhood and experience, as represented in Buddhism, are fundamentally dynamic and are never essentialised as being attached to something self-identical or soul like. Here, Western philosophers, like Rorty or Clarke, again seem to be advancing a similar view. Indeed some, Parfitt for example, explicitly acknowledge Buddhism as an influence.

Such resemblances between Eastern and Western thought are now being explored in many areas of science, psychology and philosophy. This is helping to refine the contact made during the 1960's and 1970's which was all too often superficial and over-generalised. The Western scientific worldview is, independently, undergoing a major shift towards indeterminacy and emergence. In the vacuum left by the collapse of simple reductionism are appearing the ideas to which Guenther points in his discussion of mental and physical causality. This is helping to narrow the separation of mainstream science and the phenomenological lineage of Husserl, Heidegger and Merleau-Ponty. Psychology is becoming increasingly open to qualitative methodology and to direct inquiry into experience itself.

Complementing these trends, Guenther's chapter demonstrates the systematicity of Buddhist psychological teaching. In discussing Buddhism using the vocabulary of set theory, he reminds us that much Buddhist thought has the formalised character of science rather than the intuitive character of mysticism. Perhaps it would be more accurate to say that what the chapter offers is an insight into a different balance between the rational and the intuitive. The opposition of these factors as poles of human understanding is a restrictive leftover from modernism. In the postmodern spirit of informed eclecticism we can find a new and non-oppositional balance between them. In doing so, we can recover the project of Husserl and Merleau-Ponty: to return to the phenomena themselves. For psychology, this is the appropriately ironic self-referring project of using experience to understand experience.

★　★　★

Basic Features of Buddhist Psychology

Herbert Guenther

From the outset the socio-cultural-spiritual phenomenon that became known as Buddhism insisted on its being a way with the implied connotation that the going is the way. This going somehow presupposes a territory in the vastness of which the wayfarer attempts to find his way. Finding one's way and travelling it would not be possible if there were not already some intelligence at work. This intelligence is customarily called a mind and, for the above stated reason, is of primary importance. Unfortunately, the term 'mind', even in its Western context, is not precise, because it reflects two conflicting trends. One trend is to elevate it into a metaphysical principle, the other is to reduce it to a metaphor for neurophysiological processes of the brain. Either trend poses more problems and questions than it can solve or answer.[1]

If our term 'mind' is already vague, its application to what in Buddhist texts is called *citta* (without taking into account what the Buddhists themselves understood by this keyword or how they interpreted it), makes one doubt whether the current interest in Buddhism is not some kind of infatuation with some misunderstood, if not unununderstood, novelty, rather than a serious attempt at coming to grips with a phenomenon that was meant to have an immediate impact on one's life. In view of the fact that Buddhism not only claimed to be a way of life, but also made it abundantly clear that this way of life was a way of learning, where learning, in the words of Erich Jantsch,[2] was 'not the importation of strange knowledge into a system, but the mobilization of processes which are inherent to the learning system itself and belong to its proper cognitive domain,' should suffice to show that Buddhist thinking was pre-eminently process-oriented with structural patterns subordinate. However, speaking of something being subordinate to something has its dangers. It may be understood as just another misplaced vindication of a widely held, egologically inspired, dominance psychology or as a perpetuation of a rational(istic) approach to 'reality' (whatever this may mean) that bases itself on the quite irrational premise of an either/or. The fact is that wherever something alive is involved, process and structure intertwine such that what we call 'mind' is a *process structure* or dynamic régime.[3]

It was this dynamic character of what the Buddhists called *citta* that distinguished their thinking from the static and rigidly defined world view of their contemporaries. In order to understand the full import of this difference in perspective and of what it may hold for modern man, a few words about this keyword become necessary.[4]

According to Vasubandhu, one of the foremost representatives of the Sanskrit tradition, *citta* is 'that which builds up' as well as 'that which has been built up by healthy and/or unhealthy building blocks,' and according to Buddhaghosa, the foremost representative of the Pali tradition, *citta* is 'called so because it intends its referential terminus; ... as the outcome of specific forces, *citta* is so called because it has been built up by action programs and affective processes; ... *citta* is called so, because it generates variety.'[5] All this goes to show that *citta* is not some isolated phenomenon, some 'static' entity or thing, but derives its meaning from the context in which it operates 'dynamically.' Context is another important feature of Buddhist psychology. In one of the oldest canonical texts it is introduced by the words: 'When a healthy attitude (*citta*), belonging to the sphere of human activity where desires hold sway, accompanied by and permeated with serenity, and associated and linked up with [the experiencer's] intellectual-spiritual acumen (*ñana*), has arisen...'[6] The context, 'the sphere of human activity where desires hold sway,' is, in modern phenomenological-psychological terminology, our *Befindlichkeit,* 'a primordial, bodily felt sense-of-being-in-the-world.'[7]

Lastly, the Buddhist conception of *citta* as a dynamic régime prancing back and forth in feedback loops and its relation to health seems to have anticipated Henri Bergson's notion of the formation of memory through repeated interpretation in such feedback learning processes, and Erich Jantsch's statement that 'even microorganisms, in probing their environment and selecting 'good' directions for their next movement, seem to develop a memory and the capability of comparing.'[8]

Just as process and structure are inextricably intertwined, so models and myths are interdependent,[9] and the history of Buddhism unequivoclly supports this claim. Three movements and three levels are discernible in man's building a model of man and his mind.

The first mode of model building reflects the early Buddhist thinkers' pride in their analytical acumen that reduced man to a bundle of complex patterns, called 'groupings,' of which the last topic in their enumeration, 'consciousness' or, more precisely, 'perception' attracted a sustained interest. In other words, the early Buddhists were epistemology-oriented: *what* do we perceive, and how do we organize our world on the basis of our perceptions? Theirs was a world based on the separation of the experiencer and the experienced, the observer and the observed, the one as impersonal as the other. Its organizing principle was *logic* and its overall impression was one of mere quantity and structure.

The second mode of model building reflected man's appreciation of what he perceived in both his external and internal world. Its organizing principle was *feeling* and the overall impression was one of quality and of *how* to get along with the images through which the forces of life and nature manifest themselves and in which we encounter them on our way. This second mode that involves a significant change in one's attitude from an impersonal point of view to a participatory engagement in what can be said to be the origin of any creative act, imperceptibly fuses with what in its practical application was termed 'leading one's life by tuning-in to the life force' (*yogacara*). Here 'fixation-concentration' has given way to 'creative experimentation.'

A third mode of model building, considered to surpass the above mentioned two modes, was the much misunderstood discipline of Tantra. The original meaning of this Sanskrit term is a 'loom' and, in its extended meaning, the 'weaving of one's life.' The tantric mode is holistic and existential in the sense of Karl Jaspers' notion of Existenz:[10]

> Existenz is the never objectified source of my thoughts and actions. It is that whereof I speak in trains of thought that involve no cognition. It relates to itself, and thus to its transcendence ...

Since another meaning of Tantra is 'continuity' it evinces a close affinity with Henri Bergson's notion of *durée* (duration) and Martin Heidegger's notion of the *Dasein* as the being that we ourselves are.

From among these three modes of model building the first two lead to the myth of objectivism, be this of an epistemology type or value theory type with materialism thrown in for good measure, and subjectivism, be this also of an epistemology type or value theory type and often identified with idealism (sometimes called mentalism or immaterialism) in its almost innumerable nuances.[11] What these two myths have in common is their reductionism that emphasizes a one-sided confirmation of what is basiclly speculative. In the words of Erich Jantsch:[12]

> Just as there is a 'downward reductionism' to materialism, there is also an 'upward reductionsim,' corresponding to a purely spiritual life which remains without consequences.

More poetically and experientially this pernicious dualism has been castigated by Klong-chen rab-'byams-pa (1308-1364):[13]

> As to the ultimate energy that we are
> A chain of gold and a rope of hemp are alike in fettering it/us;
> Meaning and nonmeaning are alike in fettering our mind;
> White and black clouds are alike in obscuring (the light of the sun);
> Good and evil are alike in obscuring (our) supraconscious ecstatic intensity;
> Therefore for a yogi who understands
> It is important that he passes beyond good and evil, cause and effect.

We have already noted that the Buddhist term *citta* has wider connotations than our 'mind' and that as an operator, a sort of feedback/feedforward mechanism, it requires and presupposes an environment that, in the human context, is a sociocultural milieu, the sphere where, at the lowest level, desires hold sway. I have added the phrase 'at the lowest level' to indicate that the Buddhists conceived of man in terms of a triune hierarchy of levels of which each had its own self-organizing dynamics.[14] Furthermore, in view of the fact that the operator *citta* is the principal among other operators, called *caitta*,[15] we can speak of all feedback/feedforward mechanisms – each individual being such a mechanism – as forming a set, which we can write

{all feedback/feedforward mechanism}

Letting *x* stand for feedback/feedforward mechanism, we can rewrite the same set as

{*x*|*x* is a feedback/feedforward mechanism}

which reads 'the set of all x is such that x is a feedback/feedforward mechanism.' Since we can specify a set by some property such that there is only one item (entity or object) with that property, it is possible to allow sets with just one member and write $\{x\}$. This excursion into modern set theory, a branch of mathematics, is not fortuitous. First of all, the Indians have always been and still are excellent mathematicians, and secondly, the idea of a mandala, having become well known through the work of the late Swiss psychologist Carl Gustav Jung, is, as a centered four, the psyche's self-geometrization throughout its triune hierarchy.[16] As we shall see later, this theory can account for the (later) Buddhists' claim that there is only one *citta*, which was developed into the '*citta-* only thesis' *(cittamatra)* without falling into the trap of a speculative and static monism because of the dynamic character of *citta*. Lastly, historically speaking, the development of Buddhist psychology coincided with the flourishing of Indian mathematics. It would be presumptious on our part to assume that the Indian *intelligentsia* lived in utter isolation and in blissful ignorance of what went on in other disciplines.

It will be helpful to remind ourselves of the fact that the Buddhists used their keyword *citta* with reference to a set with only one member, namely *citta*, and the term *caitta* with reference to sets with several members. There are two closely related sets with several (that is, five) members that in each set again are closely related to each other so that they can be summed up in the formula $(1+1) +/\rightarrow (1+1) +/\rightarrow 1$. This set is said to be present with or accompanying every attitude or *citta*. The Pali tradition, represented by Buddhaghosa, and the Sanskrit tradition, represented by Vasubandhu and his commentator Sthiramati, are so similar that it suffices to outline the internal logic in the Sanskrit tradition. The first member in this ever-present set is called *sparsa*. Literally rendered, it means 'touch,' primarily of a physical kind, but then also meaning what we express by the phrase 'to be in contact or in touch with' that may be understood physically and/or mentally.[17] In any case, just as, from the Budhist perspective, the eye is in contact with the 'visible,' so the mind is in contact with 'ideas.' In other words, as human beings we are tactilely programmed with the implication, developed in later Buddhist thought as the third mode of model building, that the human body is not to be despised because it is the vehicle of the instincts as well as of the spirit. (Are we not lived by our emotions, our *libido*, not necessarily in the narrow, oversimplistic, and misleading Freudian sense, and are we not in touch with what, for want of a better term, we call our spirituality transcending its enframement, called our body?).

If it were not for the fact that we are tactilely programmed, we would not only not feel anything, we would also not be able to set up a subjective relationship with the outside world and explore not only the near-infinite spectrum of flavors the external world holds for us, but also the immense wealth of our inner world. Both Buddhaghosa and Sthiramati were well aware of the relationship between 'touch' and 'feeling' (*vedana*).[18]

While feeling may be said to provide the 'climate' of the situation, judged to be pleasant or unpleasant or neutral, 'sensation' (*samjña*) serves to form images, the stock and trade of psychic life, and sets the scene for acting on what is being sensed by having mirrored, as it were, an outer reality which it rebuilds in the inner world. Inasmuch as the members in this ever-present set are not granular and isolated entities in themselves but as psychic operators or functions intertwine, it is possible to relate them to aspects of C.G. Jung's typology in such a way that feeling can be said to constitute a rational function, because it is decisively influenced by reflection, and that sensation constitutes an irrational function, because it is beyond (the dictates of) reason, all of which goes to show that the Buddhist analysis of psychic life is closer to modern thinking than has been surmised.[19]

Within this five-member set two other members are closely related to each other. The one is called *cetana*, which Vasubandhu defines as a 'setting-up of an attitude'[20] and equates with *manaskara*, defined by Yasomitra as a 'tilting of one's cognitive apparatus in the direction of an objective reference.'[21] Broadly speaking, *cetana* corresponds to a cognitive intentionality of a normally mature ego. The other is implied by the term *manaskara* which Buddhaghosa explicitly replaces by *citta* that he lets operate as having a thematic focus and as reflecting on what is found in the experiential situation and what, consequently, is fitted into an already existing cognitive domain. Whatever the subtle nuances in these definitions may have been, it is obvious that the general trend was the same: what we call 'world' is presented as an external ('objective') totality of entities with clearly definable contours, somehow presented to an internal ('subjective') mind. In modern Western phenomenological studies this is called 'representational thinking.'

This ever-present five-member set is followed by another five-member set that is defined as being 'object-specific.' This sequence of sets allows us to think of the first set as a human being's pre-program of his thinking and of the second set as the actualization of this pre-program in specific operations, all of which again shows that the early Buddhists could be proud of their analytical acumen, for which reason they were also known as Vibhajyavadins, that is, 'analysts.' Still, speaking of a sequence of sets must not be construed as an act of serialization, but rather as an intensification of the underlying process-oriented thinking.

This second five-member set is specific to the Sanskrit tradition and its internal logic continues that of the first five-member set. The first member of this set is called 'predilection' (*chanda*) and implies a strong liking and a predisposed preference for certain kinds of things.[22] As such it reflects and reinforces the individual's situatedness (*Befindlichkeit*) in his world of sensual desires.

The second member is called 'conviction' (*adhimoksa*). It adds to the preceding member's selectiveness a dimension of restriction so that that which has been selected becomes the sole focus of attention to the exclusion of everything else.[23] Restriction can work in two different directions. It can aid a person in developing and deepening his understanding of a given topic, including himself, in which case it links up with the following member (*smrti*) in this set. Or, it can make a person intolerant and dogmatic when the overall attitude is negative or unhealthy.

The third member (*smrti*), defying any 'definitive' reductionist translation, operates in two ways. The one is what is commonly referred to as 'memory' or 'recollection.' As such it is only mediately involved in a person's spiritual growth that is the ultimate aim of Buddhism as a way. In the strictly Buddhist context *smrti* is not the futile running after fleeting memories through which one may lose sight of the present exigency, but a function to keep the objective constituent as steady and constant before the mind's eye and to learn more about it (which ultimately means to learn more about one's self). In Western psychology, C.D. Broad has aptly called this operation 'inspection.'[24] It is interesting to note that, because of its overall importance in concentrative exercises, Buddhaghosa deals with it in terms of its being part of a controlling system,[25] which should not come as a surprise since representational thinking is not only objectifying, but also *manipulative* thinking.

Closely related to inspection is *samadhi*. It is an operator that ensures successful concentration and thus is both a process and an (end-)state.[26] But being an end-state does not mean that it is an absorption in something undefinable, grandiloquously called the

Absolute, rather it is an 'in-depth appraisal' that is still tied to an egological premise. The Tibetan rendering of *samadhi* by *ting-nge-'dzin* clearly brings out its egological implication. The term *'dzin* ('holding/grasping') is always correlated to the term *gzung* ('that which is to be held/grasped' or 'that which solicits the holding/ grasping'), but in this case that which is the objective reference in one's customary subject-object structure is (temporarily) suspended and no longer projected into something supposedly external, rather it is a ringing vibration (*ting-nge*), sensed deeply within one's self. The upshot of the matter is that it pays well to pay closest attention to the linguistic expression within the context in which it is used.

The last member in this five-member, object-specific set is called *dhi*.

This term is an archaism that dates back to the Vedic period of Indian literature. In course of time it was replaced by Vasubandhu by the term *mati* 'intellect' or 'judiciousness' or even 'opinion,' and by Sthiramati by the term *prajña* 'discriminative-appreciative awareness.'[27] Sthiramati's insight that this operator can also operate in an improper manner, should be ample evidence that the rendering of this term by 'wisdom' is wholly inappropriate. As a matter of fact today's 'wisdom'-addicts are guilty of a double crime (if ignorance is a crime and not a virtue). They are ignorant of the use of this technical term in the original literature (Sanskrit and/or Tibetan), and they are ignorant of the meaning of the word 'wisdom' (which they confuse with one pet notion in the welter of their personal idiosyncrasies) in English.[28]

Within the framework of representational thinking that permeates Buddhist presentations of philosophical and psychological problems, set-theoretical considerations played an important role and also were instrumental in the attempt to rediscover the unity and uniqueness of the mind that had been lost in the welter of operators conceived entitatively. While there are sets with a plurality of members, there are also sets with only one member, and it is only a matter of temperament or choice whether one subcribes to sets with many members or to sets with only one member. The Yogacara thinkers who were to become the most influential representatives of the Buddhist thought-'experiment' with their insistence on 'mentality/ mind-only' (*cittamatra*) opted for a set with only one member. This left them in a quandary. What to do with the many other operators that continued to make their presence felt?[29] Again set-theoretical considerations turn out to be very helpful. Often one set can be a subset of a set. That is to say, a set S is said to be a subset of a set M

81

provided that every member of S is a member of M. Every member of the set S of cognitive (and/or sociocultural) operators is a cognitive (and/or sociocultural) operator, hence a mentalistic operator (*caitta*), hence a member of of the set M of all mentality/mind (*citta*). Space does not allow a discussion of the various sociocultural operators that played such an important role in interpersonal relationships and prevented the Buddhists from falling into the trap of one of the most reductionist 'sciences' ever developed in the Western world – behaviorism.

But if there is only mentality/mind, materiality (or what we associate with a material world) is out of the question. And this is precisely what the mentalistic Yogacara thinkers claimed: the external material-physical world is a fiction of the mind. This claim again shows that the Indian Buddhist thinkers were excellent logicians. The only trouble is that logic is a tool of representational thinking and, because of its restricted applicability, not very useful in dealing with other modes of thinking that involve or pertain to other realms of being. Although the Yogacara followers retained much of their predecessors' and contemporaries' structure-oriented thinking, their emphasis on mentality/mind as the sole reality forced them to take into account this reality's ontological dimension.

The ontological character of this one-member set was indicated by the term *alayavijñana* which, departing from its traditional mechanistic (and hence not quite appropriate) rendering as 'storehouse consciousness' with its suggestion of the mind being a container (not necessarily in the Freudian sense of its subconscious aspect (a highly dubious postulate) being a garbage bin for repressed and suppressed notions), I prefer, in line with what the original texts (Sanskrit and Tibetan) have to say, to render as 'foundational cognitiveness,' where 'foundational' intimates its ontological dimension and 'cognitiveness' continues the traditional epistemological operation. As a matter of fact, the Sanskrit word *alaya* basically means a 'substratum' in the sense of that which underlies, maintains, or supports. Its specification as being of the nature of being the totality of all experientially initiated potentialities of experience has little to do with the Western idea of a 'storehouse' or 'container.'

The truly innovative idea was that this foundational cognitiveness was understood as a process involving a triune transformation (*parinama*) that ensured its ontological continuity in what was to become one's ego-dominated individuality. The first transformation was termed 'maturation' in the sense of being both process and outcome of the process. In its former aspect it corresponded to the older notion of 'cause,' but in this newer perspective it was understood as the 'momentum' imparted to the process emerging from the 'experientially initiated potentialities of experience' that as pervasive microstructures were figuratively called 'seeds.' These were of two kinds: (1) pure potentialities that as sediments of operations reflecting the nature of their origin – whether their operations had occurred in a valuative (moral) context that allowed itself to be described as healthy, unhealthy, and neutral and as having operational consquences or not – were themselves amoral; (2) potentialities-in-the-process-of becoming-actualized that matured into healthy and/or unhealthy operations with distinct consequences. To a certain extent these two microstructures correspond to the Jungian idea of archetypes.[30] While Jung's understanding is basically correct, his choice of the term 'archetype,' going back to Saint Augustine, is unfortunate, because it reflects and perpetuates the Westerner's obsession with an 'origin' (Greek *arche*). By contrast, the Buddhists with their insistence on process knew that a process (like going one's way) has no beginning and no end, it is always in the middle. Hence they could call their way the Middle Way.

The second transformation, concurrent with the first one, marks the emergence of the subject-object structure. Its 'thinking' is of two kinds: (1) 'factual' it moves in the dualism of affirmation and negation; (2) 'affective' it is concerned with acceptance and rejection. Whether factual or affective, this thinking is objectifying thinking that because of the ego's limited horizon leaves out a lot and prejudges what does not suit its interests as of little or no significance.

The third transformation, concurrent with the first and second transformations, was known as 'information' in the sense of announcing the self-organization of the system 'mind' as brought into a specific form – in the present case, the human individual. To be precise, information is *in* – formation. It covers the six perceptual operations. Of these, five correspond to our sensory perceptions that in the framework of our psychology are both physical and psychic. To these the Buddhists added a sixth perceptual operation performed by the *manas* that dealt with ideas. To give an example of the Buddhists' keen observation that antedated Kant's observation by centuries: the eye perceives a colored patch, it is the *manas* that perceived this colored patch as, say, a tree. But then, what for analytical purposes may be said a to be a fusion of sense-specific impressions and meaning-specific assertions (the 'factual' side of perception or so-called epistemological object), is suffused with feelings about what is so perceived (the 'affective' side of perception).

As is so often the case, the Buddhists, specifically those of the Yogacara persuasion, were fully aware of the limitations set by objectifying thinking and anticipated Martin Heidegger's somewhat cryptic statement that

Objectification blocks us off against the Open.[31]

Thus they moved away from restricting and restrictive 'transformations' (*parinama*) to what in the Western context Heidegger was the first thinker to note and to insist upon – the *Kehre,* the turning, the 'moment of vision' or, to give it its Sanskrit name *paravrtti* . We shall return to this 'moment of vision' later on.

In Buddhist psychology the idea and treatment of what we call the emotions or emotionality has little in common with the Western conception of its standing in sharp contrast with rationality. The Western rationality-emotionality dichotomy goes back to Plato who in his famous lecture *On the Good* correctly noted the presence of two ground principles in the nature of things. One was the rational and formal principle which he called *logos* and deemed to be male and investigated in his *Republic*.[32] The other was the emotional and aesthetic principle which he called *eros* and deemed to be female (in spite of the fact that *eros* is a masculine noun) and investigated in the *Phaedrus* and the *Symposium*. Failing to note an important distinction he quite arbitrarily in the *Timaeus* branded the male as good and the female as evil. This arbitrary judgment and misconception reflecting his personal, if not the ancient Greeks' general attitude of misogyny, was to have disastrous consequences for the evolving Western sociocultural-political institutions that in the wake of this thinking and under the impact of an equally male-oriented Judaeo-Christian ideology became increasingly hostile and contemptuous of women. This attitude of marginalizing women is still rampant today in the widely believed-in myth of psychoanalysis whose main representatives and protagonists were the Austrian Sigmund Freud and the French Jacques Lacan. Both have been severely criticized, Freud for his peniscentrism and Lacan for his phallocentrism.[33] Both fail miserably in recognizing and taking seriously Gaston Bachelard's suggestion that we should honor both maleness and femaleness and that our goal should be 'to live at both poles of our androgynous being.'[34]

For the Buddhists *both* rationality *and* emotionality are obscurations of the individual's original luminous being. Rationality obscures this natural light by attempting to deal with the complex nature of reality through introducing a separation between subject and object and, then, through imposing on the allegedly 'objective' world his 'subjective,' ego-logically and ego-centrically circumscribed speculations that reflect the metaphysical assumption that the model of the world so created is absolutely valid and what is not represented in it is of liitle or no relevance. Emotionality obscures this natural light by responding instinctively to the demands of the rational mind by either aiding or curtailing them. Both rationality and emotionality are, in our ideology and terminology, biological phenomena and differ from each other in the sense that rationality is a kind of intellectual obscuration and that emotionality is a kind of instinctive obsuration that, in particular, refers to the quality (or lack of quality) in human activity. In its failure to arrive at an understanding of that which concerns a human being most, the meaning of his life, rationality becomes indistinguishable from emotionality. This indistinguishability is sensed as an abysmal darkness and dullness, that can be summed up in the formula *avidya* ('diminished cognitiveness,' 'diminished excitability') equals *moha* ('bewilderment,' 'infatuation').

Again I have intentionally avoided the commonly accepted rendering of *avidya* by 'ignorance,' because this rendering reflects the persistence of a mechanistic-reductionist science, called linguistics (that, to be fair, was not always mechanistic-reductionist, but became so by its infection with the virus of the prevailing reductionism in all disciplines). The *a-* in this word does not denote the negation of what is called *vidya* 'knowledge' as it does in the word *ahimsa* 'non-violence.' We know that every living is capable of becoming excited and keep its level of excitation, in which process fluctuations play a significant role The implication for the system called 'man' is that its level of excitation may be low or high, but never absent, which for *avidya* as a characteristic of a living person then means that this term describes a particular person's state of cognitiveness as being *not quite* at its optimal level of excitation. Hence, the *a-* in *avidya* functions quite differently from the *a-* in *ahimsa* . This difference is clearly brought out in the Tibetan equivalents of these two terms: *ma-rig-pa* (*not quite (ma)* the supraconscious ecstatic intensity of a person's Existenz) and *'tshe-ba-med-pa* the *non-existence (med-pa)* of violence. Perpetuations of past misinterpretations will not help a serious student of Buddhism.

There is one other important difference between the Western and Budhist notions of emotionality. From Plato onward in the West, emotionality and the welter of discrete emotions have been viewed as agitating forces that disrupt the static image of the cosmos as postulated by reason that cannot allow the intrusion of such sensibilites as kindliness and concern into its impersonal world-view that, in the words of Erich Jantsch, sets 'man against the world minus man.'[35] By contrast, Buddhism distinguished between emotions-proper as obscuring forces that, to make matters worse, quite literally were 'poisoning' and 'polluting' the relationship between individuals, on the one hand, and what I have called 'catalysts.' There were four of them: (1) love in the specific sense of kindliness and partnership, not in the sense of passion with which love is often confused and which is an emotion or, in Buddhist terms, a pollutant; (2) compassion in the sense of an active or participatory concern, not in the sense of some sentimentality or sympathy (with its implied co-suffering);[36] (3) joyfulness in the sense of a felt happiness in seing someone succeed in his quest, not in the sense of a mere feeling of elation; and (4) equanimity in the sense of an impartial gaze, not in the sense of indifference. From a practical point of view we can witness how, to give an example, a kind word can change the whole atmosphere or situation.[37]

The claim put forward by the Buddhists that what they had to offer for practical living was a way in the sense of a *going,* was only too often forgotten by themselves and led to stagnation in many guises. One such forgetfulness can be attributed to the Buddhists' succumbing to the prevailing Indian preoccupation with epistemology- and structure-oriented thinking that was numerically restrictive-reductionist. The focus was on the *what*, and the way's outstanding characteristic, concentration on some pre-existent 'goal,' was referential, that is, having an objective reference, be this an external object or an internal (mental) state. The technical term for this procedure was *dhyana* and its description in the original texts reveals the limitations of representational thinking. However, this impoverishing mode of thinking was challenged by a different kind of thinking that allowed experience to have a say in one's going one's way. This experience-rooted intuitive thinking was intimated by what was technically known as *jñana*. It had been there all the time, but was overlooked, if not to say, dismissed by the preoccupation with the so-called 'objective.'[38]

The exercise of this experience-rooted, ontological-existential thinking was variously known as *yoga*, meaning a 'harnessing (of one's inner potential)' and interpreted by the Tibetans as *rnal-'byor,* meaning a 'linking backward to the level of quietness (where evolution is poised and a new start is made possible),' or as *bhavana*, which, literally translated, means 'to cause to exist,' 'to bring into the open.'[39] As the cultivation of the experiencer's inner potential it is akin to what C.G. Jung has called 'active imagination,' and as kind of creative experimentation, as which I would like to render this technical term, it is a far cry from the static-fixational *dhyana*.

Within the framework of the Buddhist Way in its totality, 'active imagination' or creative experimentation as a way in its own right, follows, as it were, the way of seeing, in Heidegger's words, 'the moment of vision' in which the experiencer has achieved a different vision and enjoys an openness from which his normal, that is, pathological egocentricity and logocentrity has barred him. This moment of vision involves, analytically speaking, the awareness that everything is impermanent, that what is impermanent is felt as frustrating, that what is impermanent and frustrating defies the assumption that it has an essence (or 'self') by which something is what it is, and that beyond these restrictive forces there is a dimension of sheer joy. Divesting this experience of sheer joy of the mystifying verbiage of the cultists of every persuasion, it can be likened to the aha experience of inner creativity, the cry of *eureka* by Archimedes, and Abraham Maslow's peak experience, for which the term *enlightenment*, itself a rather misleading term, is often used, and which is considered to be an achievement. But as the Buddhist texts make abundantly clear, this moment of vision is not an achievement. As a break-through it is the threshold to a shift in self-identity, the discontinuity of the ego-level tendencies. This 'felt' shift in self-identity needs disciplined practice in order to have this experience of sheer joy translated into action. This disciplined practice is summed up in what is termed *bhavana*, involving ten levels of which its first one is named after the joy experienced in the moment of vision.[40]

There is a marked shift in terminology concerning what referred to the non-self (*anatta/anatman*) specification of the moment of vision. The new terms, reflecting the more process-oriented mode of thinking and superseding the older static structure-oriented mode of thinking, were the (adjective) *sunya* and the (noun) *sunyata* which led the non-Buddhists to refer to the Buddhists as *sunyatavadin* s 'those who profess (the metaphysical notion of) *sunyata*.' This term, usually translated as 'emptiness' is one of the most misunderstood and misrepresented terms in the whole of Buddhist thought and, even in Tibet, has created an unprecedented intolerance and fanaticism that, in recent years, has spilled over into the West where it is aided and abetted by those who reject the historical Buddha's advice of 'find out for yourself' and are content with voicing what some dogmatist has told them.

Let us find out what this controversial term actually means. By way of preamble let us point out that 'empty' or 'emptiness' are container metaphors. There are empty boxes, empty dishes, and, why not, empty minds. After all, like a box or a dish, a mind is a noun and nouns stand for things (like boxes and dishes).[41] However, 'empty' and/or 'emptiness' as descriptors are something quite different from a metaphysical principle to which the 'emptiness'-fanatics attempt to raise these descriptors (of, probably, their own minds).

Now let us briefly trace the history and usage of the word *sunya*. Firstly, it derives from the Indo-European root *su*, meaning 'to swell,' 'to increase in size,' out of which the idea of 'strength,' on the one hand, and the idea of 'hollowness' (Latin *cavus*), on the other hand, developed. The word, therefore, conveys a basically positive notion. This is also evident from the fact that, in view of the global *horror vacui*, whenever we speak of something negative, we tend to weaken this negativity by using not one, but several words, as is done in the Pali scriptures or, in the case of architectural forms such as the friezes of Greek temples, filling empty spaces with garlands and or other ornamental devices. When we say that someone comes with empty hands and thereby emphasize negativity, the Indian equivalent of this phrase is 'he comes with his hands still there.' Lastly, when referring to an 'empty-headed' person, the current Hindi phrase positively states that 'there is chaff in his head.' Nowhere is there any talk of *sunya* or of our cherished emptiness. Secondly, in the field of mathematics, the Indians were the first to conceive of zero and coin a term for it – *sunya* or *bindu*. The Indian zero is not an empty shell. Rather, it embodies the calm center of the swirling and whirling tornado of life. The Indian zero may be 'empty' of numerical value, but it is 'full' of non-empirical possibilities. This paradox of a nothing that is everything which no logician (steeped in and constrained by his rational-representational-reductionist mode of thinking) has ever been able to understand, is central to an experiential mode of thinking in which experience as *Erleben* (lived-through reality) antedates experience as *Erfahrung* (reflected-on experience). This important distinction goes back to Wilhelm Dilthey (1833-1911) whose primary concern was with lived experience (*Erleben*) and the understanding (*Verstehen*) of its expressions. Formerly called *hermeneutics*, Dilthey's

Verstehen freed it from its theological restrictions. As J.J. Clarke has pointed out:[42]

> Dilthey's conception of the human sciences as a form of hermeneutics has had a considerable influence on certain twentieth century thinkers, most notably on Heidegger, the central figure of modern phenomenological and existential philosophy, and on his follower, Gadamer.

It is therefore quite conceivable that Dilthey's conception will prove to be very important for psychology in general and for a serious study of Buddhism in particular.

This paradox of a nothing that is everything was in the Western world first formulated by Basilides of Alexandria (middle of the second century of the CE), the greatest Gnostic thinker, and taken up centuries later by C.G. Jung in his *Septem Sermones ad Mortuous*.[43] It occurs again in the artist-philosopher Arturo B. Fallico's statement that 'the indifferently possible confronts us with something-which-is-nothing, and with nothing-which-is-something.'[44] This is precisely what in the Indian-Buddhist context Maitreya-Asanga (fourth century of the CE) had called 'the nothingness-that-has/is-everything.'

In the Tibetan context Maitreya-Asanga's dictum[45] became the source of violently fought-out arguments. To understand the background of this quarrel that has plagued philosophically minded Tibetans to this very day, it is important to note that the Tibetan word *stong-pa*, used to render the Sanskrit word *sunya*, is primarily a verb and not an adjective (according to our Aristotelian categories). Its verbal character could be best expressed by the now more or less obsolete German verb *nichten*, or paraphrased by Alfred North Whitehead's 'not allowing permanent structures to persist.' This verbal character led to the claim of a *rang-stong*, on the one hand, and a *gzhan-stong*, on the other hand. The former claim, thought through to its logical conclusion, means that what is under consideration *cancels itself out* and thus, in modern terms, is a plain case of nihilism. It is the avowed position the once all-powerful Gelukpa (*dge-lugs-pa*) faction and their modern Western adherents or 'emptiness'-fanatics.[46] By contrast, the followers of the *gzhan-stong* claim maintain that, in the words of C.G. Jung. everything else but what Karl Jaspers had called Existenz and to what Jung himself had referred to as a psychic reality lying on a supraluminous level of frequency, is *irrealized*. [47] This allows us to state unequivocally that the *rang-stong* claim is a dead-end street littered with trash, while the *gzhan-stong* claim is more like an alpine meadow bursting with flowers in bloom, suggesting infinite possibilities. So we shall leave the 'emptiness'-fanatics with their nihilism and their trash (*rang-stong*), enjoy the immense and dynamic richness of the *gzhan-stong*, and follow up that line of thought in which experience-as-lived is of primary importance.

This is the little, if not to say, largely unknown rDzogs-chen teaching.[48] It is rooted in the immediacy of experience before it is turned into a reflected-on experience and, hence, holistic in the strict sense of the word, for which reason it is best rendered in English as 'wholeness' and/or 'completeness (*rdzogs*) in an ultimate sense (*chen*).' Here it becomes imperative to distinguish between wholeness or a 'whole' and a 'totality' as succinctly elucidated by David Michael Levin:[49]

> A totality can be mastered, dominated, controlled; it can be grasped and possessed; it can be fixed and secured; it can be known with certainty; it is absolutely complete. A whole has its own completeness, but this completeness remains open. ... The difference between a whole and a totality is an ontological difference which cannot be understood by a reductively calculative rationality; it can only be understood aesthetically, that is to say, in an experience grounded in our sensibility, our capacity for feeling. We need, to begin with, a familiarity with the feeling of wholeness, we need to consult our deepest *sense* of wholeness.

Apart from its insistence on the immediacy of experience, rDzogs-chen teaching starts with the question any thinking person will ask some time or other, 'how did it all begin?' And the answer is: it all begins with the paradox of a nothingness-that-is-everything, This is summed up by Padmasambhava, the enigmatic sage from Urgyan (an ill-defined area extending from the Iranian plateau into Central Asia, now known as Chinese Turkestan), in the aphorism of 'Being and Being's lighting-up,'[50] where 'Being' (*gzhi*) corresponds to Jakob Boehme's idea of an *Ungrund* and to Martin Heidegger's Being (*das Sein*, to be, as (for purely analytical reasons) contrasted with *das Seiende*, that which is). Just like Boehme's *Ungrund* and Heidegger's *Sein* Padmasambhava's *gzhi* is not a 'thing.' His frequent use of the term *gzhi-med* 'the ground/Being-that-is-not' echoes the radical 'No' of the Gnostic Basilides.[51] Padmasambhava's 'the ground/Being's lighting-up' (*gzhi-snang*) corresponds to the late physicist David Bohm' idea of the whole's 'implicate order' becoming 'explicate.'[52] Its immediate experience is circumscribed by three 'in-depth appraisals' (*ting-nge-'dzin*).[53] The first is an 'in-depth appraisal of an as-is or just-so' (*de-bzhin-nyid-kyi ting-nge-'dzin*), a nothingness (for want of a better word), bubbling with energy that is nowhere and everywhere and on the verge of bursting forth in the second 'in-depth appraisal of a lighting-up of a light that is light through and through' (*kun-tu snang-ba'i ting-nge-'dzin*), touching and permeating all aspects of our being and about to become sound. This, then, is the third 'in-depth appraisal of a phonemic momentum' (*yi-ge rgyu'i ting-nge-'dzin*).[54] This last in-depth appraisal reminds us of what Arturo B. Fallico has called a first '*utterance* which asserts nothing and demonstrates nothing, but which nonetheless initiates everything by making it possible for us to speak at all.'[55] And what we say and what we speak about, are, in the words of Alfred North Whitehead, instances of 'misplaced concreteness' and, in the words of the *mahasiddha* Saraha, 'damned lies.'[56]

All these in-depth appraisals are pre-personal and point to a person's pre-ontological understanding of his belongingness (*Zugehörigkeit*) to the coming-to-presence and lighting-up of Being as a whole. It would go far beyond the scope of this essay to detail the psychological-philosophical riches of this so far neglected and often suppressed teaching.

In view of what has been said so far, one important question has been raised and demands an answer. The question is: 'Has Buddhism still something to offer in this modern or, if you prefer, postmodern age?' The answer is already provided by Buddhism itself by its admonition to find out by ourselves what life means. For us Westerners this, in the first instance, means a *zurück zu den Dingen* (back to the things themselves) as insisted upon by Edmund Husserl, the father of modern phenomenology. In the case of Buddhism this means *back to the original texts* and to look at them with 'fresh eyes.' Opened by phenomenology as initiated by Husserl and developed by Maurice Merleau-Ponty who, drawing on empirical psychology, illuminatingly describes our relationship with our own bodies in perception and action, our eyes will 'see' the phenomena as they 'come-to-light,' which is precisely what the Greek verb *phainesthai* means, the word ':phenomenon' being a participle of it.While phenomenology deals with what comes-to-light, hermeneutics as developed by Wilhelm Dilthey and deepened by Martin Heidegger deals with the 'unconcealment' of meaning. Both disciplines are the *sine qua non* for gaining a fresh vision of reality, against which the emptiness-nihilism reductionism rages, and for letting the light of our Being shine in all its splendor – 'darkness has gone, light has spread' were the words of the historical Buddha at the moment of vision. In this laconic statement the secret of Buddhist process thinking is encapsulated. To probe and follow it up needs courage. The image that guides us in our endeavor is again provided by Buddhism itself. It is the image of the *byang-chub-sems-dpa'* 'the person who has the courage *(dpa')* to think *(sems)* how to refine his being *(byang)* so that everything may fall into place *(chub)*.' Rather than coming up with half-baked notions in which we believe only because we have concocted them or with preposterous claims to boost our self-importance, we better heed the words the historical Buddha uttered before he passed away:

Strive incessantly!

NOTES

1 A good survey is presented in Arthur S. Reber, *The Penguin Dictionary of Psychology*, s.v. For greater details see Richard L. Gregory (ed.), *The Oxford Companion to THE MIND*, under 'Mind and Body,' 'Mind and Brain: Luria's Philosophy,' and 'Mind-Body problem: philosophical theories.'

2 Erich Jantsch, *The Self-organizing Universe*, p. 196. Compare with these words of a modern author the historical Buddha's injunction 'Do not say so, because I said so, but find out for yourselves.'

3 I have taken the neologism *process structure* from Erich Jantsch, *The Self-organizing Universe*, p. 21.

4 I regret that in the attempt at assessing the Buddhist ideas I have to use the original terms. To talk about Buddhist ideas with no substantiation from the original source material is as intelligent or absurd as to talk about Shakespeare's creative genius wthout referring to or quoting from his works.

5 For a complete translation of Buddhaghosa's lengthy disquisition see Herbert V. Guenther, *From Reductionism to Creativity*, p. 21. Buddhaghosa's innocently looking 'intends its referential terminus' would need a study of its own from the perspective of the Buddhist author or authors. The traditional (Western) mechanistic rendering of one Sanskrit or Pali term isolated from its context by some English word whose semantic implications are not clearly understood, is more harmful than helpful. In academic circles, particularly in Germany, the supposedly profound controversy between translation and interpretation is purely 'academic' (replacing the more or less outmoded 'scholastic'). It fails to recognize the fact that every translation is already an interpretation made by a person who thought about what he translated, and that 'objectivity' is a myth. Buddhist thinkers knew all the time that subject (subjectivity) and object (objectivity) are complementary to each other – you cannot have the one without the other. Here again, Buddhist thinkers are closer to modern ways of thinking.

6 *Dhammasangani*, p. 21. By rendering *ñana* in the above mannner I attempt to capture its connotation of spirituality, which under the impact of a growing analytical-representational mode of thinking, was more or less lost sight of, as may be gleaned from a parallel passage (Buddhaghos *Atthasalini* III 177), and replaced by *pañña* (Skt. *prajña),* which is thoroughly 'intellectual-analytical.' The mistranslation of *prajña* by 'wisdom' has become a fetish word for all those (Westerners and Easterners alike) who have none.

It may not be out of place to refer to Buddhaghosa's exegesis of the little word 'when' in one of its connotations of 'momentariness' and to link Buddhaghosa's insight with Martin Heidegger's clarification of Nietzsche's 'moment of vision,' the *Augenblick,* about which he wrote in *Nietzsche,* vol. 2, pp. 182-183:

> ... thinking in terms of the moment ... implies that we transpose ourselves to the temporality of independent action and decision, glancing ahead at what is assigned us as our task and back at what is given us as our endowment.

7 David Michael Levin, *The Body's Recollection of Being,* p. 62.
8 Erich Jantsch, *Design for Evolution,* p. 25.
9 An excellent account of this interpenetration has been given by Erich Jantsch, *Design for Evolution,* chapter eleven 'On Models and Myths', pp, 191–205.
10 *Philosophy,* trans. E.B. Ashton, I, p. 56.
11 A good summary of the limitations of the myth of objectivsm and of some of the inadequacies of the myth of subjectivism has been given by George Lakoff and Mark Johnson, *Metaphors We Live By,* pp. 210–225.
12 Erich Jantsch, *The Self-organizing Universe,* p. 295,
13 Klong-chen rab-'byams-pa, *gNas-lugs rin-po-che'i mdzod,* p. 69.
14 In addition to the sphere of desires there was the sphere of aesthetic forms and the sphere of no-form or, as some Buddhistsscholastics sharing with their Western colleagues the thingness of thought (a Jungian term) ideology maintained, the sphere of traces of form still present. This extension of a binary mode (sphere of desires/sphere of aesthetic forms) into a ternary mode may be seen as a recognition of the principle of creativity that underlies all levels of man's being.
15 Linguistically speaking, *caitta* is a derivative of *citta* and, therefore, may be rendered as 'mental event' or 'mental operator,' provided we do not understand 'derivative' mechanistically. Rather, it points to a necessary connectedness such that there is a *caitta* only when there is a *citta.*
16 For details about this program and its graphic presentation see Herbert Guenther, *Ecstatic Spontaneity : Saraha's Three Cycles of Doha,* pp. 67–75.
17 Excellent discussions of the role of touch are presented by Diane Ackerman, *A Natural History of the Senses* and Constance Classen, *Worlds of Sense.*
18 *Atthasalini* III 183 and *Trimsikavijñaptibhasya,* p. 20.
19 How useful Jung's typology is in the realm of mathematics, may be gleaned from its application by Rudy Rucker, *Mind Tools,* pp. 17–21.

20 *Bhasya* ad *Abhidharmakosa* II 22.
21 *Sphutartha* ad *Abhidharmakosa* II 22.
22 *Trimsikavijapti* 10bc.
23 *Trimsikavijñaptibhasya*, p. 25.
24 *The Mind and its Place in Nature*, pp. 299ff. The reasons for why *smrti* (Tib. *dran-pa*) cannot and must not be mechanically rendered by 'memory' I have given, on the basis of original Tibetan tetxs, in my *sGam.po.pa – Jewel Ornament of Liberation*, p. 230.
25 *Attasalini* III 220–222,
26 *Trimsikavijñaptibhasya*, p. 26.
27 The paraphrase of this term by *dharmanam pravicayo dharmapravicayah* 'the sorting of entities/meanings' by Yasomitra in his *Sphutartha* ad *Abhidharmakosa* II 24 clearly shows *prajña* to be an aspect of representational thinking.
28 For an in-depth study of this word see Robert S. Sternberg, *Wisdom – Its nature, origins, and development*, and Ted Honderich (ed.), *The Oxford Companion to Philosophy*, s.v.
29 As a matter of fact they continued to be the topic for profound thinkers. In particular, I refer to the famous *Chos mngon-pa mdzod-kyi thig-le'ur byas-pa'i 'grel-pa mngon-pa'i rgyan* by 'Byams-pa'i dbyangs of mChims (ca. 1267); the encyclopedic *Thar-pa 'jug-pa'i gru-bo zab-don chos-kyi gter-mdzod* with its commentary, the *Thar-pa 'jug-pa'i gru-bo'i dka'-'grel rin-po-che'i gter-mdzod*, by 'Ba-ra-ba (prob. 1310–1391); and the *mKhas-pa'i tshul-la 'jug-pa'i sgo zhes-bya-ba'i bstan-bcos* by 'Ju-mi-pham 'Jam-dbyangs rnam-rgyal rgya-mtsho (1846–1912). None of these works has attracted the attention of Western scholars of Buddhism. *Sapienti sat!*
30 For a brief survey of the Jungian idea see Daryl Sharp, *C.G. Jung Lexicon*, s.v., and for a detailed assessment see Dr. Anthony Stevens, *Archetypes – A Natural History of the Self*.
31 Heidegger, 'What Are Poets For?' in Hofstadter (ed.), *Poetry, Language, Thought*, p. 120.
32 Plato's conception of the *logos* as male is a clear intrusion of mythological-affective thinking into the rational mode of thought, which goes to show that Plato was rather muddleheaded. This statement may seem to be shocking; it is meant to be shocking so as to rouse people from their blind acceptance of dogmatic statements based on insufficient knowledge.
33 The relevant literature is enormous. Here I mention only two major works: Richard Webster, *Why Freud was wrong – Sin, Science, and Psychoanalysis* and Page duBois, *Sowing the Body – Psychoanalysis and Ancient Representations of Women*. On the negative image of women in ancient Greece, lapped up with gusto by both Freud and Lacan, see Eva C. Keuls, *The Reign of the Phallus – Sexual Politics in Ancient Athens*.
34 See Joanne H. Stroud, *The Bonding of Will and Desire*, p. 64, where she quotes Gaston Bachelard.
35 *Design for Evolution*, p, 85.
36 There are two words for this quality in Sanskrit: *krpa* and *karuna* . The *u*-element in *karuna* points to its numenous quality. This word does not imply any sentimentality or other dishonesty. The Tibetan language also has two words for our single notion: *snying-rje* which literally means that

the heart (*snying-rje*) is master (*rje*). We can paraphrase this by saying that one's heart goes out or takes over. The other is *thugs-rje* which, in view of the paucity of terms in our language pertaining to the spiritual, is best rendered as a 'suprasensual concern.'

37 For details of the interrelationship of these four catalysts see Herbert V. Guenther, *Kindly Bent to Ease Us*, vol. 1, chapter seven.

38 See above p. 75 n. 6.

39 The Tibetan equivalent *sgom-pa* means 'turning over in one's mind' (which does not say much).

40 This numerical presentation has created strange associations with some people interested in Buddhism. I remember, when after a lecture-seminar I had given in Berkely, California, a person who introduced himself as a psychologist, asked me whether during my long stay in India I had met someone on the tenth level (*bhumi*) of the Buddhist path. I was rather taken aback by this naive concretization and, after having recovered, could only said that I had met many people, but none who wore the label 'I am a tenth-level person.'

41 It does not matter whether we call this 'thing' a *res cogitans* or a *res extensa*, as was done by René Descartes – a thing (*res*) remains a thing, and it certainly will not do to perpetuate the influential, though fallacious, thinking of this French savant. See Antonio R. Damasio, *Descartes' Error – Emotion, Reason, and the Human Brain*.

42 *In Search of Jung*, p. 44.

43 For a detailed study see Stephen A. Hoeller, *The Gnostic Jung and the Seven Sermons to the Dead* and Robert A. Segal, *The Gnostic Jung*.

44 *Art & Existentialism*, p. 53.

45 It is found in his *Mahayanottaratantrasastra* (in its short form, *Uttaratantra*) I 92

46 It is a historical fact that the Gelugpas not only did not allow works professing the *gzhan-stong* thesis in their monasteries, but even persecuted the adherents of this thesis, the Jonang-pas, and, whenever they had a chance, even destroyed their monasteries.

47 For details see Marie-Louise von Franz, *On Dreams & Death*, p. 146.

48 The popular rendering of the term *rdzogs-chen* by 'Great Perfection' is wrong for several reasons. Firstly, *rdzogs* does not mean 'perfect' in the Kantian sense of the word as which 'perfect' is generally understood, but 'complete,' 'whole' as evinced by its Chinese equivalent term. Secondly, 'perfection' pertains to a powerful but difficult tradition in philosophy and theology. For details see Simon Blackburn, *The Oxford Dictionary of Philosophy*, s.v. Thirdly, how great is great?

49 *The Opening of Vision*, p. 79.

50 *sPros-bral don-gsal*, sDe-dge edition, vol. 1, fol. 5a.

51 In all fairness to the Indian thinkers it must be admitted that in the early Upanishads the idea of an 'is not' (*asat*) is voiced, but its ontological connotation never caught on.

52 For a detailed presentation of what David Bohm so aptly has called the holomovement (which unbeknownst to him had already been stated by Padmasambhava in his *gzhi-snang chen-po*), see his *Wholeness and the implicate order* . See also David Shainberg, 'Vortices of thought in the

implicate order and their release in meditation and dialogue' in B.J. Hiley and F. David Peat, *Quantum Implications. Essays in Honour of David Bohm.*

53 On the meaning of this term see above p. 81.

54 The use of the preposition *of* in the rendering of the Tibetan term(s), suggesting what seems to be a genetive case according to the Aristotelian categories in which our Western languages are steeped, is one of the many traps a language sets for its users. It is not so that the appraisal is one thing and that what is appraised is another thing. The one *is* the other. In this context see Arthur Zajonc, *Catching the Light. The entwined history of light and mind.*

55 *Art & Existentialism*, p. 64.

56 See Herbert Guenther, *Ecstatic Spontaneity. Saraha's Three Cycles of Doha*, p. 92 stanza 10.

Section 3

Towards Therapy

Chapter 5

EDITOR'S PREFACE

The description of the Buddha found in many traditions is that of the physician. The doctor with a cure for the ills of the world. All forms of Buddhism, whether we are dealing with Zen meditation techniques, the Pali Canon or Tibetan sacred art and for all that they are diverse and at times contradictory, are united and given a common meaning by this simple fact: they are there to reduce suffering. This end is at the heart of Buddhism, the means are primarily directed at the mind.

In the West, therapy is the means to end mental suffering. That is, if people experience suffering, it is seldom accepted as part of what it means to be alive, as it might have been in previous era. For Elizabethans, Jaques' speech in 'As you like it' on the seven ages of man, finishing with the gloomy depiction of inevitable sad decline, was not the musings someone in a state of disorder but the characteristic attitude of a type – the melancholic, someone who is inclined to mournful low spirits.

Now, however, such a malaise of the feelings is taken to be a condition requiring treatment rather than part of what a person might be like. Counselling, analysis and remediation are available in abundance. The range of therapeutic theory and practices has grown enormously in the latter half of this century. Indeed, the growth has been so great that the credibility of therapy has been brought into question. How can there be this variety of ways to help people? Are they really all distinct techniques? Is one form of therapy more appropriate to use than another form particular types of disorder?

In the more established therapeutic practices, psychoanalysis would be one, answers to questions like these can be given. Enough experience has been gained and the underlying theory has been critically developed for long enough for there to have emerged some fundamental ways to describe what effective therapy is. Among the most broadly accepted factors required for effective therapy is that the therapist will have undergone the therapeutic process themselves and that the emotions that a client brings are played out with the therapist. Here the authority of and trust in the therapist is crucial. If therapists are able to keep their own feelings under control this creates the trust needed for clients to hear things they do not like, or to acknowledge difficult things that have been denied. Through the openness and control that comes from self knowledge, therapists may gain the authority to ask difficult questions and to expect honest replies.

Joy Manné here reviews books by David Brazier and Mark Epstein and shows how these issues arise and are dealt with from a Buddhist point of view. In particular, Brazier points out the striking resemblances between the 'emptying' of the therapist in many Western traditions and the calming of the mind of the teacher in Eastern ones. In encountering Buddhist teachers questions of trust and authority also arise. Meditation can bring important personal matters to light. Without proper training and without the moral grounding that authentic traditions provide, superficial teaching can be damaging.

There are significant contrasts though between Buddhist meditation training and the training of, say, psychoanalysts. Psychoanalytic training is more concerned with the past and with accepting and working through the psychic configuration of the analyst. Moral considerations and the development of personal insight through inspection of the everyday workings of the mind are incidental. In Zen traditions, the problems of living, for both teacher and pupil are ethical aporias, moral koans that need open contemplation and acceptance rather than analysis.

Epstein too takes central elements of Buddhism, selflessness especially, and explores how they relate to Western psychotherapy. Buddhist images of human existence are taken as metaphors for the different states and conditions of emotional life. He is aware of the dangers of superficial comparisons and of the care that has to be taken in encouraging people to give up their conventional notions of selfhood. Here Freud's remark about psychoanalysis being for the psychologically healthy seems particularly relevant. Manné points out the interesting notion that skillful contemplation of the mind is in itself therapeutic. This is another significant contrast with Western techniques, where the emphasis is on the analysis of mental content, rather than on experiencing and attending to it.

This last matter links to Mannés' own work with meditation and with breathing techniques. These can at first experience seem insipid to people used to therapy that encourages talk, disclosure and the analysis of personal histories. To merely have or be with states of mind can seem unproductive by comparison. With Epstein and Brazier, Manné feels this is to underestimate the effectiveness of such techniques. They move psychotherapy beyond an inward tracing of emotional difficulties into the past. Starting in the present, the aim is more to help clients know their present state and to move outward towards a fuller awareness of their interdependence, both on others and on the the world around them.

Joy Manné's own work as a Buddhist scholar and as a psychotherapist come together here. She is well placed to recognise both the therapeutic work with which these books deal and to assess the accuracy of the use they make of Buddhist ideas. For example, there are the problems, central to the present book, of the authentic transmission of traditions on the one hand and on the other the need to use them in ways that address the needs of people living as we do now. Just how far can Westerners go in eclectic re-assembly from Buddhist sources and still claim that what they do has anything to do with original teachings and practices? For another example, there is the question of what provides authority for the therapist. This is a particularly important question in the light of the abuse of power that occur, both in spiritual teaching and in therapy. People seeking help are vunerable. Whether this help concerns psychological troubles, personal growth, meditation practice or spiritual development, they may be harmed by those who are not sufficiently developed themselves to carry out the helper's role. Apart from simply being unskillful or corrupt, many people who would genuinely wish to help may be unable to do this and thereby run the danger of doing harm.

Effective therapy requires that therapists are not only well versed in the theory underlying their practice but also self aware enough not to project things from their own psychological makeup onto the the client. Many Buddhist traditions likewise recognise that teachers cannot simply adopt the role by virtue of knowledge of texts, but must be skillful enough to teach in a non egotistical way. Joy Manné's chapter explores this similarity as part of creating a psychotherapy informed by Buddhist sensitivities.

★　★　★

Creating a Contemporary Buddhist Psychotherapy

Joy Manné

THE BACKGROUND IN BRIEF

Shortly before his death, the Buddha was asked whether he would appoint someone to succeed him as leader of the Order. He advised his monks rather to be a lamp or an island (there is a problem in translation here)[1] for themselves, and to take the Dharma or Teaching as their lamp/island, or inspiration and refuge. The books I am reviewing here, David Brazier's *Zen Therapy* and Mark Epstein's *Thoughts without a thinker: Psychotherapy from the Buddhist Perspective*, have truly taken the Teaching as their inspiration.

We do not know a great deal about how the Buddha's Teaching was promulgated during his lifetime. He himself engaged in debates with other religions leaders, preached sermons to his monks and was consulted by them about aspects of his Teaching, his method and its practice.[2] Throughout its development Buddhism has continually been reinvented, consistently with the tradition of having the Dharma for inspiration. Each of the great teachers and schools of Buddhism has selected elements and explored them philosophically and psychologically and the process of reinventing Buddhism goes on to this day. Each scholar chooses one or several aspects to elucidate according to his personality and interests and so brings these into prominence. Each meditation teacher emphasises what s/he finds most relevant. What we often have today are meditation teachers who encompass more than one tradition of Buddhism and synthesise elements of these different traditions into their own Buddhist psychology. When this is well done, when it is faithful to and honours the tradition and at the same time reinvents it for the present time, we are enriched. It is because Buddhism is so rich and so capable of reinvention that it continues to be relevant today.

102

David Brazier's *Zen Therapy* and Mark Epstein's *Thoughts Without a Thinker* provide a psychotherapeutic version of the Buddha's Teaching for our time. DB's Western Psychology is inspired by Carl Rogers and the humanistic tradition. DB practises and teaches Zen Buddhism. He has drawn his Buddhist psychology widely, and has based part of his book on an Abhidharma text in Pāli. Abhidharma is a form of Buddhist literature made up mainly of lists. ME is a Freudian psychoanalyst. He draws the Buddhist psychology in his book from a part of the Wheel of Life, and from the Four Noble Truths, an essential element in Buddhist Teaching. These are both very good books. I am going to have to discipline myself with regard to quoting as DB's has something wise, profound and inspiring on every page, and the way ME relates Buddhist psychology to Freudian psychoanalysis is intriguing and often surprising. Is he the first humanistic Freudian psychoanalyst?

Paul Williams, in his excellent book *Mahāyāna Buddhism*, has said, 'One tradition will only ever influence another if the tradition which is influenced is capable of making sense of the influences in terms of its own tradition.'[3] These books show how our humanistic and psychoanalytic traditions of psychotherapy are absorbing and integrating various influences, ideas and practices that belong to the Buddhist Path to Enlightenment.

THE BOOKS

David Brazier, Zen Therapy

DB divides his book into three parts: 1. Foundations, 2. Buddhist Psychology, 3. Therapy as a Zen Way. In Foundations he shares with us (yes, really shares, no pretentions, no facade, no boasting or specialness: his warmth, integrity and simplicity pervade the book) his first encounter with 'the therapeutic power of Zen' and explains some aspects of Zen therapy, especially 'the idea of helping people to find freedom from conditioning. ... The freedom referred to in Zen is the freedom which is experienced when one lives from one's deepest inner necessity, or, we could say, from the true reality of our lives.' (p.21). Throughout the book DB is concerned with the qualities of the therapist. He explains the importance of *Clear Space* created in the external space in which therapy takes place through rituals, and in the therapist's own inner space through meditation: 'The therapist ... empties themselves so as to have room for the client to fill them. It is our own emptiness which begins the therapeutic process.' (p.24)

'When the therapist has space within themselves, then they can be at one with anybody. This is the path of the *bodhisattva* who cares for all sentient beings, not just the ones they or society approve of.' (p.28) DB explains Buddha Nature and the importance of ethics 'as a liberation. ... Moral codes are simply an approximate description of the life of a fully realized being,'(p.36). In a section called *Core Ethics* he is uncompromising, 'In Zen, ethics are not simply a matter of setting boundaries to life, or to the therapy process. They are, rather, the central nub of the therapeutic problem. To be psychologically healthy is to return to and live from our core ethics.' DB presents this inspiring re-vision of psychotherapy: Many of the "problems" which clients present to therapists boil down to ethical dilemmas: "Should I stay with my spouse even though he/she treats me badly?" ... "My parents were cruel: should I hate them or forgive them?" ... These are not the sort of problems which can be dismissed with a simplistic moralizing answer. They are koans. ... Koan is a Japanese word for the tests life presents us with: problems not amenable to simple logical solution. Koan practice is meditation in which one holds such a dilemma in mind with great intensity, trying to break through to new clarity. "New clarity" does not necessarily mean a solution. It means a new view of life when the blocked energies within us find a way of release.' (p.46) DB has chapters on Tranquility and Mindfulness. Perhaps the Buddhist meditation best known to Western meditators is that based on the breath. This is how DB explains it, 'Mindfulness of breathing is one of the best starting points for the cultivation of the mind. The breath is a clear indicator of our inner life: a bridge betweeen body and mind. ... Learning to pay attention to the breath is the beginning of meditation. It is a means of noticing that we are alive, calming ourseles and returning to the here and now. Studying the breath makes us aware of our bodies and of their inter-dependence with the world. A little time devoted each day to conscious breathing ... will improve health and calm one's life.' (p.67)

In the second part, Buddhist Psychology, DB presents a version of Buddhist psychology based on the Abhidharma text called *Paṭṭhāna*, which he transliterates *Pattana*. This part of his book explains the process of conditioning, 'The key to Buddhist psychology is the analysis of conditioning. All ordinary mental states depend upon conditions. If conditions change, then the mental state also changes. To identify with conditioned existence is unsatisfactory (*dukkha*) since within it nothing can be relied upon. One is at the mercy of forces beyond one's control and simply goes round in circles under their influence. Real satisfaction depends upon breaking the hold of conditioning. .... The aim of therapy, from a Buddhist perspective, is to liberate the mind by enabling it to let go of the conditioned states.' (p.77) 'In Buddhist psychology, the word 'self' is the collective noun for all our conditioning.' (p.81) DB presents one model of the mind in Buddhist Psychology (p.82; several are possible and ME's book contains a different one). He points out that our word 'consciousness' is inadequate to render the various types of consciousness recognised by the Buddhists. He explores various elements of Buddhist Psychology, showing their similarities to and differences from Western psychology: 'The ordinary mind is obscured. The obscurations are called kleshas. A klesha is any mental factor which produces turmoil in the psyche. Kleshas are whatever seems to prevent us thinking clearly or acting sensibly. Collectively they constitute what Freud called the Id. In Buddhism, Freud's Id is represented by 'basic ignorance' (*avidya*).' (p.87)

DB then goes through eighteen theories of conditioning from the *Paṭṭhāna*, relating each to concepts in Western psychotherapy. '.... The first three propositions, Root Relations, Object Relation and Predominance ... constitute a complete theory in their own right. The foundation for a complete system of phenomenological psychotherapy is revealed ...' (p.80) Each chapter begins with an exposition in bold type in an adaptation of the style of Abhidhamma texts. I will limit myself to three examples here. The chapter begins with the definition: 'The theory of root relations states that all dukkha (mental suffering) can be traced back to three bitter roots, greed, hated and delusion, and that all wholesome states can be traced back to three sweet roots which are the opposites of the bitter ones.' DB coherently uses these bitter roots for diagnosis, relating them to eating disorders, melancholic manifestations and functional disorders. He relates their opposites, which are also their antidotes, to Roger's '"three necessary and sufficient conditions" of therapeutic personality change': empathy instead of hatred, unconditional respect instead of greed, and congruence or genuineness instead of delusion. (p.91) About Body Zen, he begins his chapter, 'Nissaya [previously translated as 'dependence'] theory highlights the fact that everything depends upon or grows out of something as its base or source. In particular, the mind has the body as base, just as later generations have ancestors as base. This is the relationship of one thing growing out of another.' He says: 'The mind's job is to harmonize with the body. What the body is doing is the reality of our lives. It is for the mind to harmonize with the reality of our life.' (p.139) In this chapter he explains grounding and its importance, including various techniques he uses. The chapter on *Dhyana* and *Path*, begins 'The dhyana theory states that it is possible to tame the mind. The marga theory states that everyone creates a path for themselves. for those who follow the way of Zen, taming the mind and following one's chosen path coincide'. Dhyāna is the Sanskrit word for meditation that has become 'Zen' via Chinese translations. DB observes, 'Enlightenment is not generally obtained by seeking it since the unenlightened person does not know where to aim. Enlightenment is a by-product of doing what reality gives us to do.' (p.180)

The final part of DB's book, *Therapy as a Zen Way*, begins with a chapter on Compassion, 'Compassion is to understand the other person's subjective world without stealing anything. Stealing means taking over.' (p.195) In a chapter on Love, pointing out that it seems to have become a central tenet of therapy that we should learn to be more selfish, he says 'The way to increase people's confidence is not by turning them into more selfish individualists, but by helping them find dignity in the qualities of love and compassion which they already have.' (p.203). Wisdom is fourfold: 'generosity, loving words, goodwill and identifying ourselves with others.' (p.218). There are chapters on Secret Way: 'being true to one's secrets: the secret essence laid up in our hearts to which it is impossible to do full justice, save through our manner of being itself'; on death, Loss as Teacher, which contains DB's gentle and simple account of his own encounter with death; and grieving, Letting Go: DB calls grief, 'our collision with reality' (p.242). Zen Therapy encompasses society and our planet. The book ends with a chapter called Coming Home, 'Ecology is the study of our home in the external sense. It is about how all sentient beings can make a home together, benefiting one another. Therapy, on the other hand, is about helping a person return to a state which they inwardly recognise as home. It is about the 'home' within us: harmonizing outer and inner. ... from a Zen perspective, it is not possible to create a comfortable niche for ourselves isolated from others. Peace of mind includes harmony with the world ...' (p.255f)

DB introduces Buddhist terminology and analysis without heaviness. He includes Japanese adaptations of Rogers' theories, and modern Japanese psychotherapies: Morita psychotherapy (p.108–110) and Naikan therapy (p.131–135). Case histories, personal experiences and reflections are shared – that word again. DB is sharing his knowledge and wisdom and I am a willing participant.

Creating a Contemporary Buddhist Psychotherapy

Mark Epstien, *Thoughts Without a Thinker*

ME too divides his book into three parts: I. The Buddha's Psychology of Mind; II. Meditation; III. Therapy, preceding these with an introduction in which he gives a brief history of the relationship of Freudian psychology to Buddhism. Some delicate juggling takes place in this introduction. ME says:

> 'Freud described the 'oceanic feeling' as the prototypical mystical experience: a sense of limitless and unbounded oneness with the universe that seeks the 'restoration of limitless narcissism' and the 'resurrection of infantile helplessness'. This equation of the meditative experience with a return to the womb has gone virtually unchallenged within the psychoanalytic community since Freud's commentary. While it does capture some truth, it takes no account of the investigative or analytical practices most distinctive of Buddhism and most related to the psychodynamic approach.' (p.3)

It is a most crushing indictment of the psychoanalytic community, (which is extremely influential in universities in America,) that it has taken 30 or more years longer than humanistic psychologists to make this discovery. Does it really isolate itself from other psychological and psychotherapeutical thought so effectively? ME says further:

> 'While Freud's concepts have become dominant, completely taking over the language of psychology, and while psycho-analysis has continued to evolve as a forum for exploring the nature of psychological experience, virtually none of the modern popularizers of Buddhism in the West, whether translators, authors, or teachers – have been fluent in the language of psychoanalysis.' (p.5)

Are Freudian analysts truly so monolingual that they can only understand Freudian jargon? Science is plurilingual!

This is ME's explaination of how the meeting between psycho-analysis and Buddhism took place:

> 'As the emphasis in therapy has moved from conflicts over sexual and aggressive strivings, for instance, to a focus on how patients are uncomfortable with themselves because, in some fundamental way, they do not know who they are, the question of the *self* has emerged as the common focus of Buddhism and psychoanalysis.' (p.5f)

In Part I, The Buddha's psychology of Mind, ME introduces 'the Buddha's psychological teachings in the language of Western psychodynamics.' (p.7) He begins with a chapter on The Wheel of life: A Buddhist model of the neurotic mind. ME uses a different model of the mind from DB. The Wheel that ME uses depicts the six realms of existence 'through which sentient beings are said to cycle endlessly in their round of rebirths': the Human, Animal, Hell, Preta (Hungry Ghosts), Asura (Jealous Gods or Titans) and the God Realm. (p.15) 'As long as beings are driven by greed, hatred and delusion ... they will remain ignorant of their own Buddha-nature.' (p.16) 'Each realm (is) ... a metaphor for a different psychological state, with the entire wheel becoming a representation of neurotic suffering' (p.17) The Wheel represents both the problem and its cure: in each part of the wheel mandala, there is a Bodhisattva who symbolically 'teaches us how to correct the misperceptions that distort each dimension and perpetuate suffering.' (p.16) ME relates the different expertise of schools of Western psychology to particular realms: 'Freud and his followers insisted on exposing the animal nature of the passions; the Hell-ish nature of paranoid, aggressive, and anxiety states (Melanie Klein); and the insatiable longing of what came to be called oral craving (which is depicted in picture of the Hungry Ghosts). ... Humanistic psychotherapy emphasized the "peak experiences" or the God Realms (Rogers, Maslow); ego psychology, behaviourism, and cognitive therapy cultivated the competitive and efficient ego seen in the Realm of the Jealous Gods; and the psychology of narcissism was specifically about the questions of identity so essential to the Human Realm (Winnicott, Kohut).' (p.18, p.20) 'Reich tried to move from the Animal Realm of desire to the God Realm of satisfaction.' (p.51) Each realm is discussed and illustrated with case histories.

The next chapters of Part I are devoted to the Four Noble Truths, usually translated, 'The Noble Truths of Suffering, of the Arising of Suffering, of the Cessation of Suffering, and of the Path leading to the Cessation of Suffering.' For the first Noble Truth, ME uses the word 'Humiliation' (Ch.2), 'In his teaching on suffering, the Buddha made clear that some kind of humiliation awaits us all. ... No matter what we do ... we cannot sustain the illusion of our self-sufficiency. We are all subject to decay, old age, and death, to disappointment, loss, and disease. We are all engaged in a futile struggle to maintain ourselves in our own image.' (p.44) ME is a Freudian analyst; for him the Buddha's teachings about the self are a way of penetrating our own narcissism, 'All of the insults to our narcissism can be overcome, the

Buddha proclaimed, not by escaping from them, but by uprooting the conviction in a "self" that needs protecting.' (p.45) Although on historical grounds, I am surprised – the historical context of the Buddhist teaching about the self is the philosophical and religious discussion about the existence of a permanent self or soul[4] – I nevertheless, appreciate this example of how Enlightenment and the path towards it can be successfully culturally defined: the culture being that of a contemporary American Freudian analyst who is reframing the Buddha's Teaching. This is a new and valuable contemporary perspective. ME proposes, 'We might rewrite the Buddha's words as the following: "Birth is suffering, decay is suffering, disease is suffering, death is suffering, the search for ultimate satisfaction through sexuality is suffering, not to be able to love is suffering, not to be known is suffering, to not know oneself is suffering."' The chapter concerns dealing with narcissism in a Buddhist way.

For the Second Noble Truth (Ch. 3) ME uses the word 'Thirst.' 'Thirst' or 'craving' is the conventional translation. The anecdote that begins the chapter illustrates cunningly what is meant, 'A wealthy patient confided to me that after having a gourmet meal, he craves a cognac. After the cognac, a cigarette; after the cigarette he will start to think about making love; after making love, perhaps another cigarette. Soon, he begins to crave sleep, preferably without any disturbing dreams. The seach for comfort through sense pleasures rarely has an end.' (p.60) ME relates the thirst for sense pleasures to Freud's Pleasure Principle. The Third Truth is 'Release' (Ch 4): 'The Buddha is suggesting something very radical here: that it is possible to isolate the forces of craving in one's own mind and become both liberated from them and unattached to them merely from seeing that craving for what it is.' (p.77f) He describes this as the kind of sublimation that Freud did not often consider. (p.79). This is what ME says about wisdom and compassion, 'the two qualities of the enlightened mind: Wisdom is, after all, sublimated ego libido; it is investment in the self turned inside out, the transformation of narcissism and the eradication of ignorance about the nature of self. . . . Compassion, it follows, is sublimated object libido: desire and rage transformed through the vision of there being no separate subject in need of a magical reunion with either a gratifying or a frustrating Other.' (p.83) – Quite different from DB!

The Fourth Truth is paraphrased 'Nowhere standing' (Ch 5), a phrase taken from a Zen story is used to illustrate it. (The same story is used in DB pp.140–142 to different ends.) ME says of the Buddha's Middle Path, 'it was said to avoid the two extremes of self-indulgence and self-mortification, or, in more contemporary terms, of idealization and denial.' (p.91) The Path to the Cessation of suffering, known as the Eightfold Path comprises Right View, Right Thought, Right Speech, Right Bodily Action, Right Livelihood, Right Effort, Right Mindfulness and Right Concentration. ME uses this chapter to talk about emotions and feelings in relation to the Buddhist concept of no self. 'I often have the experience as a therapist of helping someone discover a difficult feeling like anger and then hearing them ask, "What do I do now? should I go home and have it out?" Sometimes we feel that the only solution is to act out every emotion that we get in touch with. We feel as if we must express it to whomever it is directed or that we are somehow cheating ourselves. The idea of simply knowing the feeling does not occur to us.' (p.93) He astutely shows how meditators can become confused 'and mistakenly strive to rid themselves of what they understand to be their Freudian-based egos ... and equate selflessness with (liberation) from all constraints of thought, logic, or rationality, and ... (the acting) out (of) emotions.' (p.93) As ME so clearly states, 'Rather than encouraging a consolidated self sure of its own solidity, the Buddhist approach envisions a fluid ability to integrate potentially destabilizing experiences of insubstantiality and impermanence.' (p.94) ME refutes the view that selflessness is 'some kind of oneness or merger.' (p.94) He calls the view that the self should be subjugated to a higher power 'masochism', and makes some perceptive remarks about the relationship between masochism and attachment to gurus. (p.97) ME also refutes the idea in transpersonal psychology that egolessness is a developmental stage beyond the ego. (p.98) Anybody practising meditation would do well to study this chapter.

Part II, *Meditation*, 'is meant to explain the basic Buddhist attentional strategy of *bare attention* and to show how the meditative path may be understood in psychodynamic terms.' (p.8) ME explains the point of *Bare Attention* (Ch 6) in this way, 'Much of our interior life is characterized by this kind of primary process, almost infantile, way of thinking, "I like this. I don't like that. she hurt me. How can I get that? More of this, no more of that." These emotionally tinged thoughts are our attempts to keep the pleasure principle operative. Much of our inner dialogue, rather than the "rational" secondary process that is usually associated with the thinking mind, is this constant reaction to experience by a selfish, childish protagonist. ...

Buddhist meditation takes this untrained, everyday mind as its natural starting point, and it requires the development of one particular attentional posture – of naked, or bare, attention. ... bare attention takes this unexamined mind and opens it up, not by trying to change anything but by observing the mind, emotions, and body the way they are. It is the fundamental tenet of Buddhist psychology that this kind of attention is, in itself, healing... ' (p.110) He compares this with ' "evenly suspended attention," the attentional stance that Freud recommends for practicing psychoanalysts.' (p.114) ME compares bare attention to Winnicott's transitional space (p.122) He says interesting things about resistance, 'From a Buddhist perspective, there is really *nothing* but resistance to be analyzed: there is no true self waiting in the wings to be released.' (p.121)

In Ch. 7, *The psychodynamics of meditation*, ME makes the following contrasts: 'Psychoanalytic psychotherapy tends to lead to experiences that reenact earlier and more formative emotional relationships so that the person's history can be, in effect reconstructed. Buddhist meditation tends to intensify certain ego functions so that the sense of self is at once magnified and deconstructed. Psychotherapy often involves the creation of a narrative to explain a person's history, while meditation is a process of questioning the most basic metaphors that we use to understand ourselves. The most moving emotional experiences in therapy are those of the transference, in which it is revealed how earlier relationships are still shaping and defining present-day interactions, as demonstrated in the actual relationship with the therapist. The most moving experiences in meditation are those that enable the meditator to come face-to-face with various cherished images of self, only to reveal how ultimately lacking such images are.' (p.129) This chapter explores the mutual contribution of meditation and psychoanalysis, their overlap and their limitations. This is useful information. There are sections on the importance of the body (p.144) and of the breath (p.145).

Part III, *Therapy*, 'takes Freud's treatise on the practice of psychotherapy, "Remembering, Repeating and Working-Through," and uses it as a template for considering how the Buddha's teachings can be integrated into the practice of psychotherapy.' (p.8) It begins with a chapter on *Remembering* (Ch. 8) which compares the remembering that Freud described and contrasts this with the Buddhist practice of mindfulness. It is interesting to observe that word for 'mindfulness' in Pali, *sati*, comes from the Vedic and Sanskrit root *sm* – to remember. With regard to the mutual contribution of meditation and psychoanalysis, in his chapter on *Repeating* (Ch. 9) ME points out that meditation masters are not trained to handle the transference. (p.184) This is a very important point and I will come back to it.

The book ends with a chapter on *Working Through* (Ch 10). From the perspective of the Buddhist Wheel of Life, 'it is the perspective of the sufferer that determines whether a given experience perpetuates suffering or is a vehicle for awakening. To work something through means to change one's view,' (p.204) and we can only do this if we own what we are feeling. ME helps a client to do this, 'You say, "This anxiety was welling up" ... What if you say, "I got anxious?"' (p.208) This is a Freudian analyst discovering Gestalt! He continues, 'the crucial step, from the Buddhist view, is to shift the perspective from the reactive emotions to the feeling of "I" itself. In so doing, one's investment in outrage is gradually withdrawn and replaced by interest in exploring the nature of "I".' (p.212) For ME, 'Buddhist ... meditation is not just about creating states of well-being; it is about destroying the belief in an inherently existent self.' (p.222)

This book, too, contains many case histories.

COMPARISONS

Each book has chosen a different aspect of Buddhist psychology as central. For DB, it is conditioning and how that comes about; for ME it is the self-concept and how to go beyond it. Going beyond an identification with a permanent self is part of the Buddhist teaching on how to go beyond conditioning.

These books cope with the similarities and differences between Buddhist and Western psychology in different ways. DB is willing to explore these without attachment: '... although there can be important similarities between western and Buddhist psychology, we have to be careful that we are not being deceived by similarities of language which do not represent similarities of substances, and that we are not simply projecting our favoured ideas onto eastern material. An integration of east and west will be best served by clarity about what the real differences are.' (p.37) ME is relating Buddhist psychology to Freudian psychoanalysis, so he finds in Buddhist psychology elements he can relate to humiliation, narcissism, the pleasure principle, the false self, the primary process, the basic fault, sublimation, subjugation and masochism, neurosis and psychosis. DB barely uses such terminology, although he obviously is familiar with it. His wise view is that 'conventional psychological terminology ... betray(s) underlying prejudices.' (p.174)

DB uses Buddhist technical terms explaining them clearly in words, through the use of tables and with case histories and examples. I am familiar with the vocabulary of technical terms in Buddhist psychology, but I did wonder how a reader for whom most of the words are unknown would cope, and so I got some friends to read the book. People for whom this is an introduction to Buddhist Psychology tell me that the explanations are so clear that there is no problem with the Buddhist terminology. There is, in any case, a glossary. The transliterations introduced were the one major fault in this book. I found them painful – like spelling 'knowledge' 'nolij'! An 'ā' and an 'a', for example, are completely different letters in Sanskrit and Pāli as well as different sounds; similarly for 'n' and 'ñ' (pronounced 'ny'), 't' and 'ṭ' or 'ṭh,. DB's logic is that he has selected the spelling that seems to him likely to beome the standard Anglicized term. (p.8) The Buddha described his Teaching as *ehipassika*: one is not required to believe, but to test it, to 'come and see' for oneself. The problem with these new spellings is, how can discerning readers who wish to read Pahana for themselves ever be able to trace the text rendered in this book, Pattana? or if they want to acquire further information about the various concepts, how can these be identified when all the scholarly – meaning knowledgeable – books transliterate according to a different standard? Anglicization is justifiable, but it should contribute to knowledge and not to confusion. The fact that DB has not consulted textual scholars amd linguists on such a serious problem as transliteration illustrates the problem of the gap between scholars and meditation teachers, psychotherapists using meditation, and meditators. This gap is also illustrated in the bibliographies of both books. If the pursuit of knowledge has any meaning, it is important to find bridges across this gap. I hope the transliteration problem will be remedied in a second edition of this book.

ME uses Freudian technical terminology and elucidates it – he really makes it lucid; he does not take it for granted that we are familiar with it. He takes familiar elements in Buddhism such as the Four Noble Truths and translates them with terms from his Freudian vision. He looks with painful realism at the human condition. Yes, it can be humiliating.

Both DB and ME use Buddhist psychotherapy in inspiring and convincing ways. It is interesting to observe how they interpret the same concepts differently, each according to his own tradition of

Western psychology. I have quoted the example of wisdom and compassion above. The books are rich in case histories. Both draw attention to the importance of the body in Buddhist meditation and in psychotherapy. In DB, ethics and morals are given their rightful place. It is a pleasure to read the phrase, 'our fundamentally ethical nature' (p.36). For DB, too, people are naturally loving (p.227f).

Both books pay attention to the training and qualities of the therapist. In DB in almost every chapter there are requirements with regard to the qualities of the Zen therapist. The healing of the client takes place through the therapist modelling the Zen way of life, which has so much in common with Carl Rogers' empathy, unconditional respect and congruence. ME is critical of the training he received, 'When Freud imagined how to make the therapeutic relationship a vehicle for working through ... repetitive emotions, he said some interesting things. The emotions must first be given the right to assert themselves "in a definite field," he maintained. The relationship must then become like a "playground" in which "everything that is hidden" can reveal itself. What happens in therapy must be like an "intermediate region between illness and real life" a kind of twilight zone of the soul. While many would consider Freud's musings overly idealized, his major omission lay in his failure to teach his followers how to create the kind of environment he imagined. Meditation is indispensable in demonstrating to both therapist and patient how to maintain Freud's "intermediate region"[5] ... The Buddha's vehicle of bare attention is one means by which Freud's playground can be constructed.' (p.201f) Further, ME points out that meditation teaches how to stay in the present, and makes this observation, 'Just as the therapist is never really taught how to pay attention in the most effective way, the patient is never taught how to pay attention either.' (p.193) The moral of this story is: make sure your Freudian analyst has learned how to meditate!

ME, as I pointed out above, makes pertinent remarks about the training of the meditation master, 'meditation practitioners and their generally psychologically untrained teachers are often unambiguously unable or unwilling to handle the transference material that will inevitably emerge ... Meditation ... can bring up lots of emotionally loaded material, which, if not dealt with efficiently, may suffuse the entire meditative experience without ever being effectively put to rest.' (p.184) The ideal meditation master and the ideal therapist are bodhisattvas (DB). In the real world, meditation masters have the same problems as any other therapists with regard to boundaries and many transgress them.[6] Abuse is abuse, whether it is carried out by a therapist or a meditation master.

DB criticises humanistic psychology, 'There is very little written in the person-centred literature about death, disease, loss, guilt, tragedy and the other basic existential dilemmas we are prey to. The optimistic spirit prevails over all. People, however, are not omnipotent. The confrontation with powers greater than oneself, and with the simple fact of otherness, is the making or breaking of a person. If the universe is in some sense a whole, then we are part of something greater than self.' (p.33) The moral of this story is: make sure your humanistic psychotherapist can handle suffering.

What about problems in the way these books treat Buddhism itself? The main problem in DB is that of transliteration mentioned above. Otherwise he has done a quite excellent job. He has respected the Buddhist tradition, presenting his version of Buddhist psychology in an interesting and readable way without making compromises. He has not shied away from ethics, which are fundamental in Buddhism[7], however unfashionable they may be these days. He has taken a complex text, the Pahana, respected its meaning and made it understandable and relevant to Western psychology. He has made many challenging remarks about the qualities of a therapist, including proposing the bodhisatta, the ideal being, as a role-model. Bravo!

ME has shown how his version of Buddhist psychology: the Wheel of Life, The Four Noble Truths, the concept of no self, bare attention and emptiness; can improve Freudian psychology. The Wheel of Life he describes is simplified from a much larger mandala, and although his description is inspiring and poetic, an illustration would have been useful or at least some reference where one could find it. I would also have liked him to say that he has simplified the original mandala(s). A discerning reader who may wish to 'come and see', and to follow up what s/he has read, cannot through want of references.[8]

ME has what I think of as a freudian tendency towards dogmatism and absolutes. He says, 'In our culture, it is the language of psychoanalysis, developed by Freud and carefully nurtured by generations of psychotherapists over the past century, that has seeped into the general public awareness. It is in this language that the insights of the Buddha must be presented to Westerners.' (p.7) 'Must'? To Western Freudians perhaps, but the rest of us are not so confined. There are further examples of his globalising, but not so many as to spoil the book.

ME invents absolutes about Buddhism. He claims, 'It has become a fundamental axiom of Buddhist thought that nirvana is samsara ...'

(p.18) Some schools of Buddhism teach this, but I doubt that all teach it today and certainly not all the schools originally did. ME asserts, '... The accepted Buddhist strategy of the search for identity.' (p.37) No, there is no search for identity in Buddhism. Quite the contrary, the search is to go beyond conditioning to reach the unconditioned which is called Nirvana. The Buddha taught that there is no absolute Self, only conditions in flux. ME's book shows perfectly well that he understands this. Another of his absolutes: '... craving, ignorance and anatta (no-soul or no-self) – are ... the most difficult concepts in all of Buddhism ...' (p.85) It is a bad habit to talk for everyone. ME's tendency to speak for all is the antithesis of DB's humanistic approach.

ME has understood parts of the Buddha's life story in a strange way. He says, 'The Buddha appears to have been embarrassed by his discovery. ... His inclination was to assume that no-one would take him seriously.' (p.43) There is no textual evidence whatsoever to support this interpretation (projection).[9] The Buddha thought people were not sufficiently wise or developed to understand, as ME's quote on p. 43 illustrates! And about the Buddha's first sermon, 'It was as if he was testing his ability to explain his understanding to his old friends and fellow renunciates ... ' (p.45) A Buddha is omniscient (in ways defined differently by different schools). The idea that a Buddha could be 'testing his ability' contradicts what a Buddha is. This is how the Buddha announced himself to these old friends:

> 'Monks, do not address the Tathāgata either by name or by the word 'friend'.[10] I am an arahat, a Tathāgata, a Completely Enlightened One. Listen, monks. I have attained the Imperishable. I instruct. I teach the Dhamma (Teaching). By following the method as instructed, after a short time, you will live in that incomparable perfection of the religious life for whose sake sons of family go forth from living at home to becoming homeless wanderers. (You will have) seen it for yourselves through your own higher knowledge in this very lifetime.'[11]

I do not see how these can be interpreted as the words of someone 'testing his ability'. Further, ME perceives an image in the Dhammapada: 'Oh housebuilder! ... All your rafters have been broken, Your ridgepole shattered,' in the following way, 'The whole of Buddhist psychology is encapsulated in this seemingly simple verse, and yet, the Buddha's message has never been easy to fathom. What is the Buddha alluding to in his verse? What was he seeking, what has he broken, what has been shattered? To what do we owe this unusual expression of naked aggression from a man so renowned for his equanimity,' (p.77) Each person is free to interpret imagery in their own way, using it as a support for their own imagination, inspiration and projections – there is a certain amount of 'violence' in ME's vocabulary ('meditation is 'ruthless',' p.109; the 'brute strength' of a difficult emotion, p.207). The smallest incursion into any good translation would have given him information about the meaning of the verse. As Radhakrishnan observes in his translation, 'The builder of the house is craving, taha. It is the cause of rebirth. If we shake off craving there is nothing to bind us to the wheel of existence.' (p.110)

Finally, ME makes the mistake many people make who do not read the scholarly literature. He does not respect the immense cultural difference between the Buddha's times and our own. He asserts, 'While no psychological language as we know it existed in the Buddha's time – no talk of narcissism, no grandiosity, no abandonment depression or mirroring – there were highly developed philosophical systems that in many cases espoused similar psychological concepts.' (p.64) He would have to convince me of this. DB is better on appreciating how different Buddhist psychology is from Western psychology, and therefore better at seeing the many and diverse ways it can contribute to our psychotherapy.

These mistakes in ME are disappointing and could easily have been avoided by some reference to the scholarly literature and particularly to translations of the original texts, a minimum requirement, I think, if one purports to write about Buddhist psychology. They detract from an otherwise very interesting and challenging book.

Is there anything in these books that might offend me as a Buddhism-influenced psychotherapist (who reads the Pāli texts in their own language, others in translation)? Absolutely not. These are books that can inspire any therapist. DB's book is a classic to draw on for education and inspiration for clients and therapists alike. He is pure acceptance, tolerance, openness, empathy and unconditional respect. ME's book will not be too threatening for Freudians, and for others, who find that contemporary Freudian psychotherapy is mostly irrelevant theorizing and 'being in the head,' it provides a humanistic perspective.

What do these books have in common? Very little – their bibliographies share only two books. This is the great pleasure in reading both of them, why they are worthy of so much attention, and why it is unnecessary to choose between them. They are exemplary of the richness of Buddhist Psychology and of its potential contribution to Western psychology. There is room for many more books as good as these.

CREATING A BUDDHIST PSYCHOTHERAPY

Buddhist Psychotherapy has existed in the West for a long time. One seminal book was Zen Buddhism and Psychoanalysis, edited by Fromm, Suzuki and De Martino in 1960. Fritz Perls, was influenced by Zen,[12] among other things,[13] and I think it is fair to say that all recent psychotherapy has been influenced by Gestalt. The Esalen Institute has promoted various forms of Buddhist psychotherapy including meditation through programmes offered for over 30 years. Why, then, am I talking about the creation of Buddhist psychotherapy when it has existed in the West since before 1960 and been growing ever since? The diversity of these two books, is just one reason. The other is that many methods and practices that exist in the Buddhist texts have not yet been explored in any depth as psychotherapeutic tools.

Meditation, as taught in the West, is primarily a form of Breathwork. The Buddhist texts contain many exercises based upon the breath.[14] Breath is used to aid concentration (DB, p.56). It is used for exploring the self-concept, '... one might start to ask, "Who breathes?" One observes the air come in, the abdomen rise, the air go out, the abdomen fall. "Who is doing the breathing?" One starts to become aware of the space between the breaths, and space within the breath itself. "Who breathes?" We become happily absorbed.' (DB, p.59) There are several forms of psychotherapy that use the breath[15] among which the one that is the most centred on breathwork is Concious Connected Breathing or Rebirthing. I practise an adaptation of this which I call Conscious Breathwork or Conscious Breathing Techniques.[16] I would like to comment briefly on what DB says about using the breath, and on a case history in ME from this perspective.

DB says, 'Mindfulness of breathing is one of the best starting points for the cultivation of the mind. The breath is a clear indicator of our inner life: a bridge between body and mind. The therapist notices the client's breathing. Is it shallow or deep, long or short, rough or smooth? How does it change as the client tells their story? By synchronizing one's own breath with that of the client, it is often possible to understand the client's suffering more deeply. Drawing attention to the breath can sometimes be helpful. As the client breathes into their pain, some relief may occur or an insight be triggered.' (DB, 66f) This would qualify as a description of the use of Conscious Breathing Techniques in psychotherapy,[17] and that is hardly surprising, as meditation is the Conscious Breathing Technique that influenced my own adaptation of Rebirthing. Besides, I can hardly imagine that Leonard Orr, who invented Rebirthing and taught at Esalen, was not familiar with various meditation techniques – although he does not easily reveal his sources of inspiration.[18] In a Conscious Breathwork session, the breathing of the therapist tends naturally to synchronise with that of the client, and indeed provides information as to the clients mental, emotional and physical state. This phenomenon was already observed in the first Rebirthing book.[19]

This is the case history in ME that I wish to comment on. ME provides it as a demonstration of 'how the practice of meditation can act in a manner most reminiscent of Freud's hypnotic technique.' (p.167)

'Joe ... found himself quite fearful of watching his breath. It did not feel like the neutral object his teachers described it as; it felt dangerous and made him anxious. He avoided attending to the breath, concentrating instead on simply listening to the sounds that surrounded him for the first three days of the retreat, until he felt composed enough to approach his breathing once again. Developing the qualities of tranquillity and peacefulness that come with increasing concentration, Joe then had a particularly blissful sitting ... This was immediately followed by the feeling of an iron band constraining his abdomen, hurting him and restricting his breath.

So intense and unpleasant were these sensations that Joe felt unable to work with them meditatively. Nevertheless, he tried to watch the pain with bare attention, although he found it necessary to walk around, lie down, and stretch out, changing his position constantly. No amount of attention, no change in position, no associated thoughts or feelings, no advice from his teachers seemed to affect the intensity of the sensations, which lasted for the better part of the day. Finally, Joe lay in one position and found himself overcome with sadness. He sobbed and shook for several hours and then had a childhood memory that was new for him. He remembered hiding in the closet from his raging father, filling his mouth with rags to stifle his sobbing out of fear that his father would hear him and become even more angry. Attention to the breath had evoked the memory of choking in the closet, where his efforts had been not to attend to the breath, but to hold it so he would not provoke his father's wrath.' (ME, p. 168f)

This is the kind of case history that could have come from any Rebirthing book, except that the episode would have been over in a shorter time. It reminded me that when I discovered Rebirthing, 20 years after I began meditating, it seemed to me to be meditation made more efficient because there was someone present to support awareness. DB observes that sometimes, 'therapy is rather like meditation for two.' (p.61) In ME's case history, through Conscious Breathwork, the meditator/client finds himself engaged in a lengthy trauma that goes on for several days. Had there been someone there who understood conscious breathwork techniques, Joe would have been guided to breath into his pain,[20] and the whole experience would have been over in one or two hours.

This case history reminded me how I and many others tried to sit in meditation, our minds wandering, unable to keep our attention on our breathing, and unable to deal with what was happening even on those rare occasions when we could identify it. Through Rebirthing my ability to meditate – to concentrate on my breathing and be aware of what was happening – improved and become good. The literature about Conscious Breathing Techniques is often inadequate for serious therapists and clients,[21] and although there are now a few good books available,[22] people are in general insufficiently informed. Neither of the books reviewed here seem to be aware that breathing techniques are used in various forms of therapy.[23] I want to draw attention to that here and to the similarity between the results of using Conscious Breathing Techniques in psychotherapy and the experience and results of meditating. The gentlest use of breathwork of any kind, including meditation, may bring up memories of the birth-trauma, interuterine life or even conception, as well as any of the other traumas that are remembered through therapy. Therapists, meditation teachers and breathworkers of all kinds should be prepared to deal with this.

Conscious Breathing Techniques can support meditation as do the techniques of Rogerian analysis, psychodrama, art, the use of stones (p. 145, 208), etc. that DB uses, or as does ME's use of Freudian analysis. ME has no doubts that meditation needs supporting by psychotherapeutic methods. Nor have I.

BIBLIOGRAPHY

Brazier, David, *Zen Therapy*. London : Constable, 1995; 282pp including Glossary, Bibliography and Index.

Ellenberger, Henri F. (1970), *The Discovery of the Unconscious : the History and Evolution of Dynamic Psychiatry*. London: Fontana Press.

Epstein, Mark. *Thoughts without a Thinker: Psychotherapy from the Buddhist Perspective* (New York: Basic Books. 245pp including Index and a foreword by the Dalai Lama)

Fromm, Erich, D. T. Suzuki and Richard De Martino (1960), *Zen Buddhism and Psycholanlysis*. New York : Harper & Row.

Jung, C.G. (1963), *Memories Dreams, Reflections*. London: Flamingo, 1983 edition.

Radhakrishnan, S. (1950), *The Dhammapada*, Madras: Oxford University Press.

Williams, Paul (1989), *Mahāyāna Buddhism: Doctrinal Foundations*. London: Routledge.

NOTES

1 Bareau, André (1963), *Recherches sur la biographie du Buddha dans les Sūtrapiṭaka et les Vinayapiṭaka anciens: de la quète de l'éveil à la conversion de Śāriputra et de Maudgalyāyana*. Ecole Française d'extreme-orient, Paris. Page 145.

2 Manné, Joy (1990), 'Categories of Sutta in the Pāli Nikāyas and their implication for our appreciation of the Buddhist Teaching and Literature.' Journal of the Pali Text Society, XV (1990), pp.29–87.

3 Williams, Paul (1989), *Mahāyāna Buddhism : Doctinal Foundations*. London : Routledge. Page 100.

4 Bronkhorst, Johannes (1993), *The Two traditions of Meditation in Ancient India*. Delhi : Motilal Banarsidass. [1st edition 1986]; Bronkhorst, Johannes (1993), *The Two Sources of Indian Asceticism*. Bern: Peter Lang.

5 Epstein is quoting from p.154 of Freud, Sigmund, 'Remembering, Repeating and Working-Through,' Vol. 12, pp.146–156, *Standard Edition of the Complete Psychological works of Sigmund Freud*, ed. and trans. James Strachey. Londond: Hogarth Press and Institute of Psychoanalysis, 1958.

6 Anthony, Dick, Bruce Ecker and Ken Wilbur (1987), *Spiritual Choices : the problem of recognizing authentic paths to inner transformation*. New York : Paragon House Publishers

7 Gombrich, R. (1996) *How Buddhism Began: the Conditioned Genesis of the Early Teachings*. London: Athlone.

8 This information can be found on p.14f and Plate 3 of Snellgrove, David L. (1987), *Indo-Tibetan Buddhism : Indian Buddhists and Their Tibetan Successors*. London: Serindia Publications.

9 See pages 135–143 of Bareau, André (1963), *Recherches sur la biographie du Buddha dans les Sūtrapiṭaka et les Vinayapiṭaka anciens: de la quète de l'éveil à la conversion de Śāriputra et de Maudgalyāyana*. Ecole Française d'extreme-orient, Paris.

Joy Manné

10 The usual greeting among monks who are equals.
11 Majjhima Nikāya I 171f. My translation.
12 Shepard, Martin (1975), *Fritz*. Sagaponack, NY : Second Chance Press. p.65.
13 ibid, Chs. 1, 14.
14 Manné, J. (1995,a), 'Rebirthing – Marvelous or Terrible?' *The Therapist : Journal of the European Therapy Studies Institute*, Spring 1995.
15 Manné, J. (1994), 'Rebirthing, an orphan or a member of the family of psychotherapies?' *Int. J. of Prenatal and Perinatal Psychology and Medicine*, Vol.6 (1994) No. 4, 503–517 ; Manné, J. (1995,b) Report by a Breathworker for Breathworkers on the *International Society for the Advancement of Respiratory Psychophysiology (ISARP) Conference*, Toronto, 9–11 October, 1995. Available from the International Breathwork Foundation, Secretary Gunnel Minett, 6 Middlewatch, Swavesey, GB – Cambridge CH4 5RN, Tel. 0044 1954 230 250, Fax. 0044 1954 232 019 ; Minett, Gunnel (1994), *Breath & Spirit : Rebirthing as a Healing Technique*. London : Aquarian/Thorsons. pages 131–135.
16 Manné, J. (1995, a) *op. cit.* ; Manné, J. (1997, a) Soul Therapy. California: North Atlantic. ; Manné, J. (1997, b) 'The use of conscious breathing techniques in psychotherapy,' in Rapp, H. (Ed.) *Experiences of Difference*. British Institute of Integrative Psychotherapy New Controversial Discussions Series. London: British Institute of Inegrative Psychotherapy.
17 Manné, J. (1997, b) *op. cit.*
18 Manné, J. (1994), *op. cit.*
19 Orr, Leonard and Sondra Ray (1983), *Rebirthing for the New Age* (Revised edition. First edition, 1977.) California : Trinity Publications. Page 42f.
20 See Minett, *op. cit.* Ch. 9, *The Role of the Therapist in a Breathing Session*.
21 Manné, J. (1995, a) *op. cit*
22 Minett, op. cit. ; Morningstar, Jim (1994), *Breathing in Light and Love: your call to breath and body mastery*. Transformations, Inc. Morningstar is particularly rich in case histories. ; Taylor, K. (1994) *The Breathwork Experience: Exploration & Healing in Nonordinary States of Consciousness*. California: Hanford Mead. ; Talylor, K. (1995) *The Ethics of Caring: Honoring the Web of Life in Our Professional Healing Relationships*. California: Hanford Mead.
23 Timmons, Beverly H. & Ronald Ley (1994), *Behavioral and Psychological Approaches to Breathing Disorders*. New York : Plenum Press.

Chapter 6

EDITOR'S PREFACE

Padmasiri de Silva was educated in Sri Lanka and taught philosophy and psychoanalysis in a number of countries. Thus when writing on Buddhism and Western ideas he not only has his academic background on which to call but also his earliest experiences. As Jung pointed out, this is a powerful combination. In this chapter, he compares Buddhist and Freudian frameworks for psychotherapy. More specifically, he deals with how the two systems approach emotion and feeling.

Here, 'feeling' refers to affective experience that arises in direct response to a particular event, while 'emotion' refers to the affective response to feelings. In the case of a sudden noise for instance, the feelings arising would include auditory sensations, the startle and orientation responses, a state of arousal and the disruption of previous objects of attention. Subsequently, the emotional experience might be of anger, fear, amusement or bare attention to external and internal conditions. In this particular illustration, feelings relate more to what the noise does to the hearer while emotions are more a function of what the hearer does with the feelings. Both emotions and feelings are hard to control, though perhaps for different reasons. However, with practice, more control may be possible than is generally supposed. The development of this control is one focus of this article.

For anyone who undertakes a phenomenological investigation of their own mental life, the primary and perhaps more fundamental encounter is with feeling and with emotion rather than with thought. For Buddhism, this is axiomatic. For Western psychology, particularly those traditions modeling themselves on science, the primary emphasis is on rational thought. Of course, this does not apply to all Western traditions, phenomenology and psychoanalysis being exceptions to this implicitly Cartesian rule. The investigation of feeling and emotion is central to psychotherapy and discovering how they arise and hence how they may be better managed is the goal. In this respect, this chapter is less about resemblances between Buddhism and psychoanalysis than it is about differences. For example, the Freudian attitude to memory is to treat it as deceptive; a conundrum whose solution may reveal hidden sources of anxiety and distress. A similar but more pragmatic line is taken in early Buddhism. Here the focus is more on the role of memory in the immediate arising of feelings and emotions. Once this is recognised, the source of the memory and its meaning is less relevant.

Authority is expressed differently in psychoanalysis and in Buddhism. The authority of the psychoanalyst is that of the doctor: an expert acting on a disorded patient to cure them. In Buddhist traditions the authority is that of the teacher who imparts skills for managing emotion. Of course, this is to oversimplfy both traditions', which in any case share the objective the discovery of hidden emotional difficulties. The methods for achieving this objective overlap, but have distinct differences of emphasis. For example, the role of anger in psychoanalysis is, potentially at least, curative. In Buddhism, anger is harmful in any form; what helps is to make friends with it and thus pacify it. Psychoanalysis proceeds through conversation. Buddhist teaching is primarily discourse and meditation proceeds in silence

These differences may suggest that resemblance is as far as any overlap between Buddhist and Western systems may go. Meditation, for example, might not seem a practical therapeutic tool. For example, a lot of skill and time are required to both determine if it is suitable and to monitor its effects. However, research on the use of simplified forms of meditation as an adjunct to western medical and psychological therapy has indicated that it can be cost effective, and humanistic traditions of psychology and psychotherapy find much in Buddhism that is useful.

More challenging differences between the two systems arise at deeper levels. Freudian ideas are fundamentally in line with the Western world view as it stood in the late nineteenth century. Some ideas in Buddhism, that of previous lives being an obvious case, are hard to bring into line with this worldview. Later developments of Freudian insights, for example by Jung and by Assagioli, go some way to resolving such discrepancies, but even so, difficulties remain. If Buddhism is misinterpreted and used inappropriately when dealing with people made vunerable through mental illness, the results could be harmful. Jung warned this was likely to happen without the proper insight into Eastern traditions. In this chapter, given that Padmasiri de Silva speaks both as a philosopher and as someone who has grown up in a Buddhist culture, we can find a properly informed insight into how far Western and Buddhist therapeutic practices may overlap.

★ ★ ★

Exploring the Vicissitudes of Affect and Working with Emotions: An Early Buddhist Perspective

Padmasiri de Silva

INTRODUCTION

This chapter attempts to do a study of what may be called 'Buddhist Experientialism', through an analysis of the Buddhist techniques of meditation dealing with feelings and emotions. As the practice of Buddhist meditation is greatly focused on the present moment, it is necessary to unravel the temporal dimensions of the past, present and future in dealing with the management of emotions or affects and to understand the kind of dynamic changes they undergo. This paper will also place in comparative perspective the contributions of Sigmund Freud to understanding the psychodynamics of emotion and their implications for therapy. While most of the basic concepts like the Buddha's focus on suffering, impermanence and the doctrine of the non-self are common to all the Buddhist traditions, the scriptural resources used in this paper are from the early Buddhist tradition.

This analysis also goes beyond an earlier study that we did on Buddhism and Freud,[1] where we were more struck by the similarities between the two systems than the more interesting differences. In dealing with the psychodynamics of emotions according to Buddhism, we need to free ourselves very much, from the spell of the 'drama of neurosis',[2] and look patiently at more pedestrian and prosaic routes taken by human consciousness in routine life. It is true that Freud did focus attention on the psychopathology of normal life, hinted at the notion that all humans are partially neurotic, and above all paved the way for the concept that 'analysis is not merely a method of treatment, but a way of life.'[3] But it appears that Freud's understanding of the normal mind was greatly coloured by his highly concentrated study of the workings of the neurotic mind. It has been even said, in a lighter vein, that Freud was worried that he began to 'look more and more like his patients'. That was the universe in which he lived, so much so, that he even said that if he has to devote his whole life to one patient, that itself would be a worthwhile venture.

Apart from the gap between the normal and the neurotic, a second issue that will concern us in this paper is the point that Freud was basically focusing on the past of the patients rather than the present. The past of an individual is important and is certainly a central strand of psychotherapeutic exploration. But an endless preoccupation with one's past, may not be the only way to get out of the interminable neurotic cycle, a point which Freud stumbled on, when he wrote one of the most significant contributions of his life time, 'Analysis Terminable and Interminable'.[4] Margaret Donaldson has highlighted this point well: 'This is not to deny the value of reflecting on how one came to be as one is and trying to be free of old self-deceptions. The hard acknowledging this entails – the kind of established honesty with the self that may result from it, if it succeeds are no mean achievements.'[5] She also says, 'But there are dangers. "Interminable analysis" may mean endless absorption in one's past of a kind that narrows the vision and is not desirable.'[6] In looking at the vicissitudes of affect and working with emotions in Buddhism, in this paper, the focus on the 'present' and the immediate past will be maintained. In general, a central theme that will link up our discussion on therapy, emotions and experientialism will be the Buddhist perspectives on time.[7]

A third concern is to look at Freud's concept of affect and how he looked at the psychodynamics of emotions. Though he was a pioneer in exploring emotions, his perspectives were limited by his own metapsychology of psychic energy. To a great extent Freud equated affect with psychic energy in his early attempts to understand the nature of affects. Though there was an evolution in Freud's theoretical perspectives on this issue, the initial Freudian claim that hysteria was due to the strangulation of affect, that their origins are found in traumatic events and abreaction was the technique to deal with them – are claims that always persisted with the development of Freudian theory. Freud later in his study of dreams introduced the 'wish model' of psychological functioning, and with the integration of this idea to his theory of instincts, Freud had a more broader basis for understanding affect. In developing the thesis that a patient's emotional life may· be transformed through an understanding of its causes rooted in the past and its meanings, Freud was giving an ideogenic interpretation of neurosis rather than a physiogenic interpretation.

We cannot in fact understand concepts like 'abreaction' unless we give an important place to thoughts. Jerome Neu has even made a case for a strong cognitivist strand in the Freudian perspectives on emotions.[8] Freud did not integrate these rich strands of thought into a comprehensive theory of emotions. Of course, it may be unfair to expect a pioneer who charted out a new territory of the human mind to offer such a comprehensive understanding of the nature of affects. But in the final analysis, the Freudian claim is that the key to understanding of emotions is the Unconscious and its residual strains in trauma and the patient's past. Buddhism while attempting to integrate the different strands of an emotion like the instinctual, physiological and the cognitive would also focus on the present moment, in addition to the past. The Buddha also emphasises the transformative power of positive emotions like compassion, loving kindness, sympathetic joy and equanimity.[9] This is again an aspect of emotions Freud did not develop.

By contrast, Jung, in drawing inspiration from Eastern thought, saw the transformative power and the therapeutic efficacy of positive emotions of compassion and love. Also, it has to be emphasised that while Freud's concepts of the pre-conscious, conscious and the unconscious were some what compartmentalised, the Buddha saw a broader spectrum ranging from clear awareness to areas of dim awareness, self-deception and ignorance.

The last point that lies implicitly in our discussion of Buddhist experientialism, but may need some brief discussion in our introduction of the central concerns of this paper, are the Buddhist perspectives on 'authority' as contrasted with experience. The discussion in the discourses of the Buddha, on the concept of authority, range from the epistemological, metaphysical and the ethical to the psychological and therapeutic.

At an epistemological level the Buddha was critical of authoritarian creeds and admonished his own followers to accept even his own doctrine only after critical examination and reflection. In a celebrated discourse, The Kalama Sutta, the Buddha says that one should not accept anything because it is mere rumour, a traditional belief, it is the opinion of the majority, it is found in the scriptures, it is a product of mere logic, it is the teaching of a prestigious teacher etc.[10] Though critical reflection is a useful tool, ultimately it is the test of experience that is the guide. The Buddha in fact mentions three groups of thinkers of his time- the traditionalists who upheld only the authority of the scriptures, the speculative metaphysicians who used mere logic and the experientialists who practiced meditation.[11] The Buddha said he belonged to the third group. At an ethical level the Buddha was critical of both determinism and indeterminism and upheld the concepts of freewill and responsibility within the framework of the law of dependent origination.

In the area of psychology, we discover in the teachings of the Buddha a tremendous psychological space for personal autonomy, self-restraint, self-definition, as well as personal effort and endurance.

It is within this framework that one could develop the Buddhist therapy for the management of emotions. Meditation includes a set of practices that train people to develop powers of attention, with the aim of bringing mental processes under greater voluntary control. It also becomes possible to develop understanding and insight into the emergence of negative emotions like lust, malevolence, envy and the way to develop the positive emotions of compassion and loving kindness.

Critics who have seen a strong coercive strain in the Freudian analyst and emphasised the need for a more open space may find the Buddhist setting of compassion attractive for developing psychotherapy. The ideal norms of Buddhist therapy would be a kind of non-directive therapy, where the skills may be learnt under an experienced teacher. The monks were trained by the Buddha to impart his teachings as well as the meditational practices to the followers. While the monks and the nuns took the obligation to teach and preach seriously, the lay community supported them through gifts of food and clothing. Thus the lay people went to the monks when they had personal problems. While there were restrictions for monks getting involved in the secular art of medicine, the monks continued to function as 'Doctors of the Soul'. Thus though a discipline like psychological counselling did not exist at the time of the Buddha in the modern sense of the term, some sort of psychological counselling for the average person with normal problems was not completely absent. The discourses of the Buddha are rich with advice to people who were struck by bereavement, sickness, loss of meaning in their lives, anxieties, fears and rage. These problems were basically existential than pathological. The advice that was given by the Buddha, the monks and the nuns following the Buddha are not of an authoritarian nature. The heart of the Buddhist practice of meditation is contained in the Discourse on Satipatthana.[12] It is the best guide to

128

the systematic cultivation of right mindfulness in daily life, as well as for it's highest goal of the liberation from the wheel of suffering. It is the indispensable foundation for right living, for overcoming sorrow, and the destruction of pain and grief.

EMOTIONS AND THERAPY

Now that we have introduced the central themes of this paper, we shall first look at issues concerning the model of therapy in Buddhism, then do a detailed look at the Buddhist perspectives on time in relation to therapy and thirdly the management of feelings and emotions.

The Buddhist model of therapy depends on a number of strands of thought on mental health and sickness in the discourses of the Buddha. First there is the notion that ideal mental health is only attained after perfection by the arahant. Perhaps we may understand this way of thinking in terms of the following words of Abraham Maslow: 'What we call "normal" in psychology is really a psychopathology of the average, so undramatic and so widely spread that we don't even notice it'.[13] The Buddha would say that this pathology is rooted in greed and addiction, in anger and aggression, as well as our existential confusion of the nature of the self. Secondly, there is the concept of the well adjusted householder who lives the righteous and harmonious life, who has not completely mastered the roots of sickness mentioned earlier. If we accept the idea that psychotherapy is a way of life than a therapy for sickness, we see interesting linkages between these two Buddhist ideals.

The third strand of thinking is that Buddhism has resources to deal with those who have breakdowns. If we look at a spectrum of deviations from average mental health, like drug addiction and alcoholism to severe neurosis, it must be said that Buddhist techniques would work only with those who have the normal powers of memory and reasoning, and would not work with those with extreme psychotic and neurotic breakdowns. The point at which Buddhist techniques will work well is to deal with the pathogenic qualities of the normal mind. Writing on the subject of the management of emotions, Margaret Donaldson makes a fitting observation: 'I shall not be talking about disturbances of the kind we call "mental illness" but rather about human suffering with which each of us must some how deal. Of course the line separating mental illness from "normal" trouble is not sharp. It partakes of the general fuzziness of category boundaries.'[14]

Padmasiri de Silva

In the West today meditation is used with good results for stress management and relaxation. Also it has been observed that in areas like depression, anxiety, addictions and fixations, Buddhist techniques have great therapeutic potential, specially if they are designed for particular clients. It can also be used as a primary, secondary or a supplementary part of a programme.[15] In this paper we are basically concerned with emotions and the practice of mindfulness in relation to feelings. Mindfulness is concerned with attention and awareness and these are qualities needed by all of us, but society takes the presence of these qualities for granted. Meditation helps us deepen and refine these qualities so that they become part of our daily life. It is not that they are exactly time consuming, but that we fail to integrate them to our routine lives. Those who practice meditation makes a greater commitment to a life lived with awareness, insight and a more resilient, flexible and authentic emotional life. To extend these possibilities to those struck with emotional problems, anxieties and depression needs imagination, experience and hard work.

There are areas in our lives, with which we are out of touch and into which we do not care to probe. Emotions are an important area for study, as some of causes for the absence of psychological well being is that we have lost contact with our emotions. The Buddhist contributions to the management of feelings and emotions is a neglected area of study.

The term 'Sati' refers to the practice of awareness or attention in the present moment, and in the context of Buddhism would mean good or skilful attentiveness. The discourse called the 'Satipatthana' deals with four areas for the practice of awareness, the body, feelings, states of mind and mental contents. The present analysis is basically focused on feelings, with some reference to the body and thoughts.

The linkage between the practice of mindfulness on the body and the feelings is very important, as this link may be used to understand the ailment referred to as 'alexithymia'. The term refers to an ailment where people loose contact with their emotions. In fact the word comes from the Greek, a: 'without', lexis: 'word', thumos: 'heart' or 'affectivity'.[16] It can refer to difficulties people have in describing their affective states or emotions, and also the difficulties of distinguishing one emotion from another. Regular practice of mindfulness of feeling would indicate that this quality would also be found in people leading a normal life, but who have developed instrumental, operational and mechanical types of relationships with others. A very loose and diffused form of 'alexithymia' seems to be endemic to the kind of highly urbanised and industrial cultures in which people live today. This loss of affectivity may find its inroads to negative kinds of affects like pain, animosity and anger. That is apart from the failure to develop the more positive emotions like joy in work, love, compassion and gratitude, we may loose access to the even more negative emotions in us through repression and denial. Buddhism advocates a non-judgmental receptive attitude to understand these emotions, so that they may be handled well. Living in a culture of this sort, it would be apparent that, large numbers would loose their finer powers of discrimination for the nuances of assertive anger, depressive anger, narcissistic anger and moral anger.

BUDDHIST PERSPECTIVES ON TIME

In this short paper, I am limiting the comparative focus on psychotherapy and practice of mindfulness training in Buddhism to the subject of affects or emotions. The focus on the present to which I referred earlier in dealing with emotions in Buddhism has been explored in a very stimulating study by Margaret Donaldson.[17] According to her, there are four modes of concern, in terms of our space-time dimensions. They are described as (I) The 'point mode', with a focus on the present, here and now; (II) The 'line mode', with a focus on the past, then and there; (III) The 'construct mode' without any specific locus; (IV) The 'transcendent mode', which is not in space-time.

We do not intend to deal with the details of this schema here, but against the background of her distinction between encountering the present and looking at the past, to explore how Buddhist perspective on the spatio-temporal dimensions are related to the management of emotions. A great deal of human suffering, especially the facets that have to deal with our thoughts and emotions, are, according to Donaldson, the product of the line and the co-construct modes. Western culture often tries to escape out of the tribulations caused by these two modes by escaping to the point-mode. It is an escape mode which may be described through a poem of Kipling:

> ... not to sit still
> or frowst with a book by the fire;
> but to take a large hoe and a shovel also,
> and dig till you lightly perspire.[18]

She observes that Freudian analysis attempts to redeem the line and co-construct modes by a process of reconstruction, based on understanding what had originally gone wrong. Cognitive therapy on the other hand aims at reconstruction without paying heed to the developmental history of patients. In the next section of this paper, We shall also explore the Buddhist perspectives on the present, past and the future in relation to different types of contexts.

While the Buddhist makes limited use of understanding the past without getting obsessed with it, and do not project excessively into the future, while one can have healthy aspirations for the future, one is also asked not to get 'drawn into the present' by developing attachment. By understanding the present as it is through the development of attention, it is possible to gain an insight into the nature of things. Thus the Buddha's analysis may be referred to as a critical use of the temporal categories rather than a transcendence of it. As Donaldson points out, 'bare attention' is the clear and single-minded awareness of what happens to us and in us at the successive moments of perception. She also observes that, in the Buddhist traditions, there is movement from the line and co-construct modes to the detached observation of the present. But one has to be careful of speaking about a transcendent mode beyond this experience of the nature of suffering, impermanence and non-self. The Buddha in fact was silent on the question about what happens to the perfect one after death.

The practice of mindfulness calls for persistent effort and disciplined practice, as we tend to cling to mental habits and automatic responses. But once a certain degree of regular practice is established, we de-automatise the well trodden habits and bring a fresh perspective on things and events we encounter in life. As we expand and deepen our awareness that we discover areas in our lives with which we were out of touch, areas completely neglected and submerged by the routine demands of our lives. An important area thus neglected is the realm of emotions, moments of pain and anger, distress, discontent and depression. On the positive side we loose the moments of peace and joy in life. In developing awareness to the moment to moment flow of experience, we virtually 'open our hearts'. The phrase 'opening our hearts' is a metaphor which captures the idea of non-judgmental receptivity and acceptance. It is the moment to moment focus on sensations, feelings and thought which we consider as the focus on the 'present'. Very often, our minds are buried in the 'past' or projected towards the 'future'. The following lines from the discourses captures well the Buddhist perspective on time:

> Let one trace not back the past
> Or yearn for the future – yet-to-come.
> That which is past is left behind
> Unattained is the 'yet-to-come'.
> But that which is present he discerns-
> With insight as and when it comes.
> The Immovable- the-non-irritable.
> In that state should the wise-one grow
> Today itself should one bestir
> Tomorrow death may come- who knows?
> For no bargain can we strike
> With 'Death' who has his mighty hosts.
> But one who dwells thus ardently
> By day, by night, untiringly
> Him the Tranquil Sage has called-
> 'The Ideal Lover of Solitude'.

The context for this verse is important, as it is considered as 'The Discourse on the Ideal Love of Solitude'.[19] Commenting on this poem, Venerable Nanananda says, that '... it is not so much the mere recollection of the past that is the bondage, as the element of delight(nandi) or "desire-and-lust" (chandaraga), one finds therein. It is the tendency to retrace, revive, relish the past, that has to be eliminated and hence there comes in the necessity of detachment even with regard to thought processes.'[20] This comment may be confirmed by a reference to another discourse:

> Mind is not the bondage for ideas; ideas are not the bondage for the mind; but whatever desire-and-lust arises wherein dependent on them both – that is the bondage therein.[21]

The Buddha's main emphasis in this discourse on solitude is that 'tracing back the past', 'yearning for the future' and being 'drawn to the present' interferes with the practice of following the path, when the 'consciousness is bound fast by desire-and-lust'. What this reference indicates is that the Buddha does not make a kind of blanket statement on our norms for the perception of time. In the light of the discourses of the Buddha, there is a need to contextualise the Buddhist perception of time, specially if we need to look at possible time orientations for therapy. For instance, one should not be drawn into the present, but use the focus on the present moment, as a key to understand the nature of reality; one should use the knowledge of the past, so long as this can illuminate our lives without being obsessed with it. In fact the Buddha points out that even if one enters the forest for meditating in secluded surroundings, if one has lust and attachment within, it is like entering the forest with a companion. So physical solitude is not real seclusion, unless the mind is free from the chatter and noise of lust and attachment. Physical solitude where one does not see any one 'before' or 'behind' one self works only in terms of a state where one frees from the framework of 'past' and 'future'. That is the space-time orientation for the practice of mindfulness. In fact, even regarding the future, it is the desire and lust which gives rise to anxiety and longing that is unwholesome. Even for an arahant (the perfected one) making choices regarding future courses of action is not denied. For the lay householder and the practicing monk, being aware of the possible good and bad consequences of actions in the future is a virtue, so long as craving does not enter these reflections, even in disguised form. In fact, it would be better to be future-oriented in a constructive manner than express remorse and guilt after the evil action is performed.

An interesting study of the metaphors used for understanding the concept of time has been made by Robert Ornstein, and these metaphors may illuminate our perspectives on time. Robert Ornstein has cited four important ways of perceiving time in terms of basic metaphors:[22]

1. The notion that time is a sensory process and that there is an organ to experience time.
2. The notion that we are time keepers, and this is the notion of clock time.
3. The notion that time is a mental construction of the humans.
4. The more recent metaphor of 'storage' in cognitive processing.

Taking the first metaphor, 'If time were a sensory process like vision, then there would exist a 'real time' independent of us, and we would have an organ to experience time such as the eye'.[23] Though the mind is considered as a sense-door (dvara), it cannot function as an organ of time perception. Secondly, the Buddhist does not have to consider time in terms of the categories of 'existence' and 'non-existence', and thus avoids the intricacies of the issue whether there is an independent time. Instead of the concepts of 'existence' and 'non-existence', the Buddha uses the two terms, uppada (arising) and vaya (decay). This perspective emerges according to the way in which the Buddhist doctrine of conditionality is understood and extended to the practice of both calm and insight meditation: 'In developing samatha and vipassana (calm and insight), the mind is made to oscillate between these two terms (arising and decay) with ever increasing momentum, spurred by the by the three signata anicca(transcience), dukkha (suffering) and anatta (non-self). At the peak of intensity in this oscillation the lingering notions of existence and non-existence wane into insignificance since the mind now hardly rests on them'.[24] Thus the Buddha does not consider the experience of time as a sensory process or the mind as an organ which can experience the existence of an independent medium called 'time'.

Though the Buddha's focus is on psychological and experiential time, 'clock time' is adhered to as a conventional way of organising one's lives and the activities of the monks and society. In ancient times, people used other measures of time like the rising of the sun, seasons, movement of birds, sun dials etc. If we look at the discourses of the Buddha the notion of the 'Time Keeper' remains as a conventional mode like references to appointed time, meal time, morning and night etc. In the Dialogues of the Buddha, there is a reference to seven qualities of a good man: knowledge of the doctrine, of the meaning of the doctrine, knowledge of self, knowledge about how to be temperate, how to choose and keep time, about the nature of the individual and his role as a member of a group.[25] The notion of meal time and the biological and the physiological cycle indicating the need for food is true of even the perfected one (arahant). Very often the Buddha is critical of excessive speculative and dialectical debates on issues like the ontological status of time. What is recommended is the contextual and pragmatic use of language and concepts. On the path to liberation and contexts of meditation we dislodge them when it is necessary.

The third metaphor again emphasises the point that these concepts have no absolute status and are social constructs. While the experiencing of time is a fact, there are many ways of ordering time. Ornstein introduces this fourth metaphor as he is critical of the notion of the mind as an internal clock. He argues that remembered duration is a cognitive construction based on the storage size of the memory. He was interested in the storage of retrievable information. I wish to leave this issue open, Buddhist thought has yet to integrate the recent concerns of cognitive sciences. There is a close connection between the practice of mindfulness and the functions of memory, and the pali word sati refers to the practice of mindfulness which helps one to get rid of distorting factors like the projection of permanence in to our experience of time. Even memories which have been 'stored' may have been generated by these distorting factors and needs to be dissolved and emptied.

Buddhism is not anti-memory through being pro-awareness. Sati, the practice of mindfulness helps to deal with craving and the excitement of the senses, though the ultimate liberation is based on the faculty of panna or penetrative insight. The Buddha describes mindfulness practice: 'And what monks is the faculty of mindfulness? Herein, monks a noble disciple is mindful and is endowed with the highest prudence in mindfulness; he is one who remembers and recollects even what is done or said long ago.'[26] In fact, it must be mentioned that the denial of the rightful place of memory can lead to schizophrenic conditions.[27] The faculty of memory may be developed to a degree that knowledge of past lives is possible.[28] Thus we find that regarding what Margaret Donaldson calls the 'line mode' and 'point mode', there are legitimate contexts for focusing on the past, though the mindfulness practice has a focus on the present. Also, the kind of focus on the present is also a transcendence from the kind of the present moment depicted in Kipling's poem referred to earlier.

There are interesting contexts in the discourses where the development of an emotion over time sequence is presented. The lady householder Vedehika is supposed to be some one who by nature is gentle, meek and tranquil. The slave woman Kali who worked for her, who was a clever, diligent and careful worker, thought she should test the supposed gentleness of the lady and got up late in the morning on three successive days. The first day the lady was displeased; the second day, the lady was angry but only frowned to express the anger; on the third day the lady was so disturbed that she attacked Kali. From someone who was gentle, Vedehika became angry and later violent.[29] Using this context, the Buddha says that one is really gentle, when one is not disturbed by disagreeable situations.

Looking back, especially at the recent past is necessary to understand the emergence of types of meaning which emerge over time. The unfolding of meaning can be seen even over a larger span of time. There are also contexts, where over a larger span of time, if a person has spent an evil life, looking back on it, the person may mourn over it, grieve and become disillusioned: 'Monks as at eventide the shadows of the great mountain rests, lie and settle on the earth, so, monks, do, these evil deeds that the fool has formerly done by body, speech and thought lie and settle on him.'[30] Of course such restlessness is not wholesome or the best way to respond to the realisation of a bad slice of life one has lived. One should have a healthy attitude towards ones past. Excessive guilt and repentence is damaging.

Now, the unfolding of meaning in a time sequence is quite complex in Freudian reconstruction of the past. For him there were screen memories which were condensations of many others, and then only a thematic representation of a variety of previous experiences.[31] Freud attempts to reconstruct the past, to use it in the present. But yet as quite clearly expressed in *Analysis Terminable and Interminable*, and also shown by Donaldson, there was an excessive obsession with the past in Freudian psychotherapy. The Buddhist concern with the past is contextual and pragmatic. Though memories across several births is an accepted hypothesis in Buddhism, the Buddha discouraged excessive speculative concern about past births, but admonished his disciples to focus attention on the moment to moment flow of consciousness.

The attempt of Jung to develop the notion of the collective unconscious against the background of eastern thought deserves to be mentioned as he considers the notion of kamma as an archetype. In fact the Buddhist theory of kamma and dependent origination provide a broad background to understand the behaviour of individuals. But both Freud's notion of the 'archaic heritage of mankind' and the Jung's collective unconscious are very elusive terms and do not provide an intelligible basis to understand the early Buddhist notion of the unconscious. As I have pointed in detail in my earlier study of Freud and Buddhism, the Jungian term has some resemblance to the notion of 'storehouse consciousness', in some of the later Buddhist tradition.[32] But the early Buddhist position which has a different logical system in which the notion of the unconscious is in terms of dispositions rather than as a store.

Elsewhere I have attempted to analyse both the Buddhist and the Freudian notion of the unconscious in dispositional terms. If the message of Freud's *Analysis Terminable and Interminable* implies that certain case histories are problematic in the light of one life, there are interesting questions to explore. Freud's notion of the ambivalent structure of instinct which continually prepares the ground for further conflict and his notion of the repetition compulsion, some what reminiscent of Schopenhauer's will to live are closer approximations to understand the Buddhist theory of becoming.[33]

WORKING WITH EMOTIONS

In the formulation of the notion of dependent origination, feeling is the potential condition for craving and subsequently of the more intense fixity on objects, situations and persons, referred to as 'clinging'(upadana). When receiving a sense impression from the external world or an ideational stimuli from the mind, if one can pause and stop at the emerged feeling, sensation or hedonic tone (vedana) with mindfulness, the feeling will not give rise to craving, clinging(upadana) and negative emotions (best understood in terms of the concept of sankhara).[34] Negative emotions like lust, anger and conceit are rooted in greed, hatred and delusion. Delusion refers to the existential confusion regarding the 'self'. Negative emotions are also fed by the craving for sensual gratification, for egoistic pursuits and self-annihilation.[35] Feelings are also more closely associated with dormant tendencies (anusaya) towards lust, resistance and ignorance: 'In the case of pleasant feelings, the dormant tendency towards lust should be given up; in the case of painful feeling the dormant tendency towards resistance should be given up; in the case of feeling that is neither pleasurable-nor painful, the dormant tendency towards ignorance should be given up.'[36] Positive emotions emerge on the roots of non-greed or liberality, non-hatred or compassion and non-delusion or wisdom. The following verse sums up, the Buddha's attitude towards feeling well:

> If one feels joy, but knows not feeling's nature,
> bent towards greed, he will not find deliverance.
>
> If one feels pain, but knows not feeling's nature,
> bent towards hate, he will not find deliverance.
>
> And even neutral feeling which as peaceful
> the Lord of Wisdom has proclaimed,
> if, in attachment, he should cling to it,
> he will not be free from the round of ill.
>
> But if a monk is ardent and does not neglect
> the practice of mindfulness and comprehension clear,
> the nature of all feelings will he penetrate.
>
> And having done so, in this very life
> will he be free of cankers, free from taints.

Mature in knowledge, firm in Dhamma's ways,
when once his life-span ends, his body breaks,
all measure and concept he has transcended.[37]

The contemplation on feelings is one of the four Foundations of Mindfulness, along with working with the body (including breathing), thoughts and the mind and body at work together. (kayanupassana, vedanaupassana, cittanupassana, dhammanupassana). But it is very necessary that this contemplation is remembered and applied in daily life, when ever situations emerge, where feelings are prone to generate negative emotions. Mindfulness should be maintained through out the short duration of the specific feeling, till its cessation. If bare attention is directed towards the arising and vanishing of these feelings, the additional factors which convert them into negativities may be held at bay, and once refinement and sensitivity to the subtle nuances of feelings get developed, one is well on the road to the education of the emotions. Non-judgmental observation, where one virtually makes friends with anger(if anger has emerged), so that it does not get converted into more deep rooted hatred, or slide into envy and jealousy, self-hatred, moral anger, bitterness and depression becomes possible by the practice of mindfulness and its extension to routine life. Extending this to clinical practice can be done with care, caution, paying heed to context and with adjustments to each individual case.

The work of Olaf G. Deetharage blending mindfulness practice and psychotherapy refers to some good examples of 'working with emotions'. He says, 'Many clinical patients, specially those we would label depressive, anxious or neurotic have problems either contacting or controlling emotions. Continued work with mindfulness techniques often yields results in these areas, because emotions and emotional states can be made the object of contemplation.'[38] He also suggests that emotions can be watched and labelled as anger, joy, fear etc and seen objectively. Labelling and non-judgmental awareness helps us to break through alexithymia, mentioned earlier in the paper. One of Deetharage's case histories is used to illustrate his point.

A 22-year old married woman suffering from what has been diagnosed as endogenous depression expresses despair at her inability to come into contact with her emotions, not 'feeling anything more'. She was asked to become more aware of her feelings, and carefully and accurately labelling them, when ever she practiced watchfulness of breathing and her routine activities. 'She then gradually became aware that she had been misinterpreting her emotions over many months, mistakenly believing that she had been experiencing depression where as strong elements of anger, hostility, self-abasement, and disappointment had been present. This recognition of the feelings she had been inaccurately labelling depression freed her to identify other feelings as well.'[39] Thus she was able to be in contact with a fuller spectrum of human emotions and it is said in this report, that her 'depression' disappeared and was replaced by a greater understanding of her own feelings and emotions. This I feel is a good example of clinical work using the Buddhist practice of mindfulness to deal with the issues of alexithymia, and the vicissitudes of affect. Alexithymia also involves a split between 'psyche' and 'soma'. As Joyce McDougall says in her, *The Theatres of the Mind* (*Illusion and Truth on the Psychoanalytic Stage*), 'Affects are one of the most privileged links between psyche and soma, between the instinctual source of life and the mind that must organise these life forces'.[40] She also observes that affects intended to bring certain messages from either the body or the mind, do get paralysed in their 'linking function'. We need more integration between body and mind for developing a vibrant emotional dimension in our lives.

The building of such a system over a life time, fortified with a defensive wall is a strong structure to break through. We need to be sure that such patients wish to learn more about themselves, and much preliminary work needs to be done before patients are able to 'recognise their defensive prison'. Also without clear insight into the nature of symptoms, the liberated prisoner may be unable to 'gather up the fractured words' and 'incapable of holding and using the strangled emotions'. Thus within the profession of psychotherapists, there are words of caution, how much more care needs to be present, in crossing boundaries from mindfulness practice to the management of neurotic ailments need no over emphasis.

Having made this point, it has to be stated that the practice of mindfulness presents a very strong focus on the linkages between psyche and soma, as would be seen in the linking of the practice of mindfulness on the body and breathing and the mindfulness on feelings and emotions. (kayanupassana and vedananupassana).

Apart from the general practice of mindfulness, there are more specific techniques of dealing with emotions in the discourses. The 'Discourse on the Forms of Thought' directs our attention to the cognitive roots of emotions. Though the practice of mindfulness is crucial to the Buddhist path, final insight is the product of cognitive transformation. At different levels the cognitive factor as thought and correct view emerges in relation to affective phenomena. This discourse mentions five techniques. The first is the method of finding a wholesome object instead of the unwholesome object, compassion instead of anger, like a carpenter driving out a large peg with a small one.[41] This indicates the notion of finding antidotes for negative emotions.

The second method deals with the scrutiny of the peril of evil thoughts This is compared to a person who in the prime of life is fond of adornment and beautifying the body, and who suddenly sees the disgusting sight of a carcass round his neck. The third is the method of not paying attention to evil thoughts that may generate bad emotions. The fourth is the method of looking at the genesis of bad thoughts. Emotions influence thoughts and thoughts influence emotions. Thus greed and hatred as roots may generate negative emotions. The fifth method is the method of restraint and control.

It is said that if the four methods already mentioned do not work, 'with his teeth clenched, his tongue pressed against the palate', the mind should subdue and restrain the mind. In general we do not find anything like the hydraulic model of dealing with emotions. This is the idea that anger for instance is the product of frustration and when this is blocked up, release of pent up energy is necessary. Freudian catharsis too has this element, though Freud later emphasises the importance of insight into negative emotions.

The Buddhist technique is critical of both repression and the sudden release of blocked up states. Mindfulness involves making friends with anger and similar states and through non-judgmental awareness coming into contact with them and realise the futility of cultivating such mental conditions. This helps us to see clearly and come into contact with facets of our personality, specially the affective side, both the negativities that block our growth and the more creative and positive aspects that need to be cultivated and nourished.

The most powerful Buddhist technique is of course the focus on the flow of cognitive and affective experiences and their complex inter-relationship in the stream of consciousness.[42] In the ultimate analysis, the practice of mindfulness with a focus on the moment-moment awareness is the key technique of Buddhism to observe the flow of cognitive-affective stream of experience. It would be most fitting to sum up the trend of thought I have been developing about emotions and therapy with the words of venerable Nyanaponika: 'One need not have fears that one's focusing the mind on the feelings and emotions, in the manner described, will lead to cold aloofness or an emotional withdrawal. On the contrary, mind and heart will become more open to all those finer emotions spoken of before. It will not exclude warm human relationships, nor the enjoyment of beauty in art and nature. But it will remove from them the fever of clinging, so that these experiences will give a deeper satisfaction, as far as this world of dukkha admits.'[43]

BUDDHISM AND PSYCHOTHERAPY ON THE VICISSITUDES OF AFFECTS

I shall conclude this paper in the light of the above analysis by summing up some significant points. First, it has to be emphasised, that Buddhism accepts different levels and gradations of awareness and lack of awareness of emotions, compared with the more compartmentalised perspectives on the consciousness and uncon- scious in Freudian psychotherapy. Also Buddhism does not have a specific notion of dynamic trauma, though the repression of incidents at different stages in life and their impact on one's psyche can be well integrated to Buddhist psychology. As I have shown in my early study on the subject,[44] there are interesting resemblances between the Freudian instincts and the three forms of craving in Buddhism.

But the spell of the ego is the most powerful motivational spring in Buddhism and the ego is in the background for the subtlest vicissitudes in our emotions. The inroads of anger into the very bosom of love, as well as envy and jealousy are well recognised in Buddhism. But the vicissitudes that the Buddha discuses are all related to those emotions which figure prominently on the path to liberation. Loving kindness (metta) has lust as the near enemy and ill-will as the distant enemy, regarding compassion (karuna) near enemy is self-pity and the distant enemy is cruelty, regarding sympathetic joy(mudita), it is said that the near enemy of sympathetic joy is joy regarding material things, and the near enemy of equanimity is indifference. Another such context would be the emotion of disgust: 'When insight is deepened and strengthened what has been called disgust(nibbida) has no longer the strong emotional tinge of aversion and revulsion but manifests itself as a withdrawal, estrangement and turning away from worldliness and the residue of one's own defilements.'[45]

These examples will again emphasise the difference of framework between psychotherapy and Buddhism for charting the management of emotions. There are undoubtedly points of intersection between the two systems, and it is in this area, that psychotherapy may be able to use Buddhist resources. In attempting to discern the distinctive normative emotions that need to be cultivated and their counterfeit emotions and distortions, Buddhism is very much concerned with the springs of motivation, but also takes into consideration other causal factors like ideational and sensory stimuli, but gives an important place to beliefs and cognitive frames.[46] Our discussion of the temporal perspectives and emotions have emphasised the strong link between emotions and excessive desires. Practice of mindfulness contributes to both the control of undesirable emotions, as well as the development of insight into the working of the affective domain. Mindfulness also helps to break through alexithymia. Emotions are the most human aspect of our psyche and to loose touch with this domain of our life is in effect is to loose our sense of our humanity.

On the subject of emotions, Freud's early attachment to the concept of psychic energy obstructed him from developing a more comprehensive theory of emotions. On the issue concerning temporal dimensions, Freud's heavy exploration of the past of the patient prevented him from exploiting the intriguing attractions of the present moment in the therapeutic setting. Buddhist practice of mindfulness offers more ground for a non-directive therapy, than the Freudian. But Freud's final goal was to restore rationality and autonomy to the patient. He even mentioned in his Analysis Terminable and Interminable that after his sense of rationality and autonomy is restored, the analysed qualifies himself to be an analyst, and then only the great journey of self-exploration begins.

If Freud's 'Analysis Terminable And Interminable' brings him closer to Buddhism, recent research by philosophers like Thomas Nagel have found ways of bridging the gulf between the Freud who was submerged by the drama of neurosis and the Freud who was trying to convert 'hysteria into common unhappiness'. Nagel says that there is a continuity in the kind of explanations used by psychoanalysis and commonsense explanations: 'I believe that psychoanalysis can borrow empirical evidence for its most important general foundations from the ubiquitous confirmation of the system of ordinary psychological explanation in everyday life.'[47] Nagel feels that psychoanalysis can confer a valuable form of self-knowledge and can be used by those who have it to 'anticipate, identify, and manage forms of irrationality that would victimise or disable them.'[48] It also helps us to develop more subtler and sensitive responses to others.

While there are clear differences between Budhist experientialism as a therapeutic resource and Freudian psychoanalysis, in the final analysis, it is these crosscutting pathways between the normal and the abnormal that makes the dialogue between Freud and Buddhism a very rewarding venture.

NOTES

1 de Silva, Padmasiri, *Buddhist and Freudian Psychology*, (National University of Singapore Press, Singapore, 1992, Third Edition)
2 Ibid. see, Chapter VI.
3 See, Storr, Anthony, 'The Concept of Cure', in, *Psychoanalysis Observed*, ed. C. Rycroft, (Constable, London, 1966) p. 53.
4 Sigmund Freud, 'Analysis Terminable and Interminable', *The Standard Edition of the Complete Works of Sigmund Freud*, ed. James Strachey, (Hogarth Press, London, 1966) 23: 216–53.
5 Donaldson, Margaret, *Human Minds*, (Penguin Books, London, 1992) p. 209.
6 Ibid.
7 Ibid p. 194. I am indebted to John Pickering for introducing the work of Margaret Donaldson to me. See, review of, *Twin Peaks: Compassion and Insight*, by John Pickering, in, Asian Philosophy, 4, 1, 1995, pp. 187–191.
8 Neu, Jerome, *Emotion, Thought and Therapy*, (University of California Press, Berkley and Los Angeles, 1977).
9 For a discussion of emotion profiles and theoretical perspectives of emotions in Buddhism, see, Padmasiri de Silva, *Twin Peaks: Compassion and Insight* (Buddhist Research Society, Singapore, 1992).
10 *Gradual Sayings*, I, 187–191.
11 *Middle Length Sayings*, II, 211.
12 See, Nyanaponika Mahathera, *The Heart of Buddhist Meditation* (Rider, London, 1975).
13 Maslow, Abraham, *Toward a Psychology of Being*, (Van Nostrand, Princeton, 1968) p. 16.
14 Donaldson, Margaret, *Human Minds*. p. 194.
15 Deetharage Olaf G., 'Mindfulness Meditation as Psychotherapy', in, Boorstein Symour and Deetharage Olaf G., *Buddhism in Psychotherapy*, (Buddhist Publication Society, Kandy, 1982) p. 17.
16 McDougall, Joyce, *Theatres of the Mind*, (Free Association Books, London, 1986) p. 159.
17 Donaldson, Margaret, *Human Minds*.
18 Ibid p. 211.
19 Nanananda, *Ideal Solitude*, (Buddhist Publication Society, Kandy, 1973) p. 19.
20 Ibid p. 27.
21 *Kindred Sayings*, IV 17.
22 Ornstein, Robert E., *On the Experience of Time*, (Penguin Books, New York, 1975) p. 23.
23 Ibid.
24 Nanananda, *Concept and Reality*, (Buddhist Publication Society, 19710) p. 79.

25 *Dialogues of the Buddha*, III, 252.
26 *Kindred Sayings* IV, 197.
27 Nanananda, *Ideal Solitude*, p. 28.
28 *Dialogues of the Buddha*, I, 81.
29 *Middle Length Sayings*, I 126.
30 *Middle Length Sayings*, III. 164.
31 See, McGuire, Michael T., *Reconstructions in Psychoanalysis*, (Butterworths, London, 1971).
32 See, de Silva, Padmasiri, *Buddhist and Freudian Psychology*. Chapter III.
33 Ibid. pp. 185–201.
34 See, de Silva, Padmasiri, *Twin Peaks*, Chapter 3.
35 Ibid, pp. 51–58.
36 Nyanaponika, *Contemplation of Feelings*, (Buddhist Publication Society, 1983, Kandy) p. 11.
37 Ibid.
38 Deetharage Olaf G., 'Mindfulness Meditation as Psychotherapy', pp. 25–26.
39 Ibid.
40 McDougall, Joyce, *Theatres of the Mind*, p. 177.
41 *Middle Length Sayings* I, Sutta 20.
42 For an interesting paper on the emergence of a series of related emotions within the continuum of the stream of consciousness, see, Michenbaum, Donald and Butler, Linda 'Cognitive Ethology: Assessing the Streams of Cognition and Emotion', in, Blankenstein, K.R., et al, eds. *Assessment and Modification of Emotional Behaviour*, (Plenum Press, New York, 1980).
43 Nyanaponika, *Contemplation of Feelings*, p. 6.
44 See, *Buddhist and Freudian Psychology*.
45 Nyanaponika, *Worn-out Skin*, (Buddhist Publication Society, Kandy, 1977)
46 For the role of cognitive factors in emotions, see, *Twin Peaks: Compassion and Insight*.
47 Nagel Thomas, *Other Minds*, (Oxford University Press, Oxford, New York, 1995) p. 41.
48 Ibid. p. 44.

Section 4

Psychological Theory

Chapter 7

EDITOR'S PREFACE

Process philosophers such as Whitehead and Bohm suggest how psychology might recast its view of selfhood. Both treat nature, including consciousness, as an organic process rather than as a mechanism. Now, the computational metaphor for the mind emphasises mechanism over process, information over meaning and rationality over feeling. However, a different style of inquiry is emerging as, with the postmodern turn in science there is a return of interest in Whitehead.[1] It points psychology back to Susanne Langer's view that meaning and feeling, rather than mere rationality are the primary experiential phenomena to which psychology should direct its attention.[2] More recently Bruner notes how the computational metaphor has obscured the original impulse behind the cognitive revolution of the 1950's, namely, to inquire into cultural meanings.[3] He recommends that psychological inquiry start from the assumption that the motor of mental life is an effort after meaning. This effort is charged with feeling and cannot be usefully considered apart from the cultural context in which the effort occurs. Now selfhood is both a precondition of making this effort and a product of it. It is a process occuring within a system involving physical, biological and psychological levels of order. Selfhood is part of the circulation of meaning between these different levels. Bohm places this organic interchange of meaning at the heart of his perspective on the mind body relationship.[4] This interchange, which dialectically causes and is caused by selfhood, has emergent causal dynamics which participate in the activity of the brain. Selfhood on this basis emphasises relation, process and meaning; here again there are obvious parallels with Whitehead.

For Whitehead, Western science and philosophy have been progressively misdirected and unbalanced by the initial success of the mechanistic world view. Whitehead's critique when applied to psychology resembles recent critiques of cognitive reductionism.[5] It is necessary to change the ontological basis of psychological inquiry into selfhood. Instead of concentrating on internal cognitive mechanisms, postmodern psychology will also need to deal with the broader system in which cognition participates. Selfhood cannot be exclusively identified with any particular level of the system, such as cognitive mechanisms.[6]

Mental life is an effort after meaning. For human beings, selfhood arises through making this effort within a cultural context. Selfhood is thus not a structure but a process, in which biological, psychological and cultural levels of order form a ecological system based on the exchange of meaning. No level of this system has either ontological or explanatory priority, as Bateson, Maturana, Varela and Bohm, have, in their different ways, indicated in their treatments of the ecology of meaning.[7]

This broader view of selfhood resembles the Buddhist notion of *anatta* in that it shows that there is nothing essential or persistent that underlies selfhood. It is a process, embodied in a web-like system. The order at the different levels of this system is evanescent, arising and passing away over different timescales. These range from the few seconds of the specious present to the millions of years of biological and cultural evolution. It is impractical to search for any strict history of causality for the way the system behaves. Nor does it help to single out a particular level as fundamental; a systems approach and a plurality of theories are required.

Pluralism is not just a postmodern slogan. The effort after unified theories is a restrictive legacy of the European Enlightenment. Science is moving away from theoretical and methodological uniformity, towards a multiplicity of perspectives. Selfhood, as something whose proper treatment requires that it be studied in parallel from different perspective and with different techniques, is a thus paradigmatic issue for postmodern psychology. Scientific inquiry into selfhood cannot rest on just one theoretical perspective. Psychology's theories and methods need to be enriched through interaction with other traditions. Here, Buddhism has a great deal to offer.

NOTES

1 Griffin, D. (1988) *The Reenchantment of Science: Postmodern Proposals.* State University of New York Press, Albany.
2 Langer, S.K. (1988) *Mind: an Essay on Human Feeling*, abridged by Van Den Heuvel, G., Baltimore: Johns Hopkins University Press.
3 Bruner, J. (1990) *Acts of Meaning.* Harvard University Press.
4 Bohm, D. (1990) A New Theory of the Relationship Between Mind and Matter. *Philosophical Psychology, 3(2):* 271–286.
5 Valsiner, J. (1991) Construction of the Mental. *Theory and Psychology,* 1(4): 477–494.

6 Sperry, R. & Henniger, P. (1994) Consciousness and the Cognitive Revolution: a True World Paradigm Shift. *Anthropology of Consciousness*, Vol. 5, no. 3, pages 3–7.

7 Bateson, G. (1980) *Mind in Nature: A Neccessary Unity.* Fontana, London.

Bohm, D. (1988) Postmodern Science and a Postmodern World. In *The Reenchantment of Science, Postmodern Proposals*, edited by Griffin, D. R., Albany: State University of New York Press.

Maturana, H. & Varela, F. (1992) *The Tree of Knowledge: The Biological Roots of Human Understanding.* Revised edition. London & Boston: Shambala.

★ ★ ★

Selfhood is a Process
John Pickering

INTRODUCTION

The idea to be advanced here is that what Whitehead called the 'fallacy of misplaced concreteness' in the natural sciences also applies to psychology. This fallacy, broadly speaking, is to treat reality as composed of things instead of processes.[1] Thereby we fail to appreciate that nature is organic at all levels. In psychology, the fallacy is most apparent in the treatment of selfhood.

Two further points will be made in advancing this idea. The first is that the postmodern turn in science and in cultural more generally, provides the means to recognise this fallacy and to go beyond it. The second, in line with the postmodern turn toward plurality and eclecticism, is that interaction between Western psychology and Buddhism can help to repair the effects of this fallacy, without compromising what psychological science has discovered.

SCIENCE AND POSTMODERNISM.

In *The Crisis of European Sciences and Transcendental Phenomenology*, Husserl protested at the exclusion of lived reality from science.[2] He saw psychology as that science which more than any other had failed in its responsibility to address human experience. Distorted by positivism, psychology had adopted natural science as its model and with it a flawed image of how to gain knowledge of the mind. The authority of science was founded on the idea that its method was uniquely reliable and complete. Without denying the powers of this methodology, Husserl found it inappropriate for psychology, being over-committed to replicability and objectivity. This operationalism, by excluding of other ways of investigating the mind, had decapitated philosophy and science and left them unable to say anything of significance about the world of lived experience. By treating feeling and meaning as if they were outside nature, psychology had lost contact with its central phenomenon, the experience of selfhood. There had arisen a gulf between theory and the lived world. This was Husserl's *Crisis*.

But, some fifty years later, if there is a crisis in science, it is not one of confidence. In disclosing physical and biological levels of order far outside the scale of human senses, science has marginalised and downgraded commonsense realism. Furthermore, the global predominance of technocracy shows how reliable and effective scientific discoveries are. Science has become an authoritative and normative cultural practice. Prediction and control have replaced the impetus towards understanding and harmonisation that launched Western science in the sixteenth century. An analytic, reductive methodology has created a totalising world view and creation myth. This has meant that science now plays a similar cultural role to that previously played by religion, whether scientists wish it or not, and many do not.

The question then naturally arises: can science fulfil such a role? After all, science is a not a normative system of transcendental beliefs and faith but a epistemological system of material facts and reason. Science therefore may have had a role thrust upon it that it cannot play. As Theodore Rosak has put it: *Our science, like our technics, is maniacal because it bears the cultural burden of finding meaning where meaning cannot possibly be found. Nevertheless science continues to thrust fanatically into ever denser regions of being, hoping to strike through to some ultimate truth which will vindicate its quest ... the Secret of Life concocted in a test tube ... the Origin of the Universe ... the Mechanism of Intelligence. But all it finds are reductionist caricatures, nihilist know-how.*[3]

This dilemma is sharper for psychology that for other sciences because of its long struggle to be accepted as scientific discipline and to gain the authority and power that science commands. This struggle reflects the *realpolitik* of the academy rather than anything intrinsic to psychology. Thus psychology is more protective of its status and resistant to the consequences of the postmodern turn than are the more establisehed sciences.

Even so, as part of the cultural self-searching that tends to happen at the end of centuries, the postmodern critique is now clearly applied to psychology.[4] Around the turn of the previous century, roughly speaking as modernism entered its final phase, the image of human progress directed by science had become a central theme in the narrative of Western culture. Approaching the turn of the present century, there is a reappraisal of all such unified cultural narratives. Postmodernism has brought the nature and the authority of all cultural practices, including science, under sharp critical scrutiny. In science, the limitations of analytic reduction have become clear, and a move beyond them is well underway. Theoretically, this is not a retrogress to naive vitalism but a move towards an organic, participatory worldview. Methodologically the move is towards a new and more equitable balance between reduction and holism. Analytic methods are now being complemented by ones that aim to describe, though not necessarily to predict, how complex self-sustaining systems of order emerge from simpler or chaotic ones.[5] This rebalancing of theory and methods has implications that reach from science's metaphysical foundations to its cultural setting.[6]

At the metaphysical level, there is a shift towards Whitehead's organic world view. This challenges the Cartesian mechanism that has so restricted modernist science. Whitehead's metaphysics are based on organic mechanism. Nature is in continual creative advance. Its reduction, either to laws or to isolated material particles, is unrealistic. Locally and in the short term reduction is possible and has proved to be highly productive. Powerful techniques for intervening in nature have been discovered through isolation and analysis. More broadly and in the longer term however it is unproductive. Moreover, since methodology begets metaphysics, it leads to an impoverished world view where irreducible particles blindly follow laws of motion. The transformation of one configuration of particles into another is merely a matter of kinematics, which renders one configuration the same as another. This view of the universe as merely the 'endless hurrying of meaningless matter', as Whitehead put it, rests on the mistake of taking as objects what are in fact processes. This is the fallacy of misplaced concreteness.

The postmodern critique has revealed that science is not as isolated from cultural values as was thought and that an interplay between knowledge and value is as inherent in both the rhetoric and practice of science as it is in other areas of human discourse.[7] In psychology especially, it is becoming clear that there has been an uncritical imitation of the methods of the natural sciences, symptomatic of psychology's need to be identified with them. In many cases it is now very clear that this may simply be inappropriate for the scientific study of mental life, especially operationalism.[8] To adopt methods because they are academic status symbols rather than because they are what the subject properly requires is a sign that psychology has slipped from science into scientism.

So, the scientific world picture is changing. It has become clear that science is not a culturally isolated system with a uniquely privileged methodology. Rather, it is one among many epistemic practices that have been developed by different cultures at different times. It therefore complements but does not supersede other systems of knowledge and value. It is in this sense that the postmodern turn, promoting as it does a plurality of methods the blending of traditions, provides a framework within which to look at the interaction between Buddhism and Western psychology.

COGNITIVISM IS MODERNISM

Cognitivism is used here as a collective term for cognitive psychology, cognitive science, artificial intelligence and kindred approaches which take the rational content of mental life to be the foundation for a complete psychological science. Cognitivism employs a computational metaphor for mental life and treats the operations of the mind as a form of internal computation that represents the external world. Since computation may be formally described, cognitivism has been put forward as the basis for a unified psychological theory, much as evolution is for biology or as Newton's laws are, or were, for physics. It has even been suggested that this bring an end to the genealogy of metaphors for the mind that have been used through the ages. The computational metaphor, since it is not actually a metaphor but the thing itself, is the last we shall ever need.[9]

Cognitivism now dominates Western psychology, much as behaviourism did some five decades ago, and has generated a vigorous research program. The computational metaphor allows theories to be framed explicitly while the methods of natural science puts them to the test. Taken together, these practices have allowed psychology to be classified as an experimental science with all the benefits that this brings. However, cognitivism is a poor foundation for a complete psychological science. Taking mere rationality as the core of mental life is unrealistic when so much more is found in experience, especially affect and intuitive thought. The computational metaphor is equally unrealistic and illustrates Whitehead's fallacy. To treat mental life as arising from mechanistic operations that can be formalised and understood independently of the situation within which they occur is to mistake a part of the system for the whole.

Cognition is incorrigibly situated and embodied in a form of life. That is, it is intrinsically bound up with experience in situations and with the history of those situations. Embodiment, broadly speaking, is the idea that cognition cannot be realistically studied apart from the form of life to which it is attached. To look at mental life as if it could be separated from the situation and from the form of life which gives it meaning is a reductive mistake. It is misleading to follow such a formalised image of what psychological science can deliver. Searching exclusively for universal rule-like principles of mental life is unproductive. It reflects both Whitehead's fallacy and psychology's need to ape the natural sciences. Such principles may be found on occasion, but this cannot be extended to all levels of mental life.

What is required instead is an appreciation of how mental life is embodied and enacted, that is, how it participates in generative patterns of biological and cultural action. This participatory view points directly to the troublesome issue of experience. Troublesome, that is, for psychology in an era when science has lapsed into scientism. The treatment of experience, or rather, the exclusion of experience, was what Husserl depicted in the *Crisis* as a misdirection of Western psychology. Although Husserl's critique was directed at the behaviourist psychology of his day, it applies *mutatis* to cognitivism.[10] In the years since the *Crisis*, the murmur that Husserl detected at the heart of psychology has become clearer. Furthermore, during this period the devaluation of the human condition and massive environmental damage both stand revealed as major consequences of scientific technocracy. The disquiet over the exclusion of experience is part of the growing dissatisfaction with an unrestrained science that seems to contribute to human alienation rather than to ease it. Heidegger presents this as a consequence of decoupling science from from human values.[11]

Such values, and the restraints that come with them, were incorporated in the normative psychological science that Husserl sought. Nonetheless, his program for a scientific phenomenology has had little impact. Psychology's commitment to reduction has been as consistent during the era of cognitivism as it was during behaviourism. Honouring this commitment means that conscious experience itself, with its entailments of selfhood, meaning and value, remains outside science and outside nature, even though cognitivism does not exclude consciousness on principle as behaviourism did. Indeed consciousness, is now taken to be a proper object for scientific inquiry, even though the relationship between science and the experiential realm remains problematic.[12] However, the reductive program, and the gap at which Husserl protested, persist. Although cognitivism is prepared to consider consciousness this is not to be done by investigating experience directly. Rather, the aim is for conscious experience to be *explained away*, by the formal description of its vehicle, the domain of supposedly more fundamental cognitive mechanisms.

An analogy might be the relationship between the concept of temperature in physics and the experience of heat. Molecular motion, formaliseable as laws, is the 'real' nature, the primary explanation, of temperature. The experience of warmth or cold is secondary, entailed as a phenomenonological consequence of motion. Likewise, cognitivism seeks a formal theory of a supposedly primary 'reality' to which experience is attached in some way. Cognitivism thus shares, with behaviourism and with the modernist phase of natural science in general, the project of accounting for experience as a product of *something else*.

Thus, Husserl's crisis persists. Cognitivism downgrades experience in favour of what is supposed to be a more fundamental level of mental life. This proposal is widely, if implicitly, accepted. In much of psychology, the assumption is made that a primary objective must be to disclose and formalise the internal cognitive basis of human mental life and action. Experience *per se* is not easily brought into any sort of relationship with this dominant paradigm unless it is first inserted into a cognitivist envelop. The decapitation that Husserl foresaw has happened. Experience is marginalised by the very science which should most faithfully acknowledge it. The gulf between psychological theory and the lived world persists.

BUDDHISM AND COGNITIVISM

However, this gulf is being bridged following the theoretical and methodological impact of postmodernism. Cognitivism is now seen to neglect both biology and culture by taking mental life as something to be abstracted and formalised. Increasingly, cognition is treated as an aspect of the broader question of how individuals act and have experiences within given situations. This promotes contact with phenomenological traditions and indicates the emergence of a more inclusive psychological science which no longer treats experience and meaning as outside nature. The conditions now exist for bridging the gulf between psychological theory and lived experience and, consequently, for investigating selfhood on a more realistic, Whiteheadian basis. It is here that interaction with Buddhism has significance since at its heart lies a systematic inquiry into selfhood.

Now bringing Buddhism and psychology together might appear inappropriate. Psychology being a science and Buddhism being a religion, there may be no reason to expect there to be any more common ground between scientific psychology and Buddhism than between psychology and the Western religions. However, this is to miss some important differences between Eastern and Western religions. Buddhism arose in a cultural context where the opposition of science and religion did not exist. The Abrahamic religions of the West are based on belief and revelation while Buddhism is not. It is not a faith but a system of mental culture based on direct investigation of the lived world.[13]

In fact, interaction between Western thought and Buddhism is not new.[14] The influence of Buddhism can be found in Greek philosophy, Judaism and Christianity. It is especially significant to note its influence on Neoplatonism, given the role that this thread in Western thought played in the emergence of science. From Schopenhauer onwards, explicit use has been made of Buddhism by Western philosophers, most notably Heidegger. Contemporary writers on selfhood and experience have made informed use of Buddhist ideas.[15] Against this background, the proposition that cognitivism and Buddhism may interact to good effect seems far less problematic, although precautions must be observed concerning what may and may not be comparable.

It has long been recognised that Buddhist teachings and practices are fundamentally psychological.[16] They encourage the systematic and critical observation of selfhood.[17] For instance, a fundamental aspect of Buddhist practice is *sati*, a Pali term meaning the skill of paying attention to experience as it happens without involvement, distortion or evaluation. It is this aspect of Buddhism that has led to the attempts which are currently being made to bring it together with Western psychology.[18] As postmodern psychology moves away from cognitive reductionism and towards the treatment of embodied experience, so new bridges to Buddhism are emerging. Here selfhood, feeling and embodiment are central.[19]

Something very like embodiment is a fundamental principle in most forms of Buddhism. This is the doctrine of *paticca samuppáda*, an important element of the *Abhidhamma*, which is an early interpretation of the teachings of the Buddha. Translations of *paticca samuppáda* include: 'co-dependent arising', 'conditioned co-production' and 'causal genesis'. Perhaps the most frequently encountered is 'dependent origination', which will be used here. In this doctrine, the treatment of causation in dependent origination resembles recent developments in Western science which treat it in a cyclic or systems perspective.[20]

Dependent origination is often presented as a cycle of twelve statements about causality. Each links two terms as cause and effect. Successive statements take the effect term of the previous one as its causal term. Terms in the cycle of dependent origination differ in how easily they may be put in relationship to those of Western psychology. When it is relatively easy we typically find statements about moment to moment determination of the flow of consciousness. A pair of such statements are: *saláyatana paccayá phasso* (literally: 'sentience causes contact') and *phassa paccayá vedaná* (literally: 'contact causes feeling'). The first of these statements holds that if external sense objects are within sensory range of an attentive perceiver then states of sensory consciousness necessarily arise. In Western psychological terms, this corresponds to the early stages of sensory processing. The second statement holds that if states of sensory consciousness arise then emotional reactions will necessarily arise. In Western terms this is harder to place since both behaviourism and cognitivism have tended to marginalise emotion. However, critiques of cognitivism note the neglect of feeling and the relationship between affect and cognition has in recent years returned as a major focus of interest.[21]

This cycle of causation underpins the Buddhist symbol of the wheel. This cycle of cause and effect is the ground of consciousness and to it the condition of selfhood is bound. The purpose of inquiring into the way the cycle works is to appreciate more fully what selfhood is and thus to manage the condition more skilfully. This reveals the psychological significance of Buddhist practices and teachings. From the Western point of view it can be difficult to see past mystical and transcendental elements that are so striking when Buddhsim is first encountered. However, once this is done, many examples can be found that treat mental life as an object for systematic and critical inquiry.

Such examples show the overlap between Western psychology and Buddhism are more than mere suggestive resemblances. They demonstrate that what makes Buddhism appear so alien to the scientific enterprise is not of its essence. Its core is an inquiry based on an explicit psycho-physical theory and on systematic methods. However, Buddhism's approach to the human condition is not merely a disinterested inquiry into the nature of things. Both theory and methods are prescriptive and normative, in critical distinction to the ethos of science. It is a practice whose purpose is the liberation of human consciousness from ignorance and suffering. This can be seen by considering the three fundamental tenets of Buddhism captured in the Pali terms *Anicca, Dukkha* and *Anatta*. *Anicca* means that all is process: nothing is permanent; it is the nature of all things to arise and to pass away. *Dukkha* means that the human condition is essentially enigmatic and unsatisfactory. *Anatta* means that nothing self-identical or persistent is essential to selfhood.

From the earliest to the most recent and derivative traditions, this tripod of *anicca, dukkha, anatta* has provided stability for theory and practice. Of these three, *anatta* is perhaps the most direct bridge between Eastern and Western psychological traditions. *Anicca*, impermanence, requires analytic consideration of the external world. It has a somewhat intellectualised and metaphysical character and depends less on personal experience. As such, it directs attention outward, away from selfhood. By contrast, *dukkha* needs honest recollection and appraisal of each moment of experience. In that sense it is highly personalised and closely linked to individual feeling. It requires disciplined attention to be directed inward, toward selfhood. *Anatta* strikes a balance between these inward and outward directions. On the one hand it shares some of the depersonalised, metaphysical character of *anicca*, but on the other, it concerns the sense of unity and continuity that underpins our experience of selfhood. This concern, however, is disconcertingly deconstructive. *Anatta* holds that while this experience is compelling it is nevertheless a misleading and pernicious mistake. There is no self-identical, persistent essence underlying the human selfhood. Here, Buddhism apparently offers a more radical rejection of the folk psychology of selfhood than does cognitive reductionism.

SELFHOOD IS A PROCESS

Cognitivism reifies consciousness, and thus selfhood, as a formalisable property of the brain *qua* mechanism. It is this that imports into psychology something similar to Whitehead's fallacy of misplaced concreteness. Whitehead's critique, that science treats nature mechanistically rather than organically, when applied, *mutatis*, to psychology, resembles recent critiques of cognitive reductionism.[22] For Whitehead matter, at what ever level of complexity is always bound up in a process of organic action. The dynamics of that process cannot be understood merely by taking snapshots of its material vehicle. In much the same way, cognitivism assumes that somewhere in the workings of the brain there is a level of mental life which, once disclosed by experiments and formalised as a mechanism, will account completely for selfhood and experience.[23]

Postmodern science promotes a different view and a different style of inquiry. Here processes both inside and outside the brain are considered within the context that supports and generates them. The accounts of experience that people can give are considered data. This means that meaning and feeling need no longer be excluded. Selfhood now may be treated as a process which is enacted and which is embodied within a form of life, an organic system. Selfhood is a dynamic condition that arises from the effort after meaning that is the motor of mental life. This effort is charged with feeling and cannot be usefully considered apart from the biological, cultural context in which the effort is situated. Selfhood is, dialectically, both a precondition of making this effort and the product of it. It is a process occurring within a system of many levels of order: physical, biological, psychological and cultural. Indeed, the process selfhood integrates these different levels since it arises in the flow of meaning from one level of the system to another. David Bohm placed this exchange of meaning at the heart of the mind-body, relationship.[24]

Instead of concentrating on cognition, postmodern psychology will treat selfhood as an aspect of the system in which cognition participates. Selfhood cannot be completely identified with any particular level of the system, such as brain function or cognitive mechanisms.[25] Selfhood is neither a structure nor is it formalisable in any way. Rather, it is a process within a system comprising biological, psychological and cultural levels of order. Activity in all levels is co-ordinated by the exchange of meaning, or formal causation. No level in this system has explanatory priority. Selfhood clearly involves cognitive mechanisms, but these are only parts of the system. They are necessary, not sufficient preconditions of selfhood.

Selfhood is not formalisable in the sense that cognitivism assumes. As Whitehead proposed in more general terms, the nature of organic systems is intrinsically dynamic and may not be retrievable from static particulars. It is indeed a mistake if psychology models itself, however distantly, on sciences where such a reductive agenda is more appropriate. Mental life is essentially a process and cannot be held still in order that constituent parts may be extracted and isolated. Such structures as may appear once mental processes are constrained and analysed may bear little relation to the generative flow of experience in the lived world. Indeed, they may not even exist at all outside the experimental situations which bring them into being. However reproducible the results of such an enterprise may be, there is no guarantee that they correspond to anything of significance in the dynamic flow of mental life.

It is as if one were to try to understand a windmill by looking at the gears alone and to ignore how the whole system is animated by the wind. Cognitive mechanisms are not causal in and of themselves. They are animated by the flow of organic action in which experience and feeling also participate. This flow is not an epiphenomenal or *post hoc* trace of cognitive mechanics. The principal guide for the flow of experience is feeling, not the cognitive mechanisms of perception, memory or thought. These, of course, are intimately bound up in the total flow, but if causal primacy has to be assigned, it is the other way round. That is, much as Buddhism proposes, the dynamics of experience are essentially affective. This affective primacy is another aspect of the effort after meaning that lies at the heart of selfhood.

In the human case, this effort is made with a world of culturally created meaning. Cognitive reductionism leads attention away from the cultural context. As Jerome Bruner points out, the Cognitive Revolution of the 1950s: ... *was intended to bring "mind" back into the human sciences ... But ... that revolution has been diverted into issues that are marginal to the impulse that brought it into being. Indeed, it has been technicalised in a manner that undermines that original impulse.* (Bruner, 1990, page 1). By contrast, when psychology: ... *concerns itself centrally with meaning, ... it must venture beyond the conventional aims of positivist science with its ideals of reductionism, causal explanation and prediction. To reduce meaning or culture to a material base ... is to trivialise both in the service of misplaced concreteness.* (Bruner, 1990, page xiii)

Bruner's partial quotation of Whitehead here is surely no accident. He is pointing to the mistake of thinking that selfhood depends, essentially, on one particular aspect or level of a complex dynamic process. What he advocates in psychology is very much in line with what Whitehead proposed for natural science more generally.

Reductive inquiry into the vehicle for a process will not neccessarily reveal anything significant about the process itself.[26] For this reason, if psychology persists with cognitive reduction, the limitations that Husserl foresaw will persist.

Husserl's project was for a systematic, empirical inquiry into the world of lived experience. For human beings, this is the world of culturally created meaning. The language, the signs, the practices and the very material structures by which we are surrounded are cultural creations. Thus, experience within this environment is likewise a cultural creation. Bruner offers this cultural creation of meaning as the proper objective of a psychology liberated from cognitive reductionism.

As common experience shows, the most central and problematic meaning with which human beings have to deal is what it means to be an individual, to be conscious and to have a sense of identity. Here there is common ground both with Buddhism and with postmodernism. Major postmodern writers have concerned themselves with the cultural production of selfhood. In doing so they continue the phenomenological thread in Western thinking and in some cases, Heidegger is one, make significant use of Buddhist thought.

EMBODIMENT AND SELFHOOD

Postmodernism is a critical deconstruction of claims to completeness or to finality in the arts, sciences or humanities. This therefore applies to psychological theories of the self. Lacan, for example, criticises Freud for being too literal in his emphasis on the biological preconditions of selfhood. Lacan moved beyond Freud's concern with desires and needs towards social interaction from which self consciousness dialectically arises, that is, without being prefigured in any essential way in the physical conditions of the body.[27] The condition of selfhood is a symbolic one, the internalisation of an image prefigured in the cultural conventions of parent – child interactions. Hence, the construction of individuality occurs within social discourse and is founded symbolic interactions. Thus deconstruction concentrates on discourse because selfhood is taken to be a cultural production involving language and other systems of signs. Human selfhood arises within a cultural context that is dialectically produced and produced by human action. Indeed, a recognition of this strange loop or closure has contributed to the postmodern condition of culture.[28]

Derrida and Baudrillard to an even more radical extent, explore this process of culturally mediated self-production. Baudrillard points to the inevitable ambiguity and groundlessness of the play of cultural signification while Derrida emphasises the contradiction and denial that are intrinsic to discourse.[29] This leads them to the rejection of selfhood as an object of inquiry. We are left with a problematic condition of being and the enigma, as Heidegger has it, of why is there something rather than nothing.

Encountering this deconstructive project can be disconcerting. Is there really no self apart from what is constituted in discourse? Are all forms of discourse in inevitably beset by hidden denials and contradictions? Is there no authentic author's voice in the books we read? Are creativity and personal responsibility merely the products of bourgeois false consciousness? Those coming from traditions of empiricism and critical realism may feel uneasy here. Surely there is something more tangible on which our sense of selfhood and individuality can be grounded?

Some critics of the nihilistic tendencies of deconstruction have pointed to embodiment in this sense. Selves are bodies too and the human condition is embedded in social practices that depend on the body itself. Development, especially early development, occurs in an environment in which those practices help in creating and defining individuality.[30] Embodiment may thus appear to provide some welcome solid ground on which to stand firm against the deconstructive flood. Since embodiment is also central to the Buddhist view of selfhood, we may perhaps expect to find in Buddhism some refuge there too.

But any sense of relief has to be temporary at best. In Buddhism the grounding of selfhood in embodiment is merely the precondition for an even more fundamental attack on it. Although selfhood might be identified with its material support, the reverse in fact is the case. The teachings of *anatta* and *anicca* are as radical a deconstruction of individual existence and its material surroundings as anything that has originated from Parisian Neo-Marxism. They go beyond cultural discourse and question the very ground of embodied existence: matter, biological and psychological structure, action and experience. At heart of Buddhism is the effort to understand this ground, its origins and how, in a process of cyclic causation, it supports consciousness. This effort ultimately demonstrates the emptiness of all levels of the ground, including, paradoxically, Buddhism itself; a deconstructive program indeed.

So, embodiment is far from a material reification of selfhood, and although Buddhism may help psychology to recover from cognitive reductionism, it will not save it from deconstruction. It leads on to a properly open inquiry rather than shifting a restricted theoretical focus from one level to another. To recognise that cognition is embodied is to recognise that it is attached to a form of life, a process. The body is the vehicle for the process. Neither body nor process can be considered separately, since they mutually constitute each other. The process is the current of organic action that flows through the body, the body is the medium through which this flow passes. Experience is the flow itself. Nowhere is to be found any material, formal or abiding essence by which the condition of selfhood may be explained.

ON FACTS AND VALUES

What has been advocated in this chapter is a view of selfhood that brings together scientific and phenomenological traditions. This would not only raise theoretical and methodological issues but also ethical ones. The modernist image of science was of an ethically neutral investigation of material reality. Science was to be an empirical inquiry in which 'right' and 'wrong' would be used in their logical rather than their moral senses. While ethical considerations become attached to scientific findings, they are not intrinsic its practice. From its inception, science had an ethical purpose, the betterment of the human condition, but its methodology was held to be strictly neutral. Facts and values, it seems, do not mix.

But this view has been profoundly weakened as part of the postmodern turn in science. The claim of methodological neutrality is part of the rhetoric of scientism. The authority given to science assumes that it functions as some sort of 'honest broker' in political and social issues. But science has never functioned like this. From its political and social origins, science's metaphysical foundations have been intimately bound up with cultural assumptions and values.

This is not to reject science but to recognise that it has to be approached hermeneutically. Science is one of many ways of inquiring into reality that have been developed in different cultures at different times. All of these have their different powers and fields of application. Clearly, science and technology have yielded more effective techniques for short term manipulation of the natural world than any phase of culture hitherto. But it is becoming equally clear that in the longer term these techniques are not sustainable. Science needs constraints that reflect human values unless it is to degenerate further into mere deep technology. Without these constraints it is destructive, as shown in the loss of biological and cultural diversity that has resulted for the globalisation of technocracy.

It is in this context that the rebalancing of psychology envisaged here may be both liberating and timely. Dominated by cognitive reductionism, psychology is poorly equipped to deal with the concerns that lead many students who choose it. Often this choice arises from a feeling that to repair the damage caused by technocratic culture requires that we study psychology rather than natural science, technology or political economy. It is an appropriately postmodern irony that what they find is a discipline that technologises the human condition.

To study mental life as if it were merely a property of some mechanism is to perpetuate Husserl's *crisis*. It is time to move beyond cognitivism's reductive image of mental life. To take embodiment and experience as the focus of a broader and more inclusive psychological inquiry is to create a science that has intrinsically to do with human feelings and values. Moreover, to investigate selfhood along these lines will bring with it more directly personal consequences than those that follow from practising psychology as it presently stands. This, again, is strongly in line with the postmodern insight that science is shaped by the personalities of those who practice it, rather than being some neutral, impersonal system.

This is to loose nothing of what scientific psychology has achieved. Postmodernism is neither shallow relativism nor mere deconstructive rejection. It is the means to create a more inclusive worldview. As Bohm has proposed: ... *postmodern science should not separate matter and consciousness, and should not, therefore, separate facts, meaning and value.*[31] Thus, postmodern psychology is postcognitive. It involves the psychologist more personally than hitherto. It offers an integrative framework that no longer treats meaning, value or experience as outside nature. Within this more open and inclusive practice sought by Whitehead and Husserl, insights into the human condition from science and from Buddhism can together help to repair the damaging separation of fact and value.

NOTES

1 Whitehead, A. (1926) *Science and the Modern World.* Cambridge University Press.
2 Husserl, E. (1970) *The Crisis of European Sciences and Transcendental*

Phenomenology, translated by Carr, D., Northwestern University Press, Evanstown, Illinois.

3 Roszak, T. (1990) *Where the Wasteland Ends: Politics and Transcendence in Postindustrial Society.* California: Celestial Arts. Page 43.

4 Kvale, S. (1992) (Ed.) *Psychology and Postmodernism.* Sage, London.
Clarke, C. (1996) *Reality Through the Looking Glass: Science and Awareness in the Postmodern World* . Floris Books, Edinburgh. Ch. 5.

5 Maturana, H. & Varela, F. (1987) *The Tree of Knowledge.* Shambala, Boston.
Eigen, M. (1992) *Steps Towards Life: a Perspective on Evolution.* Trans. Wooley, P.. Oxford University Press, London.

6 Jencks, C. (1992) (Ed.) *The Postmodern Reader.* Academy Editions, London.
Griffin, D. R. (1988) Introduction: The Reenchantment of Science. In *The Reenchantment of Science: Postmodern Proposals,* edited by Griffin, D.R., State University of Ney York Press, Albany, NY.

7 Gergen, K. (1992) Towards a Postmodern Psychology. In *Psychology and Postmodernism,* edited by Kvale, S.. Sage Publications, London.
Billig, M. (1987) *Arguing and Thinking: A Rhetorical Approach to Social Psychology,* Cambridge University Press, Cambridge.

8 Green, C. (1992) Of Immortal Mythological Beasts: Operationalism in Psychology. *Theory & Psychology,* Vol. 2, No. 3, pages 291–320.

9 Johnson-Laird, P. (1988) A Computational Analysis of Consciousness. In *Consciousness in Contemporary Science,* edited by Marcel, A. & Bisiach, E., Oxford University Press, Oxford.
Newell, A. (1991) *Unified Theories of Cognition.* Harvard University Press.
Thagard, P. (1996) *Mind: Introduction to Cognitive Science.* MIT Press, London.

10 Dreyfus, H. & Dreyfus, S. (1988) Making a Mind versus Modeling the Brain: Artificial Intelligence Back at a Branchpoint. In *The Artificial Intelligence Debate,* edited by Graubard, S., MIT Press, Cambridge.

11 Heidegger, M. (1977) *The Question Concerning Technology and Other Essays,* translated by Lovitt, W. Harper Row, New York.
Bookchin, M. (1988) Towards a Philosophy of Nature: the Bases for an Ecological Ethics. In *Deep Ecology,* edited by Tobias, M.. Avant Books, San Marcos, California.

12 Marcel. A. (1988) Phenomenal Experience and Functionalism. In *Consciousness in Contemporary Science,* edited by Marcel, A. & Bisiach, E., Oxford University Press, Oxford.

13 Johansson, R. (1979) *The Dynamic Psychology of Early Buddhism.* Curzon Press, London.

14 Batchelor, S. (1994) *The Awakening of the West: the Encounter of Buddhism and Western Culture.* Thorsons Press, London.
Clarke, J. (1997) *Oriental Enlightenment: The Encounter Between Asian and Western Thought.* Routledge, London.

15 Parfitt, D. (1987) Divided Minds and the Nature of Persons. In *Mindwaves,* edited by Blakemore, C. and Greenfield, S.. Blackwells, Oxford.

16 Thouless, R. (1992) Foreword to *Buddhist and Freudian Psychology,* de

Silva, P. Third edition, Singapore University Press, Singapore. The preface was originally written in 1972.

17 De Silva, P. (1979) *An Introduction to Buddhist Psychology.* MacMillan, London.

18 Goleman, D. & Thurman, R. (1991) *Mind Science: An East West Dialogue.* Wisdom Publications, Boston.

Guenther, H. (1989) *From Reductionism to Creativity.* Shambala, Boston.

19 Hayward, J. & Varela, F. (Ed.s) (1992) *Gentle Bridges.* Shambala, Boston.

20 Wallace, B. (1989) *Choosing Reality.* Shambala, Boston.

Rosch, E. (1994) Is Causality Circular? Event Structure in Folk Psychology, Cognitive Science and Buddhist Logic. *Journal of Consciousness Studies,* Vol. 1, No. 1, pages 50–65.

21 Damasio, A. (1995) *Descartes' Error: Emotion, Reason and the Human Brain.* Macmillan, London.

Donaldson, M. (1992) *Human Minds.* Penguin, London.

Langer, S. (1988) *Mind: an Essay on Human Feeling.* Johns Hopkins University Press, Baltimore.

Lazarus, R. (1984) On the Primacy of Cognition. *American Psychologist,* 39: 124–129.

Zajonc, R. (1984) On the Primacy of Affect, *American Psychologist,* 39: 117–123.

22 Valsiner, J. (1991) The Construction of the Mental. *Theory & Psychology,* 1991, 1(4): 477–494.

Bruner, J. (1990) *Acts of Meaning.* Harvard University Press, London.

Edelman, G. (1992) *Bright Air, Brilliant Fire.* Basic Books, New York.

23 Churchland, P. M. (1995) *The Engine Of Reason, The Seat Of The Soul, A Philosophical Journey Into The Brain.* MIT Press, London.

24 Bohm, D. (1987) *Unfolding Meaning.* Ark Paperbacks, Routledge, London.

Bohm, D. & Hiley, B. (1993) *The Undivided Universe.* Routledge, London. Page 389.

25 Sperry, R. (1994) Consciousness and the Cognitive Revolution: A True Worldview Paradigm Shift. *Anthropology of Consciousness,* vol. 5, no. 3, pages 3–7.

26 Goodwin, B. (1989) Organisms and Minds as Dynamic Forms, *Leonardo,* 22(1): 27–31.

27 Lacan, J. (1977) *Ecrits: a Selection.* Trans. Sheridan, A. Tavistock Publications, London.

28 Kingdon, J. (1993) *Self-Made Man and His Undoing.* London, Simon & Schuster.

29 Derrida, J. (1977) *Of Grammatology.* Trans. Spivak, G. C., Johns Hopkins University Press, Baltimore.

Baudrillard, J. (1988) *The Ecstasy of Communication.* Semiotext(e), New York, p 107.

Baudrillard, J. (1993) *Symbolic Exchange and Death.* Trans. M. Gane, Sage, London, p 254.

30 Burkitt, I. (1994) The Shifting Concept of the Self. *History of the Human Sciences,* Vol. 7, No. 2, pages 7–28.

31 Bohm, D. (1988) Postmodern Science and a Postmodern World. In *The Reenchantment of Science: Postmodern Proposals*, edited by Griffin, D.R., State University of New York Press, Albany, NY. This article is reprinted in Jencks, C. (1992) (Ed.) *The Postmodern Reader.* Academy Editions, London, where the quotation appears on page 385.

Chapter 8

EDITOR'S PREFACE

Historians and cultural commentators are inclined to give dramatic names to periods or conditions of society. These often use a state of mind or some aspect of human experience to catch the nature of the time. So, the Age of Reason, the Enlightenment, the Age of Anxiety... and so on. Here Brian Lancaster opens his chapter with what is now an all too familiar picture of our times as something like the Age of Uncertainty or of Confusion. The rate at which we are loosing the basis for cultural stability, a complaint made throughout the ages, seems to have jumped to an all time high.

His chapter suggests one way that psychology may respond to this condition. This is to try to bring our scientific knowledge traditions for knowing the mind *qua* object into informed correspondence with older wisdom traditions for knowing the mind *qua* subject. In keeping with the major theme of this book, he discusses how cognitive science might interact with Buddhist views of the mind and experience. However, in his conclusion, he broadens the discussion in a particularly useful way and critically notes some of the limitations there will inevitably be on such a project.

His initial focus though is the important Buddhist teaching of anatta. This is the claim that our conventional sense of self is a misguiding illusion. This doctrine, which critically distinguished early Buddhism from the Vedic traditions out of which it developed, holds that not only is there nothing soul-like, that is unique, self-identical and eternal, that animates the human condition, but also that to believe that there is leads to suffering.

Cognitive science, although not having to do with human suffering, is likewise committed to exorcising soul-like notions such as the homunculus, the computer metaphor being one way of doing this. If computers can act as if they have a sense of their own existence, then the functional architecture inside them amounts to a theory of how the human sense of selfhood may arise. Brian Lancaster assumes that people would shudder at the notion that a computer might develop a sense of self. For some cognitive scientists it is merely a research objective, albeit an ambitious one.

The mythology of anatta: bridging the East-West divide

The model of human awareness found in early Buddhism, the Abhidhamma especially, is surprisingly modern, having something like the character of contemporary information processing models.[1] Here Brian Lancaster brings the two together, focussing on the difficult notion of *javana*, by which is meant the combination of separate percepts into a unified flow of experience. To translate this as apperception is quite appropriate. This term, and it's derivatives, has been used by a number of Western thinkers, including Kant and Johannes Muller to cover a stage of processing that they felt was both very important and very difficult to understand. Brian's 'I-tag' model provides a framework within which this central concept can be considered from both Western and Eastern perspectives. The model is a conceptual catalyst: it provides a framework within which other ideas may be brought together, compared and, when appropriate, combined.

The comparison is rich indeed. Even from the brief account given here, suggestive correspondences and differences emerge. For example, on the one hand, the account of recognition given in the Abhidhamma gives a primary role to affective reactions, something seldom considered in western theories. On the other hand, both the Abhidhamma and cognitive science recognise that to bring perceptual and memory processes together into a coherent flow of experience requires some form of self-representation as a framework.

However, these similarities need to be interpreted realistically. Like Jung, Brian warns that concepts from other cultures will be distorted, re-mythologised is his term, during incorporation with Western ideas. This does not mean that the attempt to do so is mistaken even though there may be intrinsic limitations on intercultural recombination. Vaclav Havel points out that it is a characteristic of the postmodern cultural condition that ideas previously separated in space and time appear in new and lively combinations from which new meaning may emerge.[2]

The postmodern critique of totalising cultural narratives like scientific reduction or Marxism rejects claims to absolutism and essentialism. Accordingly, Brian's warning about the ways in which anatta may be taken up in the west are indeed timely. Consciously or not, many cognitive scientists take up the task of explaining away consciousness with a quasi religious zeal, presenting it as 'really' some sort of phenomenological mistake or as an acausal epiphenomen that bobs in the wake of autonomous cognitive mechanisms. Brian Lancaster points out that the re-mythologisation of anatta could

171

easily lead to it being misappropriated to this programme. Buddhism too, believes that to essentialise self consciousness as something soul-like is indeed a phenomenological mistake.

The way to guard against this misappropriation of anatta is to understand as best we may how and why the doctrine was originally taught, how it has developed and how observations made in the course of this development may be brought together with scientific data. This is an appropriately pluralistic task for postmodern psychology. Nor need we limit ourselves to importations of Easterm ideas, as Brian Lancster's concluding remarks about the richness of Western wisdom traditions show. This chapter shows how comparisons can be made between Western and Eastern psychological concepts so long as we take proper precautions. It points directly to the often overlooked question of what scientific psychology is *for* and to the fact that theories of the mind cannot be value free. In bringing together the resources of Western knowledge traditions with the insights of wisdom traditions, we help create a psychological discipline that addresses not only what the mind is, but what it may become, for the better.

NOTES

1 Johansson, R. (1979) *The Dynamic Psychology of Early Buddhism.* Curzon Press, London. Guenther, H. (1976) *Philosophy and Psychology in the Abhidhamma*, London: Routledge.

2 Havel, V. (1995) Self Transcendence. In *Resurgence*, No. 169, March, pages 12–14. (ISSN: 0034–5970). This is the text of an address given on receiving the Liberty Medal in Philadelphia on July 4th. 1994.

★ ★ ★

The mythology of anatta: bridging the East-West divide

Brian L. Lancaster

Freud reports three wounds to the narcissistic pride of human beings: Copernicus' discovery that our planet is not at the center of the universe; Darwin's that we are merely the latest step in an evolutionary chain, one rung above our primate ancestors; and Freud's discovery that we are subject to unconscious processes and therefore not even masters in our own house. There remains perhaps a final, radical step to be taken in this historical process of deconstruction: the human subject – the one to whom actions and experiences, whether conscious or unconscious, are attributed – does not exist![1]

The 'crisis of the self' which Barglow captures in the above words assails us from all sides. The relative permanence in roles and structures which previous ages have seemingly enjoyed has all but evaporated in our post-industrial day. 'Society' – and it is not even clear to what this word refers today – can no longer offer a bedrock within which an individual's sense of purpose is grounded; the workplace is subject to frequent and strategic changes in organisational structure, as if the very possibility of enduring order might threaten productivity; 'families' are frequently short-term or even 'experimental'; and the notion of 'the individual' seems to slip from our grasp into some kind of relativistic soup whenever questions of authority or responsibility are raised. Given such an external context, it is no wonder that uncertainty characterises discussion of the psychological self. Does the human subject indeed not exist, or is this view itself merely an intellectual distraction from the fundamental experience of self?

In this chapter, I focus on the value of the Buddhist concept of *anatta*, no-self, for the development of theories in cognitive

173

Brian L. Lancaster

neuroscience. As the foregoing suggests, however, there is clearly a broader context to such an investigation. Firstly, cognitive neuroscientists are products of their age and consequently the kinds of issues addressed, as well as the interpretative perspectives applied, will inevitably be reflective of the images of mind operative in the wider society. Secondly, introducing concepts from one culture into another raises questions of 'cultural compatibility'. As will be discussed, it is naïve to suggest that a concept such as *anatta*, embedded as it is within a broad soteriological context, can simply be aligned with a body of neuroscientific data for the purpose of explanation. These considerations lead me to address the deeper issue of what kind of image of mind is likely to be cultivated in western society in the immediate future. And this question is asked not only in relation to the cognitive neuroscientific quest to understand mental processes, but also in terms of the kinds of personal and collective responsibility that are thereby fostered. Indeed, the notion that 'theoretical' concerns of science may be separated from applied and ethical considerations is one which is itself at odds with the broadly 'ecological' image of mind for which I shall argue.

ABSENCE OF SELF IN BUDDHISM AND PSYCHOLOGY

The doctrine of *anatta* can simply be understood as Buddhism's central premise of impermanence applied to the person. Thus, Rahula explains *anatta* as asserting that:

> What we call 'I', or 'being', is only a combination of physical and mental aggregates, which are working together interdependently in a flux of momentary change within the law of cause and effect, and that there is nothing permanent, everlasting, unchanging and eternal in the whole of existence[2].

A classical statement of *anatta* is given in the canonical *Milinda Panha* where the monk, Nagasena conveys the point to King Melinda by reference to his own name, described as, 'this designation, this conceptual term, a current appellation and a mere name.' Nagasena continues by remarking that, 'In ultimate reality, however, the person cannot be apprehended'[3]. Similarly, in the *Visuddhimagga*, Buddhagosa writes:

> For there is ill but none to feel it;
> For there is action but no doer;
> And there is peace, but no-one to enjoy it;
> A way there is, but no-one goes it[4].

174

The mythology of anatta: bridging the East-West divide

The essence of the *anatta* doctrine is conveyed in classical texts by insisting that the appropriate response to any images arising in the mind should be, 'This does not belong to me, this I am not, this is not my self'. Realization of *anatta*, as a necessary condition of enlightenment, entails recognising both the constructed nature of 'I' and the conceit normally attaching to it.

The general assumption of cognitive psychology holds the brain/mind to function as an information-processing system. As has frequently been remarked, the workings of the mind have always been understood by reference to systems of the day, and for cognitive psychology that system is pre-eminently the computer. Not only does the language of computer function provide a powerful language with which cognitive psychology is able to describe mental functions, but it is also frequently the case that advances in our thinking about brain/mind function are generated by working with computer models. In other words, the metaphor has become proactive. To the extent that the computer plays a determining role in cognitive theorising, there is little or no place for a self in the cognitive endeavour, certainly not an enduring self. Whilst we may happily talk of input and output functions, memory and intelligence in relation to computers, we would probably shudder at the notion of the computer's self![5] Barglow comments, 'as a model of detached, ownerless cognitive processing, the machine symbolizes an *absent* subject'[6].

Cognitive theoretical models typically encapsulate the functions under examination in flow charts of one form or another, themselves owing much to information theory as developed in relation to machines. Reference to self or 'I' in such charts is rare indeed, for this would seem to entail a *homunculus*, 'the familiar theoretical bogey of psychological theory (*bad* psychological theory)'[7]. Positing some kind of inner subject – a homunculus – seems to entail an inevitable infinite regress, and therefore cannot advance the goal of explaining psychological function. Even when invoking *will* as a factor in the control of action – an apparently strongly subjective term – the cognitive approach is scrupulous in its avoidance of any reference to a subject[8]. In a nutshell, 'The cognitivist challenge does not consist simply in asserting that we cannot find the self; it consists, rather, in the further implication that the self is not even needed for cognition'[9].

The parallels between Buddhism and cognitive psychology in their rejection of any notion of an enduring self are striking[10][11][12]. Moreover, the major topic of contemporary interest to neuropsychologists – so-called dissociations of consciousness – may perhaps be best under-

175

stood from the perspective of *anatta*, as I consider shortly. These dissociations are observed in a range of cases in which brain damage results in the loss of some cognitive ability at the conscious, or *explicit*, level, whilst the ability is preserved – at least, partially – at the nonconscious, or *implicit*, level. Cases of this kind include amnesia, blindsight, prosopagnosia, unilateral neglect and alexia[13] . This phenomenon of implicit processing in the absence of explicit awareness is not restricted to such neurological cases; the same pattern may be discerned with appropriate testing of normal subjects.

The seemingly straightforward interpretation of these observations is to suggest that consciousness is essentially an 'extra ingredient' of some kind normally 'added' to the results of information processing. In one version of such a model, Schacter[14] proposes that a 'Conscious Awareness System' (CAS) interacts with modules that are dedicated to specific cognitive domains. One such module may, for example, process information relating to faces. In a normal case, the output from this module is available to the CAS with the result that the individual consciously recognises faces drawn from their prior experience. Schacter postulates that implicit processing in the absence of explicit can occur if the output from the domain specific module is cut off from the CAS. Thus, in prosopagnosia, for example, the output from the face processing module fails to reach the CAS. Accordingly, patients will have no consciousness of the meaning of any faces presented to them. Nevertheless, this output may still be able to effect some appropriate response at an implicit level, as studies of implicit processing in prosopagnosia have indicated.

In a second version of this general type of model, Moscovitch[15] has suggested that the consciousness which accompanies perception and thought becomes incorporated in the subsequent memory; it becomes 'an intrinsic property of the memory trace'[16]. When the memory is subsequently re-activated, consciousness is recovered along with other elements of the memory trace. This consciousness underlies the critical sense of familiarity felt at the time of recognition or recall. Whilst Moscovitch's approach is distinctive in stressing the centrality of consciousness to this kind of memory experience, his theory shares with Schacter's the idea of domain specific modules operating pre-consciously.

As Schacter himself notes, 'to postulate that conscious awareness depends on a specific mechanism in no way explains how consciousness is achieved or exactly what it is'[17]. Similarly, in the case of Moscovitch's theory, it remains somewhat obscure how consciousness could become incorporated in the memory trace. In effect these theories skate around what seems to be the central question for understanding the relation between implicit and explicit events, namely, what are the factors involved when consciousness arises in relation to some mental event? Ideally one would like to know how and why consciousness arises, and what role it plays.

In framing these questions in this way, I am anticipating the value of Buddhist thought in this context. Buddhism eschews the notion of some form of enduring consciousness in favour of a view of its arising in the moment. For the Buddha, consciousness arises as a conditioned consequence of specific determining factors. 'Consciousness is defined according to the condition through which it arises ... if through mind and mental objects, [it is called] mind-consciousness'[18].

A detailed analysis of the conditions through which consciousness arises is found in the Theravadan Abhidhamma tradition, and I have argued that its approach may be especially valuable in addressing the whole issue of the relation between implicit and explicit processing[19]. It is increasingly being recognised that our endeavours to understand consciousness may require a more integrative scientific approach[20]. In the present context, I hold that the fruits of disciplined introspection, as presented in the Abhidhamma literature, may usefully be studied together with those stemming from controlled cognitive and neuropsychological experiments. This seems to me the great value of the general opening up of western thought to eastern influences in our day. It is not specifically the adoption of a given Buddhist concept, such as *anatta*, which is significant. The historical significance lies, rather, in the shift in outlook which comes about with the recognition that a trained mind attains a degree of objectivity in introspection.

The Theravadan Abhidhamma applies the central Buddhist conception of momentariness to mental processes. It states that the 'sense door process' (i.e. perception) comes about through a series of moments, in each of which a consciousness arises, performs some particular function, and decays, having generally conditioned the next arising of consciousness in the sequence. These moments are grouped into a number of stages, as indicated in the lower part of figure 1. In brief, the essence of my argument is that the nature and sequence of these stages can provide a degree of illumination in thinking about perception in cognitive neuroscientific terms. My own analysis of these two strands of data, namely the stages of perception as conceived by the Abhidhamma and the experimental observations in cognitive neuroscience, has led me to advance a model of perception

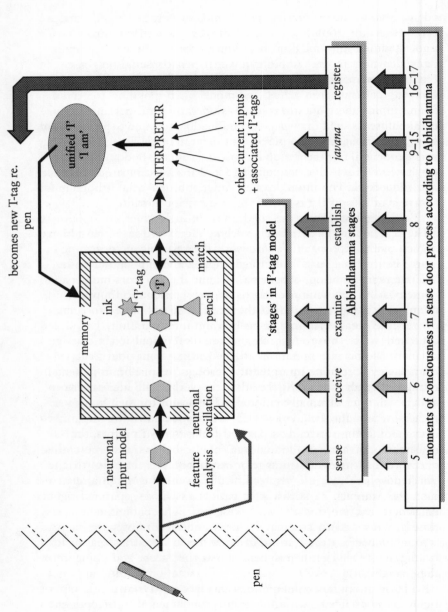

Figure 1 'I'-tag model of perception and memory illustrating correspondences with perceptual stages described in Abbhidhamma

and memory – the *'I'-tag model* – which is depicted in the upper portion of figure 1. A key point to stress here is that the proposed stages of the 'I'-tag model do not directly mirror the corresponding stages depicted in the Abhidhamma. It is not simply a case of describing one realm of thinking in terms provided by another. For example, the 'stages' in the 'I'-tag model corresponding to Abhidhamma moments 5 to 8 are viewed as operating through interactive neural pathways such that it may be misleading to think of an ordered sequence (although for the purpose of diagrammatic represenation a static, sequential representation is shown). From the Buddhist point of vew, however, each is a genuine stage and the process is quintessentially sequential. The model comes about through what I hope is a creative synthesis of the two strands of data; it is a fruitful marriage, not a one-sided take-over.

The heart of the 'I'-tag model concerns the nature of 'I' and how it interacts with memory. In accord with the teaching of *anatta*, it is recognised that there is no enduring 'I'; the model envisages 'I' to be a cognitive representation, or schema, generated anew from moment to moment[21]. But of what exactly is it a representation? Whilst it undoubtedly encompasses the body image, it seems more fundamentally to incorporate elements of agency and interpretation. This 'I' is postulated to be a product of the mind's compulsion to assign explanations and interpretations to elements of behaviour[22]. Gazzaniga[23] has explored this interpretative process in split-brain patients. A range of studies demonstrates that the verbal left hemisphere of patients will offer seemingly rational explanations for their behaviour in cases where the behaviour was actually initiated by the right hemisphere. Being surgically separated from its right partner, the left hemisphere can have no 'knowledge' of the behaviour's true cause (which will have been some image or instruction presented only to the right hemisphere), yet it finds no difficulty in offering a confabulated cause. An example is the case of a patient to whose separated right hemisphere the word *walk* was presented. The patient had been primed to respond to command words and, accordingly, he began walking away from the testing area. On being asked his reason for walking, he (i.e. his left hemisphere) answered that he was going into the house to get a 'coke'.

Evidence of similar confabulations may be drawn from any number of clinical cases. That such a function is fundamental to the way the mind operates is confirmed by everyday examples and studies on normal subjects. Nisbett and Ross[24], for example, report on several studies in which individuals give explanations for their behaviour at odds with what the experimenter knows to be the case. In one of the studies, shoppers selected a preferred pair of stockings from a choice of four identical pairs. Their choice evidently reflected a position effect, the rightmost pair proving most popular. When questioned about their choices, however, subjects strongly denied the position effect, explanations being offered instead in terms of the stockings' (non-existent) different characteristics – colour, sheerness etc. These confabulated explanations of behavioural choices were given with a clear strength of conviction. It seems that, under conditions in which the *real* explanation for some behavioural or mental event is for some reason unavailable, a drive to construct a *purported* explanation is irresistible. Gazzaniga accounts for these observations by positing a specialised module of the left hemisphere, the *interpreter*, which is dedicated to this function of generating explanations and interpretations:

> The interpreter considers all the outputs of the [brain's other] functional modules as soon as they are made and immediately constructs a hypothesis as to why particular actions occurred. In fact the interpreter need not be privy to why a particular module responded. None the less, it will take the behaviour at face value and fit the event into the large ongoing mental schema (belief system) that it has already constructed[25].

My argument is that a central feature of this 'ongoing mental schema' is 'I'. As Gazzaniga notes, '[patients] view their responses as behaviours emanating from their own volitional selves'[26]. The schematic 'I' is at the centre of the 'hypothesis as to why particular actions occurred,' for it is itself a hypothesis, one that brings a kind of final common path of unification into mental processing. It is the hypothesis of a unified subject of perceptions, thinker of thoughts, and instigator of actions. When Nisbett's subjects explained their choices in terms of the stockings' characteristics they were reinforcing their images of themselves as being in control; their behaviour is given a (fictional) controlling focus. Similarly, when the patient described by Gazzaniga explains his walking away from the test area, he construes the situation as 'I' am thirsty and 'I' am going to get a 'coke'. The illusion of choice necessarily implicates 'I' as locus of control. I refer to this schema in the focus of the interpreter's output as the *unified 'I'*. This is not to imply that it represents a unitary subject – a homunculus – as some kind of control centre in the brain or mind. The unified 'I' is a post-hoc construction which merely gives the illusion of unitary control. The term 'unified' is intended to capture the subjective sense here, for the individual generally feels him/herself to be one and continuous.

In figure 1 this process whereby the 'interpreter' generates the *unified* 'I' is shown in juxtaposition to the Abhidhamma stage of *javana*. I have left this Pali term untranslated, for the direct translation, 'running', hardly conveys its meaning in context.[27] The term is used to indicate the more active nature of this stage by comparison with earlier stages. A commentator on the Abhidhamma texts, Shwe Zan Aung, writes of *javana*, 'At this stage ... the subject interprets the sensory impression, and fully appreciates the objective significance of his experience'[28]. Collins[29] considers this stage as giving rise to 'full cognition' and notes that 'the conceit of "I am"' becomes a key factor here since the stage is *kammically* significant.

We approach here the nub of my discussion in the next section. In relating the role of the 'interpreter' to the *javana* stage, I am mindful of the soteriological assumptions of the Buddhist material. Typically, cognitive neuroscience simply attempts to describe the brain/mind *as it is*. Abhidhamma, by contrast, is interested in the mind *as it could be*. In the context of perceptual experience, unless the individual has purified their responses during the earlier stages of the process, the result in the *javana* phase will be in the form of habitual desire or aversion to the sensory object; the strings of attachment will be perpetuated. For Buddhism, of course, the goal is to overcome such attachment. I have argued that the observational strategies of cognitive neuroscience and Buddhism are complementary. The question to be addressed in the next section is, given that their goals are so disparate, are their data compatible?

First, however, some further comments relating to the 'I'-tag model are in order. I will briefly review the other stages of the perceptual process as illustrated in figure 1,[30] and continue with an examination of the implications of the model for an understanding of memory and self.

The Abhidhamma literature views moments five to eight[31] as comprising an all-or-none phase of the perceptual process. A stimulus which is 'sensed' will automatically reach the stage of 'establish'. 'Sense' consciousness implies no conceptual analysis of the properties of the stimulus, merely an impression that some entity is 'in contact' with the sense organ. 'Receiving' gives rise to a simple feeling tone in relation to the object; and 'examining' involves the mental function of

Brian L. Lancaster

recognition and labelling. 'Establishing' determines the object's properties and sets the direction in which the *javana* moments will 'run'. Finally, 'registering' may be seen as conveying the object as perceived – which means the *javana* reaction – into memory.[32]

The 'I'-tag model proposes that the first phase of this scheme comes about in neurophysiological terms via a set of processes whereby the neuronal responses to the sensory input are effectively equilibrated with memory read-out. Present evidence suggests that this equilibration – or sensory-memory *matching* process – may be signalled by means of coherence in neuronal oscillating patterns[33].

We may presume that all currently active representations generate memory traces. It follows therefore that the unified 'I' as well as the representation of the present sensory object produce memory traces. This is equivalent to the view of the Abhidhamma that the output of the *javana* stage becomes 'registered' in memory. Since any given object familiar in experience will repeatedly be accompanied by a representation of 'I', the associative bond between the memory of the object and that of 'I' will be particularly strong. This is the conceptual basis of the term *'I'-tag*. As illustrated in relation to the stage of 'examine' in figure 1, when any familiar memory trace becomes activated, this 'I'-tag will invariably be the most prominent associated trace. The 'I'-tag is presumed to underlie the phenomenal sense of possessing, or being personally engaged with, the memory. As Warnock notes, 'To count as a memory a cognitive experience, or thought, must contain the conviction that I myself was the person involved in the remembered scene'[34].

It can readily be seen how this model might account for the distinction between implicit and explicit processing. In the case of amnesia, for example, we may presume that some disturbance has interfered with the system whereby the unified 'I' becomes associated with the memory of a perceived object. There is effectively a disruption in the consolidation of 'I'. The consequence would be that any future activations of the memory will not be associated with a sense of phenomenal personal engagement with the memory, which I see as a defining hallmark of implicit memory.[35] A historical antecedent to this approach may be found in the work of Claparède[36] who noted in connection with Korsakoff patients that, 'everything happens as though the various events of life, however well associated with *each other* in the mind, were incapable of integration with the *self* itself'[37]. In a manner analogous to my hypothesis of the role of 'I'-tags, he suggested that perceived objects possess 'the characteristic coloring of this consciousness of self'[38]. However, his theory seems predicated on a view of self as stable and continuous, a view which the present approach questions.

The 'I'-tag model is advanced not only as a potential 'fit' for the neuroscientific observations, but also as an approach to the processes underlying our sense of self. It gives a framework for conceptualising the way in which 'I' arises from moment to moment. In itself, this does not seem to contradict Buddhist teaching for 'the Buddha is not denying each and every conception of "I" ... but only the metaphysical presupposition behind the statement "Such and such an aggregate belongs to such and such a self"'[39]. According to the present model, the unified 'I' enjoys no ontological status, it merely arises in relation to the need to give context to present experience. Moreover, as noted above, it may represent a false context, and therefore the idea of 'dethroning' it – as the Buddha teaches – may be seen as developmentally adaptive.

The organisation of 'I'-tags within the memory system, however, may lead us to think in terms of more traditional western notions of 'self'. It would be highly improbable that individual memories are 'stored' each with their own distinct 'I'-tag. Although each memory is associated with the 'I' constructed at the time of experience, there are presumably major continuities between successive constructions of 'I'. We may think of the 'I'-tag for a given memory as a sub-set of what Baars refers to as the 'self-system'. As Baars suggests, the self-system provides the context for experience: 'self is not in the first instance an object of knowledge; it is contextual'[40]. The 'I'-tag for the pen depicted in figure 1, for example, is not conceived to be a distinct and unique entity (as, due to the restrictions of displaying a frozen moment, the figure may imply). Rather, it would be an activated constellation within the backdrop of all 'I'-related memory structures. It is an element of the overall context given by that backdrop. Moreover, its function should be understood in these terms: the 'I'-tag enables a context of personal reference to be built up in memory, which means that memories can be reflected upon without necessarily inducing direct action.

This final point is analogous to Moscovitch's view of the role of consciousness in relation to memory: 'Consciousness may be necessary to allow us to have memories without acting on them and to retrieve them without the need of an external stimulus cue. In this way, we can think about and manipulate memories until we are ready to act'[41]. It will be clear from the foregoing discussion that I would wish to substitute the term 'I' for 'consciousness'. Indeed, such a substitution indicates precisely the distinction between Moscovitch's approach and my own.

In certain respects, however, my approach has much in common with that of Moscovitch. Where he considers the brain structures engaged in the consciousness of an experience as becoming bound into the memory trace, I envisage the unified 'I' being similarly bound into the trace as an 'I'-tag. For Moscovitch, amnesia results from the consciousness component being unavailable; in the 'I'-tag model amnesia is attributable to unavailability of the 'I'-tag. The difference, then, seems merely to be one of emphasis, my model placing emphasis on 'self' as compared to Moscovitch's emphasis on consciousness. On further analysis, however, the difference becomes more significant. The 'I'-tag model is not only directed to understanding memory function; its analysis of the origin and function of 'I' is intended to be seen in the context of spiritual traditions also[42]. All religious traditions seem to concur in insisting that progress on the spiritual path depends in some measure on changing one's view of the self. In this, then, the model shares a further, more general, feature with the Buddhist approach: it attempts to set psychological understanding in the context of the will to transcendence.

Questions regarding the nature of self certainly represent a point of contact between cognitive neuroscience and spiritual traditions. As discussed earlier, the fruits of disciplined introspection can and should be integrated with the data available through the methods of cognitive neuroscience. But what of the 'will to transcendence'? To dismiss it as an irrelevance to the cognitive perspective may actually distort the very questions cognitivism wishes to address, for I would argue that such a 'will' is not separate from processes generally interrelating self and memory. Challenges directed to expanding the repertoire of schemata to which 'I'-tags relate may be seen operating at all stages of the life-cycle. They motivate childhood play and adult explorations of their world, just as they engage the putative mystic in spiritual techniques such as meditation and ritual.

Within Buddhism, the challenge becomes that of detachment from the normally automatic sense of 'I am' which arises, as envisaged above, through the operation of the 'interpreter'. Detaching from the unified 'I', as encouraged by Buddhist practice, does not mean that 'I' disappears. If that were the case then, according to the 'I'-tag model, conscious operation of memory would be compromised (as in amnesiacs). Detachment means rather that the seemingly automatic explanation of experience in terms of self reference ('I am walking to get a 'coke' because I am thirsty') becomes attenuated. By not identifying with the immediate self-reinforcing interpretation of events, a broader framework of causation and context is opened up. The tagging system envisaged here will thereby become enriched. 'I' as a controlling element in the interfacing of sensory and thought events with memory will be maintained; but it will become a less restrictive interface, for the matrix from which it is constructed will have been enlarged.

SEARCHING FOR SELF IN PSYCHOLOGY AND BUDDHISM

The model described in the previous section has illustrated the value of bringing into some kind of rapport insights from the Abhidhamma tradition and those from cognitive neuroscience. In particular, it is the emphasis in both traditions on the microprocesses of the mind, those processes which are normally concealed from our view, which enables meaningful dialogue. Cognitive neuroscience has, over recent years, become increasingly engaged in specifying the nature and role of brain/mind processes on which the subject cannot (at least verbally) reflect. Abhidhamma is largely directed to specifying processes which a mind lacking the discipline attained through prolonged meditative practice, is unlikely to detect. As I have already implied, I believe the yoking of the two approaches can provide an especially powerful means for advancing the quest to understand the mind.

This point that the common ground for Buddhism and cognitive neuroscience is found in their respective interest in the microprocesses of the mind, masks what may be considered an underlying tension, however. For their interests are different: cognitive neuroscience lays no claims to a soteriological emphasis. Moreover, the phrase, 'those processes which are normally concealed from our view,' is itself problematic. In what sense are these processes 'concealed', and whose view is it anyway? In addressing these questions, which concern the relationship between conscious and nonconscious events and the nature of self, I wish to suggest that a simple juxtaposing of Buddhism and psychology brings some fundamental issues in its wake, which have not generally been adequately addressed.

It has frequently been noted that different authors introduce differing shades of meaning to the term, consciousness, even within a singular cultural tradition. How much more so when attempting to bridge cultures. At the outset, it is important to note a striking difference between the Abhidhamma view of perception and that of cognitive neuroscience in this regard. For Abhidhamma, each moment is a moment of consciousness, whereas cognitive neuroscience generally views only the endstage as conscious. I do not think that this is simply a question of terminology. Rather, it reflects the deeper consideration of what exactly is the purpose in specifying the stages of perception. Abhidhamma encourages its disciples to cultivate a state of equanimity in relation to the early stages of mind processes. Its interest is in the re-alignment of what we would call pre-conscious processes. By focusing on the endstage, however, and calling only that conscious, western psychology implies that there is no possibility of intercession in the unfolding of the perceptual process. In fact, this conception lies at the heart of the tradition of dualism embedded in western thought as it has been shaped through Christian theology. Moral action has been viewed as operating primarily outside the realm of embodied processes, and the path to freedom largely entailed the denial of such embodiment. It is instructive in this context to compare the central myth of Buddhism, in which 'the goal is to become embodied out of compassion for the world'[43], with that of Christianity which is essentially one of *disembodiment* out of compassion for the world. Although it is held that God 'became flesh', salvation becomes dependent on the disembodied Christ. For the disciple of the Abhidhamma, it is necessary to penetrate the intricacy of the mind. And this fundamentally entails working *with the body* in meditative practice. Ultimately, the objective is to bring about fundamental change in the operation of one's mind, and this may only be achieved by altering the early perceptual stages, before the momentum of the process is too great, as it were.

I indicated in the previous section that *javana* thought moments are considered to be *kammically* active, i.e. they may be moral or immoral and will give rise to future consequences accordingly. The forms of consciousness arising in the stages prior to *javana* are either the result of previous *kamma* or have the status of *kiriya*, meaning that they do not partake of the *kammic* process The term, *kiriya*, 'is intended to designate the spiritual sensitivity of a man of developed wisdom, who responds to every situation with appropriate activity without partiality of any kind'[44]. Within the sense door process, moment four ('adverting' to the sense door stimulated) and the stage of 'establishing' represent windows of opportunity for moral development since these are both occurrences of the *kiriya* mind. At the moment of 'establishing', for example:

there appears to be a choice or free will. If the object is determined wrongly on the false data as being permanent, of the nature of a self, with attachment or ill-will, then the ... [*javana*] thoughts will be immoral. If the object is determined correctly as being impermanent, without self, with notions of renunciation, love and kindness, then the thoughts that follow will be moral[45].

It cannot be stressed too strongly how dominant a concern this interest in the moral dimension is for Abhidhamma. The question arises, is it possible simply to jettison the moral issues and draw directly upon the depiction of perceptual stages, as I have done in the previous section of this chapter? I believe the answer to this question is 'yes', but not an unqualified 'yes'. In particular, the concept of *anatta* is critical in this regard. Is the absence of self portrayed in Buddhism *of the same kind* as that seemingly advanced by many cognitive scientists? And, more importantly, what moral implications may follow from the attempt to 'import' such a Buddhist concept into a psychology so clearly founded on western tradition?

Before pursuing these questions further, I would like to emphasise that this point about soteriology, or moral development (using the term in its broadest sense), may itself be significant in the impact of Buddhist ideas on western psychology. In the quest for objectivity, cognitive neuroscience evinces a value-free vision of the mind. There is of course no such thing. All models of the mind which take root bear implications for the society as a whole, and purvey a moral import. The Freudian model is a compelling example. Freud's image of the mind has probably had more impact on society – through, for example, attitudes to sexuality, to mythology, to religion, to criticism – than it has on any one individual undergoing analysis. 'The importance of Freudian psychology derives far less from its scientific validity than from the effects it has had on our shared image of man himself'[46].

In the cognitive sphere, the very absence of value terms in information processing models projects a cold image of what a person is, which reinforces such an image in society. In the emerging climate of re-assessing values in science, why should the kind of emphasis on moral value seen in the Abhidhamma not become integral to cognitivism, or whatever cognitivism evolves into?

The general point here could be made in relation to any number of traditional ways of knowledge. The quest for knowledge before the rise of post-renaissance science was intrinsically bound to the goal of perfecting oneself and/or the world of nature around one. In his 1981 Gifford lectures, Nasr chronicles the loss of such sacred science:

> The unifying vision which related knowledge to love and faith, religion to science, and theology to all the departments of intellectual concern is finally completely lost, leaving a world of compartmentalisation where there is no wholeness because holiness has ceased to be of central concern, or is at best reduced to sentimentality[47].

To the extent that issues of wholeness are being rediscovered in contemporary science, dialogue with such sacred traditions may be expected to grow. Is it possible that cognitive neuroscience will enjoy its own such dialogue? Of all the traditional ways of knowledge, Buddhism is probably the only one which addresses the microprocesses of mind in such a way as to be able to share a viable language with cognitive neuroscience. Earlier I made the point that Buddhism is valuable to psychology since it can help re-establish a discipline of introspection. Here is a second aspect of its possible value, to introduce an extended sense of moral purpose into the work of cognitive neuroscience. At present the discipline's value is seen largely in applications such as improved rehabilitation for patients with disease or brain damage of one form or another, and in areas of artificial intelligence. Perhaps dialogue will encourage a greater recognition of the discipline's value for ways of developing oneself in the spiritual sense that Buddhism conveys. As Goleman[48] notes, Buddhism can serve to remind psychology that the systematic study of the mind and its workings lies at the heart of the spiritual life. Varela *et al.* go further by suggesting that the dialogue between Buddhism and cognitive science can play a key part in the challenge 'to build and dwell in a planetary world'[49].

But is the dialogue as benign as it may seem? This question becomes acute in relation to the concept of *anatta*. There is perhaps a danger of 'importing' a view of no-self which, wrenched out of the context in which it was developed, simply reinforces a certain vacuousness and nihilism in contemporary society. A parallel may be drawn with an earlier phase of 'dialogue' when it was argued that metaphysics was absent from Buddhism. Rosenberg explains that such was the view of European authors on account of the worldview within which they operated: 'It must not be forgotten that the beginning of Buddhist research in Europe coincided with the collapse of metaphysical philosophy and the rise of materialistic systems'[50].

Our current interest in Buddhist research, I would add, coincides with the collapse of modernism and the rise of postmodernism with its emphasis on deconstruction of self. 'Some moderns imagine that their deconstruction of the self captures the Buddha's intention, reducing each supposedly substantial thing to a disconnected sequence of moments ...'[51]. But, as Clark argues, it may be that a wrong view of the Buddhist concept of *anatta* is being appropriated in these contexts. In general, it is not only the seed of an idea drawn from another culture that counts; the ground in which it lands will play a critical part in determining how the seed grows. As I will discuss further in the final section, ideas from a divergent culture tend to become *re-mythologised* as they become integrated in a recipient culture.

The concept of *anatta* is not simply a statement of the absence of self, as its translation alone might suggest. It is more a conceptual focus for developing a distinctive view of impermanence as this pertains to the mind. The Buddha came to the conclusion that the spiritual teachings of his day failed to inculcate a correct perspective on the nature of reality. In particular, the Brahmanical view of self as a metaphysical ultimate reality uniting the individual and the external world could become a barrier to true liberation, as he saw it. The *eternalism* inherent in this view of self inhibited the individual from seeing the essentially conditioned nature of mind as process.

When considering the value of *anatta* for western traditions in our day, insufficient attention is placed on this contextual background. The Buddha taught *anatta* as a means towards a given end, dependent on a given prevailing view. If, in our contemporary western context these givens are significantly at odds with those the Buddha had in mind, then caution in importing a Buddhist concept may need to be exercised. Varela *et al.*, for example, assert the value of *anatta* as an alternative to what they see as the prevailing view in social science, namely the view of self as 'an economic man':

> The self is seen as a territory with boundaries. The goal of the self is to bring inside the boundaries all of the good things while paying out as few goods as possible and conversely to remove to the outside of the boundaries all of the bad things while letting in as little bad as possible. Since goods are scarce, each autonomous self is in competition with other selves to get them.[52]

This 'economic' view of self is far removed from the metaphysical backdrop against which the concept of *anatta* emerged. Varela *et al.*

are effectively asserting that *anatta* is an insight which transcends its contextual milieu, which may be to stretch its value too far.

Furthermore, caution should be exercised in relation to the 'imported' view of *anatta*, since within the Buddhist tradition itself *anatta* may not imply such absence of self as is often assumed. The question really is, what view of 'self' is addressed? Pérez-Remón concludes his in-depth analysis of the concept of *anatta* in early Buddhism by asserting that, 'nowhere is the reality of the self absolutely and explicitly denied'[53]. The Buddha was directing his teaching to redress misplaced notions of what the self might be identified with. The teaching 'does not say simply that the self has no reality at all, but that certain things, with which the unlearned man identifies himself, are not the self and that is why one should grow disgusted with them, become detached from them and be liberated'[54].

According to Ramanan, Nagarjuna – one of the key philosophers in the transmission of early Buddhism – held that at root the individual is one and undivided, having an unconditioned nature. Our ignorance lies in not recognising this ultimate sense of becomingness as self. The teaching of *anatta* is directed specifically at the more fragmented, conditioned 'I':

> The sense of "I" in its true form is the sense of the real immanent in man; the true import, the ultimate, original meaning of "I" is self-being, unconditionedness. But the mind, the self-conscious intellect, under the influence of ignorance, comes to apply wrongly this sense of unconditionedness to itself in its mundane, i.e., conditioned nature, as well as to that with which it identifies itself and through that to all things that it lights upon[55].

Quoting from Nagarjuna's Maha-Prajnaparamita-Sastra,[56] Ramanan informs us in this context that the Buddha sometimes taught of self and sometimes of no-self:

> To him who understands the meaning in the teaching of the Buddha and grasps the truth of derived name [i.e. conditioned personality], He has taught that there is "I"; but to one who does not understand the meaning in the teachings of the Buddha and does not grasp the truth of the derived name, He has taught, there is no "I"[57] .

Conze quotes a text from the *Personalist Controversy* in Hinayana Buddhism, concluding with the view that:

It is only when, as is the habit of non-Buddhists, something which is not the true Self is mistaken for the true Self, that one will feel affection for that pretended self. If, however, one sees, as the Buddhas do, the Ineffable Person as the true self, then, because that actually is the true self, no affection for it is thereby engendered[58].

Nagarjuna informs us that there are two kinds of *anatta* teaching. The correct one (i.e., representing the Middle Way) in which things are seen for what they are, resulting in the denial of 'I' with equanimity. The other involves 'seizing of the determination of "no I," clinging to the denial of "I"'[59]. It seems to me that, to the extent that any precedent might be cited for much contemporary thinking about the deconstruction of self, it would be the latter view, erroneous from the Buddhist perspective, which is purveyed.

At the outset I quoted Barglow's statement of the post-modern assertion that the human subject does not exist. Such a view arises in the context of the preoccupation with surface appearances and lack of rootedness evident in much contemporary culture. 'The immediacy of events ... becomes the stuff of which consciousness is forged', writes Harvey[60]. Yet, in an understandable paradox, people are searching intensively for something to fill the rootlessness. We search out the family tree; we grasp at what may be the most tenuous links to some indigenous culture; and we enshrine the past in museums or theme parks. An appropriate model of mind for our day must clarify the individual's connection to the wider whole, both in terms of personal and collective roots, and in relation to transpersonal responsibilities. In terms of the 'I'-tag model described above, I wish to propose that focusing our notion of self not on the ephemeral and illusory nature of the unified 'I', but rather on the deeper organisation of the 'I'-tag system in memory, will help meet these contemporary needs.

THE RE-MYTHOLOGISATION OF ANATTA

I have argued that contemporary incorporation into western systems of thought of the Buddhist concept of *anatta* may be compromised by inadequate understanding of the meaning and purpose of the term within the context in which it was developed. The fact is, however, that history testifies to the way in which cultural interchange is no respecter of such an emphasis on original meaning and context. When a culture imports some concept or system of images endemic within a second culture with which it has come into contact, then we may observe forces of *re-mythologisation* at work. The concept becomes integrated into the recipient culture not as a 'new' addition but as an elaboration of existing systems, or as a vehicle for re-balancing features within its own tradition. It hardly needs emphasising that in the process, all kinds of square corners are found to fit into round holes. The recipient culture may become enriched, but not generally at the expense of abandoning long-cherished beliefs.[61]

Do we have any reason to suppose that things are essentially different as far as our culture's encounter with eastern systems of thought is concerned? I think not. We see evidence of this both in the way that eastern teachers often adapt their teachings for the western market and also in the selective treatment of eastern ideas by western authors. My concern here is not with what form of Buddhism may become further established within western settings, but specifically with the likely re-mythologisation of *anatta* in the image of mind we carry forward from our current seemingly transitional period.

I believe that the critical issue in regard to this concern is not specifically the *intellectual* idea of *anatta*, but the *moral dimension* attendant upon it. One feature of this is soteriological and has already been discussed. A second (and related) feature concerns personal responsibility. The idea of *anatta*, as Pérez-Remón notes, 'raises many questions such as the reality of the moral agent and the existence and nature of moral responsibility, the continuity of individuality ... in the rebirth-cycle, the nature of *kamma* and the way it works ...'[62]. The Buddhist teachings of *dependent arising* and *kamma* seem to me to be essential components of the framework within which *anatta* can have any social legitimacy, for without them the absence of self does seem to imply absence of responsibility. 'In any society it is clearly of importance that a man should consider himself as *one* person. Otherwise he could not be held responsible today for what he did yesterday'[63]. Parfit[64] argues that the individual is indeed not one person over time in the normal sense of the word, a position supported by reference to *anatta* teachings and psychological experimentation. He considers various moral consequences of this lack of continuity in personal identity. Thus, for example, he argues that a criminal's 'punishment' should reflect the strength of connections between his or her identity now and that at the time of the crime. Binns[65], however, questions Parfit's view of the person, suggesting that by adhering only to a (cognitive) psychological perspective he ignores biological, historical, social, spiritual and ecological dimensions, all of which need to be included to capture the essence of identity.

It seems clear that whilst the idea of *anatta* suits our current concerns with the deconstruction of self, the attendant teaching of *kamma* in relation to *dependent arising* does not. Indeed, even for those willing to embrace a spiritual path, a notable trend in western Buddhist teaching concerns the de-emphasising of the concept of re-birth. *Kamma* becomes limited to this life only. Where *anatta* is imported to bolster a more intellectual concern with changing views of personhood, the moral ballast of *kamma* as a factor in the conditional arising of incarnations of mind has little or no place.

I suggest that the re-mythologisation of *anatta* will entail a balancing of the superficiality of the personal 'I' with a deeper recognition of the ecological validity of selfhood, and the responsi-bilities attaching to it. In terms of the model discussed above, the unified 'I' is an inadequate vehicle for defining the person for, as we have seen, it represents merely a post hoc interpretation of mental and physical events. The organisation of 'I'-tags in memory, however, constitutes the matrix from which the interpretation arises. By shifting the balance in our conception of personhood from the unified 'I' to the matrix from which it is constructed, we overcome moral problems of discontinuity in self. All incarnations of 'I' are rooted in the totality of autobiographical memories.

Although the topic of autobiographical memory has recently received renewed attention within cognitive psychology, I am inclined to think that the cognitive perspective is inadequate in this context. Cognitive science has been unable to generate models which adequately relate to individuals' experiences of the profound roots of their sense of self. In proposing a shift in our conception of personhood I am especially aware of what I conceive to be the real meaning of *anatta*. As discussed above in relation to the philosophy of Nagarjuna, the parallel in the Buddhist scheme to this proposed shift in balance is that from the conditioned and fragmented 'I' to the unconditioned fount of being; a shift from an individualist perspective to a spiritual ecological one.

Cognitive neuroscience has been successful in pursuit of limited goals such as the specification of modular systems contributing to perception and memory, but when it comes to the analysis of implicit processing, self and consciousness, a more all-embracing psychology is needed. As Harman remarks in relation to scientific epistemology, 'The scientist who would explore the topic of consciousness ... must be *willing to risk being transformed* in the process of exploration'[66]. The development of *Discursive Psychology*[67] attempts to address this need. By recognising the primacy of symbolic interaction and the broad context within which the individual operates, Harré and others adopting this approach attempt to break down the restrictive boundaries which have surrounded psychology (and cognitive psychology in particular) over recent decades. Just as Harré & Gillet argue that the discursive process underlies our sense of selfhood, we may expect current east-west discourse to play a role in the kind of shift in the collective view of selfhood envisaged here.

It is often asserted that eastern views of self can help disengage us, in particular as psychologists, from a view which is increasingly seen as inappropriate for our day. The re-mythologisation of *anatta* needs to be considered in this context, for the avowed inappropriateness of this western conception of selfhood epitomises the need for change. This western conception is summarised by Ho:

> What emerges is an individualistic self that is intensely aware of itself, its uniqueness, sense of direction, purpose, and volition. It is a center of awareness at the core of the individual's psychological universe. The self is at center stage, and the world is perceived by and through it. Self and nonself are sharply demarcated. The self is an entity distinct from other selves and all other entities. The self "belongs" to the individual and to no other person: the individual feels that he/she has complete and sole ownership of his/her self. ... Rooted firmly in individualism, the Western self is, in short, the measure of all things[68].

Just as the 'eastern view' covers a range of traditions, so too does the western. In particular, the above characterisation is at odds with the picture painted by western spiritual traditions. The Talmud, for example, encourages the individual who would advance on the spiritual path to 'make himself as a desert', an apt metaphor for the kind of 'psychological decentering' which Ho sees eastern traditions as encouraging. Such ideas become more elaborated in the mystical traditions of all three major western religions, where a wide variety of techniques for annulling the personal ego (detaching from the unified 'I') may be found. Simplistic comparisons between the view of self passed on within a spiritual élite in eastern countries and the secular view held by the mass in the west, yields self-evident differences. In asking questions about the future of *anatta* in western thought, its relationship to western *spiritual* views is of primary interest. Indeed, perhaps the re-mythologisation of *anatta* (which is, of course, only one of many key eastern concepts in this regard) will take the form of a re-evaluation of pre-Cartesian western views of self.

An important dimension in western spiritual views – often overlooked – is one which today would be classed as 'ecological'. The Neoplatonic maxim, 'Man the measure of all things', did not imply an externalised, controlling relation to nature. Rather it meant that the entirety of nature is inherent within: man is the microcosm. Hints of this dimension may be found throughout the Bible and rabbinic commentaries, for example. In midrashic elaboration of the story[69] of Adam's creation, we find a view that God 'concentrated the whole world in him'. Similarly, following the famous poem in the book of Ecclesiastes indicating that all things have their time, we read 'He made the whole beautiful in its time and placed the world in their heart without which man could not find the work which God has made from beginning to end'[70].

Views similar to these are strongly represented in gnosticism, and found their way into most branches of western esoteric thought. In particular, the conception of Adam as a cosmic being interconnecting all[71] becomes a defining feature of later Jewish mysticism. And this totality is not removed from the individual person; it is very much the heritage of humankind and the means for realising our oneness with all things. For Cordovero, a major figure in the sixteenth century mystical movement in Judaism, 'man comprises in his composition all the creatures, from the first point until the very end of [the four worlds of *kabbalistic* thought]'[72]. Prayer and meditation became acts directed to promoting the harmony of this collective realm. And, of course all humans are essentially interconnected on account of their rapport with the entirety of Creation. Similarly, in arguing for a return to a Plotinian conception of self, Clark reminds us 'that the Self in me is just the same as that in you; that only the One Self attends on parallel and successive states of mind and action, separating itself out as One in Many'[73].

It is in relation to these 'ecological' views that I believe *anatta* (amongst a variety of other eastern concepts) is taking its place. 'As Buddhism's *anatta* or no-self doctrine (read: no permanent, individual self) reminds us, no hard and fast line between self and world can be drawn'[74]. When we adopt the viewpoint of *deep ecology*, as Naess[75] argues, the issue is not one of defining the self but of understanding the process of identification. We may choose to identify with an expanded 'field-like' or *ecological* self which shares many features with the mystical views I have touched on. By asserting the conditioned nature of the process whereby we identify with the everyday limited 'I', the *anatta* teaching legitimates the possibility of re-identifying at the more global level, and in the process effectively resurrects the heart of western esotericism. This western re-mythologisation of *anatta* strips it of any traces of absolutism whilst meeting the need to 'spiritualise' our responses to the ecological challenge of our day.

This is not to imply that such 'ecological' views are not intrinsic to branches of Buddhism. 'The self-existence of a Buddha is the self-existence of this very cosmos,' writes Nagarjuna[76]. In the *Yogacara* tradition, the cosmos was identified as nothing but representation, i.e. mind, and the continuity between cause and effect was attributed to a kind of cosmic *store consciousness*. Perhaps the clearest parallel to the ecological viewpoint is found in Zen: mind is 'mountains, rivers, earth, the sun, the moon and the stars,' writes the Zen master Dogen.

Returning to the 'I'-tag model, the pivotal idea here is identification. That notion of self with which the individual identifies at the time of some experience becomes the 'I'-tag relating to the experience as it is laid down in memory. The more open the individual's view of their self at the time of the experience, the less limiting will be the 'I'-tag. If the 'mountains, rivers, earth, the sun, the moon and the stars' are within one's sense of self when reaching for the pen depicted in figure 1, then they too may become engaged within the 'I'-tag system connected with the pen. And, following Velmans' reflexive model of consciousness[77], these representations are projected back onto the 'world out there'. Moreover, as Bohm[78] suggests, at root, memories themselves (which is what 'I'-tags are) may enfold into an order of reality in which any boundary between the physical and the mental disappears. Jung similarly held that the psyche and physical reality are complementary manifestations of the deeper medium of the *archetypes*: psyche 'touches matter at some point,' and matter bears 'a latent psyche'[79]. Indeed, in arguing for the integration of depth psychology with ecology, Hillman makes the point that, 'the most radical deconstruction of subjectivity, called "displacing the subject", today would be re-placing the subject back into the world, or re-placing the subject altogether with the world'[80].

In taking these steps towards an ecological perspective on the 'I'-tag model, a shift in scale is evidently called for. When the sense of self with which the individual identifies embraces 'a wide, expansive, or field-like conception of self'[81], the range of interconnections available to the memory tagging system becomes correspondingly broader. Ultimately, to borrow an aphorism beloved of Jewish mystics, the 'I' (Hebrew ani) transforms to nothingness (Hebrew ain). And, in that transformation, the 'I' of the mystic encounters the 'I' of the divine:

> Beside the formulae "He is He", and "I am He and He is I" we get the formula "I - I". . . We may then ask the intention of the author who has chosen to use the formula "I - I" in lieu of "I am He", since in both cases, the basic meaning is the mystical union. In other words, who is the real speaker, God, as in the Biblical sources, or the mystic, who may pronounce this formula as the assertion of his identity with God (perceived as the I-ness)?[82].

In kabbalistic thought, God is seen as fragmented in His emanations, and the cosmic role of humanity becomes one of promoting His unification. Describing the worldview of the Zohar – the major kabbalistic text, Tishby comments that, 'man becomes an active participant in the renewal of the unity of the divine forces'[83]. As Jung points out, the self is the God-image in man, and the fragmentation in this kabbalistic scheme may accordingly be thought of as inherent in the self. But, as the concept of man as microcosm implies, the fragmentation is also manifest in the world. The goal of the mystic is accordingly to heal the Godhead, the world and their self, each of these levels being an inseparable aspect of the others.

Here, I believe, is a valuable myth to power a spiritual ecology for our day. *Anatta* and attendant teachings, together with the data from cognitive neuroscience with which they seem to relate, lend 'scientific' credence to the primary tenet – that the everyday 'I' is an inadequate vehicle for engaging in the cosmic role granted to humanity in the myth. But it is the essentially western contemporary concern with our responsibilities to the world, and the inclusion of the divine as fellow actor in the drama, which ensure continuity with western spiritual roots.

NOTES

1 Barglow, R. (1994), *The Crisis of the Self in the Age of Information: Computers, Dolphins and Dreams*. London: Routledge. p. 82.
2 Rahula, W. (1967), *What the Buddha Taught*. London and Bedford: Gordon Fraser. p.66.
3 Conze, E. (1959), *Buddhist Scriptures*. Harmondsworth, Middlesex, UK: Penguin Books. p.149.

4 Cited in Pérez-Remón, J. (1980), *Self and Non-Self in Early Buddhism.* The Hague, Paris, New York: Mouton. p. 11.

5 In information terms, machines can and do monitor their parts and functions. Such 'self'-monitoring does not implicate a sense of self as generally understood. In particular, the psychological self implies not only autonomy and control, but also the potential for creative growth. The science fiction image of the autonomous android asserting power is compelling, of course, precisely because it evokes the idea of a machine with 'self'.

6 Barglow, *op. cit.*, p. 89, emphasis original.

7 Allport, A. (1988), What concept of consciousness? In *Consciousness in Contemporary Science,* eds. A. J. Marcel & E. Bisiach. Oxford: Clarendon Press. p. 160, Emphasis original.

8 Norman, D. A. & Shallice, T. (1986), Attention to action: willed and automatic control of behaviour, in *Consciousness and Self-Regulation: Advance in Research and Theory, Vol. 4,* eds. R.J. Davidson, G.E. Schartz & D. Shapiro. New York: Plenum Press.

9 Varela, F. J., Thompson, E. and Rosch, E. (1991), *The Embodied Mind: Cognitive Science and Human Experience.* Cambridge, Mass and London: MIT Press. p. 51.

10 Claxton, G. (1986), The light's on but there's nobody home: the psychology of no-self, in *Beyond Therapy: The Impact of Eastern Religions on Psychological Theory and Practice,* ed. G. Claxton, London: Wisdom Publications.

11 Claxton, G. (1996), Structure, strategy and self in the fabrication of conscious experience, *Journal of Consciousness Studies,* 3, 98–111.

12 Varela *et al, op. cit.*

13 For reviews, see: Lahav, R. (1993), What neuropsychology tells us about consciousness, *Philosophy of Science,* 60, 67–85; Milner, A. D. & Rugg, M. (1992), *The Neuropsychology of Consciousness.* London: Academic Press; Schacter, D. L. (1987), Implicit memory: history and current status, *Journal of Experimental Psychology: Learning, Memory, and Cognition,* 13, pp. 501–18; Schacter, D. L, Chiu, C.-Y. P. & Ochsner, K. N. (1993), Implicit memory: A selective review, *Annual Review of Neuroscience,* 16, pp. 159–82; Schacter, D. L., McAndrews, M. P. & Moscovitch, M. (1988), Access to consciousness: Dissociations between implicit and explicit knowledge in neuropsychological syndromes, in *Thought Without Language,* ed. L. Weiskrantz. Oxford: Oxford University Press.

14 Schacter, D. L. (1989), On the relation between memory and consciousness: Dissociable interactions and conscious experience, in *Varieties of Memory and Concsciousness: Essays in Honor of Endel Tulving,* eds, H. L. Roediger and F. I. M. Craik. Hillsdale, NJ: Lawerence Erlbaum Associates; Schacter, D. L. (1990), Towards a neuropsychology of awareness: Implicit knowledge and anosognosia, *Journal of Clinical and Experimental Neuropsychology,* 12, pp. 155–78.

15 Moscovitch, M. (1994), Recovered consciousness: A hypothesis concerning modularity and episodic memory, *Journal of Clinical and Experimental Neuropsychology,* 17, 276–90; Moscovitch, M. (1995), Models of consciousness and memory, in *The Cognitive Neurosciences,* ed. in chief M. S. Gazzaniga. Cambridge, Mass. & London: MIT Books.

16 Moscovitch, 1994, p. 1351.
17 Schacter, 1990, p. 369.
18 *Mahatanhasamkhaya Sutta,* cited in Collins, *op. cit.,* p. 103.
19 Lancaster, B. L. (1994), A neo-Buddhist framework for modelling implicit processing. Paper presented to the symposium on *Selfless Minds: Buddhist influences on Cognitive Science.* British Psychological Society Winter Conference; Lancaster, B. L. (1997), On the stages of perception: towards a synthesis of cognitive neuroscience and the Buddhist Abhidhamma tradition, *Journal of Consciousness Studies, 4,* 122–42; see also Claxton, 1996.
20 For recent overview see Harman, W. and Clark, J. (1994), *New Metaphysical Foundations of Science.* Sausalito: Institute of Noetic Sciences.
21 See also Blackmore, S. (1986), Who am I? Changing models of reality in meditation, in *Beyond Therapy: The Impact of Eastern Religions on Psychological Theory and Practice,* ed. G. Claxton. London: Wisdom Publications.
22 Lancaster, B. L. (1991), *Mind, Brain and Human Potential: the Quest for an Understanding of Self.* Shaftesbury, Dorset, UK and Rockport, Mass: Element Books.
23 Gazzaniga, M. S. (1988a), The dynamics of cerebral specialization and modular interactions, in *Thought Without Language,* ed. L. Weiskrantz. Oxford: Oxford University Press; Gazzaniga, M. S. (1988b), Brain modularity: Towards a philosophy of conscious experience, in *Consciousness in Contemporary Science,* eds. A. J. Marcel & E. Bisiach. Oxford: Clarendon Press.
24 Nisbett, R. E. & Ross, L. (1980), *Human Inference: Strategies and Shortcomings of Social Judgement.* Englewood Cliffs, NJ: Prentice-Hall.
25 Gazzaniga, 1988b, p. 219.
26 *Ibid,* p. 233–34.
27 In a discussion of the term *javana,* Mrs Rhys Davids comments, 'I have spent many hours over *javana,* and am content to throw apperception [the term generally used] overboard for a better term, or for *javana,* untranslated. . .' (Aung, 1972, p. 249).
28 Aung, S. Z. (1972), *Compendium of Philosophy,* revised and edited by Mrs. Rhys Davids, first published 1910. p. 29. London: Pali Text Society.
29 Collins, *op. cit.*
30 Since my primary interest in this chapter lies in the nature of self, the stages prior to *javana* are not of critical interest. I have considered them more fully in Lancaster (1997).
31 Moments one to four have not been included in figure 1 since they operate prior to the stages of psychological interest.
32 In this review of the sense door process, I have employed the English translations of Pali terms as given by Cousins (1981).
33 For details see Lancaster, 1997. See also Damasio, A. R. (1989), Time-locked multiregional retroactivation: a systems-level proposal for the neural substrates of recall and recognition, *Cognition, 33,* pp. 25–62; Damasio, A. R. (1990), Synchronous activation in multiple cortical regions: a mechanism for recall, *Seminars in Neuroscience, 2,* pp. 287–96;

Llinás, R. R. & Paré, D. (1991), Of dreaming and wakefulness, *Neuroscience, 44*, pp. 521–35; Paré, D. & Llinás, R. R. (1995), Conscious and pre-conscious processes as seen from the standpoint of sleep-waking cycle neurophysiology, *Neuropsychologia*, 33, 1155–68.

34 Warnock, M. (1987), *Memory*. London: Faber & Faber. p. 59.

35 The 'I'-tag model can be applied to a variety of different implicit phenomena, as is explored in Lancaster (forthcoming). To pursue the point further here would detract from the main argument.

36 Claparède, E. (1995/1911), Recognition and selfhood, *Consciousness and Cognition*, 4, 371–8.

37 *Ibid*, p. 375, emphasis original.

38 *Ibid*, p. 373.

39 Kalupahana, D. J. (1992), *A History of Buddhist Philosophy: Continuities and Discontinuities*, p. 70. Honolulu: University of Hawaii Press.

40 Baars, B. J. (1988), *A Cognitive Theory of Consciousness*. p. 331. Cambridge: Cambridge University Press.

41 Moscovitch, 1994, p. 1353.

42 Lancaster, 1991.

43 Varela *et al*, *op. cit.*, p. 252.

44 Cousins, L. S. (1981), The Patthana and the development of the Theravadin Abhidhamma, *Journal of the Pali Text Society*, IX, pp. 22–46.

45 Jayasuriya, W. F. (1963), *The Psychology and Philosophy of Buddhism*. Colombo: YMBA Press. p. 43.

46 Miller, G. A. (1969), Psychology as a means of promoting human welfare, *American Psychologist*, 24, 1063–75. p. 1067.

47 Nasr, S. H. (1981), *Knowledge and the Sacred*. Edinburgh: Edinburgh University Press. p. 48.

48 Goleman, D. (1991), A western perspective, in *Mindscience:an East-West Dialogue*, ed. D. Goleman & R. A. F. Thurman. Boston: Wisdom Publications.

49 Varela *et al*, *op. cit.*, p. 254.

50 Cited in Govinda, A.B. (1975), *The Psychological Attitude of Early Buddhist Philosophy*. Delhi: Nag Publishers. p. 49.

51 Clark, S. R. L (1991), How many selves make me? In *Human Beings*, ed. D. Cockburn. Cambridge: Cambridge University Press. p. 229.

52 Varela *et al*, *op. cit.*, p. 246.

53 Pérez-Remón, *op. cit.*, p. 304.

54 *Ibid*.

55 Ramanan, K. Vankata (1975), *Nagarjuna's Philosophy as Presented in the Maha-Prajnaparamita-Sastra*. Delhi: Motilal Banarsidass. p. 98.

56 There is some debate as to whether Nagarjuna is the real author of this work. For our purposes, there is no doubting the authenticity of its philosophical orientation, whether or not it is genuinely from the pen of its traditionally assigned author.

57 *Ibid*, p. 105.

58 Conze, E. (1959), *Buddhist Scriptures*. Harmondsworth, Middlesex, UK: Penguin Books. p. 197.

59 Ramanan, *op. cit.*, p. 105.

60 Harvey, D. (1989), *The Condition of Postmodernity: an Enquiry into the Origins of Social Change*. Oxford: Blackwell. p. 54.

61 A fascinating illustration of this process may be observed from the history of 'angels'. Much of the early concretisation of angelic lore in Judaism, for example, came about through its contact with Babylonian myths and its attempt to integrate the rich imagery whilst holding onto its central tenets:

By means of the wisdom of the Chaldeans ..., the Jews had become familiar with many of the old Babylonian myths – the creation, the deluge, the early generations of man, etc. – and they sought to harmonize these myths with the biblical reports of these events. Old Babylonian tales of intercourse between gods and legendary heroes, and of books containing heavenly wisdom, were thus made to concur with Jewish legends; however, in order to avoid contradiction with the monotheistic character of Judaism, they were ascribed to the world of angels (Encyclopaedia Judaica 2:961).

One can trace the many conceptions of 'angels' – their character, classifications and functions – throughout the jostlings of civilisations almost as a marker of cultural dialogue. And of course the process continues in our day, with media images of supermen and heroes, as well as surfacings in the popular imagination of encounters with numinous beings in the form of extraterrestrials.

62 Pérez-Remón, *op. cit.*, p. 2.

63 Cohen, J. (1980), *The Lineaments of Mind in Historical Perspective*. Oxford: W. H. Freeman. p. 112. Emphasis original.

64 Parfit, D. (1984), *Reasons and Persons*. Oxford: Oxford University Press.

65 Binns, P. (1994), Affect, Agency, and engagement: conceptions of the person in philosophy, neuropsychiatry, and psychotherapy, *Philosophy, Psychiatry & Psychology*, 1, 14–23.

66 Harman, W. W. (1993), Towards an adequate epistemology for the scientific exploration of consciousness. *Journal of Scientific Exploration*, 7, 133–143. Harman, W. & Clark, J. (1994), *New Metaphysical Foundations of Science*. Sausalito: Institute of Noetic Sciences. p. 139, emphasis original.

67 For recent overview see Harré, R. & Gillett, G. (1994), *The Discursive Mind*. Thousand Oaks, CA: Sage Publications.

68 Ho, D. Y. F. (1995), Selfhood and identity in Confucianism, Taoism, Buddhism, and Hinduism: contrasts with the west, *Journal for the Theory of Social Behaviour*, 25, 115–39. p. 27–8.

69 *Midrash Avkir*, cited in Idel, M. (1988a), *Kabbalah: New Perspectives*. Yale: Yale University Press. p. 118.

70 Ecclesiastes, 3:11.

71 It has generally been argued that this vision of Adam as world-filling in scale entered the rabbinic worldview from gnostic sources. For an alternative approach see Niditch (1983).

72 Cited in Idel, *op. cit.*, p.119.

73 Clark, *op. cit.*, p. 232.

74 Smith, H. (1994), Spiritual personality types: the sacred spectrum, in *In Quest of the Sacred: The Modern World in the Light of Tradition*, eds. S.H. Nasr & K. O'Brien. Oakton, VA: Foundation for Traditional Studies. 1994. p. 55.

75 Naess, A. (1987), Self-realization: an ecological approach to being in the world, *The Trumpeter*, 4, 35–42.

76 Cited in Loy, D. (1992), Avoiding the void: the *lack* of self in psychotherapy and Buddhism, *The Journal of Transpersonal Psychology*, 24, 151–79. p. 171.

77 Velmans, M. (1990), Consciousness, brain, and the physical world, *Philosophical Psychology*, 3, 77–99.

78 Bohm, D. (1980), *Wholeness and the Implicate Order*. Routledge & Kegan Paul.

79 Jung, C. G. (1969), *The Structure and Dynamics of the Psyche*, CW vol. 8, 2nd edn., transl. R. F. C Hull. London: Routledge & Kegan Paul. p. 234.

80 Hillman, J. (1995) A Psyche the Size of the Earth: A Psychological Foreword. In *Ecopsychology: Restoring the Earth, Healing the Mind*. Edited by Roszak, T., Gomes, M. & Kanner, A., San Francisco: Sierra Book Club. P. xxi.

81 Fox, W. (1990), Transpersonal ecology:ˆpsychologizing¤ ecophilosophy, The *Journal of Transpersonal Psychology*, 22, 59–96. p. 68.

82 Idel, M. (1988b), *Studies in Ecstatic Kabbalah*. New York: State University of New York Press. p.11.

83 Tishby, I. (1989), *The Wisdom of the Zohar*, vol. 1, transl. D. Goldstein. Oxford: Oxford University Press. p. 240.

Section 5

Knowing and doing

Chapter 9

EDITOR'S PREFACE

What is the relationship between experience and knowledge? In this chapter, Elizabeth Valentine addresses this question through the issue of validation. This helps to avoid the unproductive metaphysical issues to which such questions point. These are fundamental matters, but they are difficult and even rather arid. Somewhat easier, since it is a more practical issue, is the matter of how we decide whether what we know, or just as importantly, what we are told, is true.

The chapter points out that, although various sources of knowledge have been recognised by different cultures at different times, there has been a recurrent distinction made between external and internal validation of experience. In Western terms, albeit somewhat simplified, this is the distinction between empiricism and rationalism. Empiricism holds that the senses not only provide us with our basic knowledge of the world but also the means to test any more advanced hypotheses about it. Rationalism places greater reliance on thought and knowledge that arises within the mind rather than being acquired via the senses. No strictly comparable distinction is made in Eastern traditions, at least not explicitly, although there is much discussion of the difference between experiential, rational and intuitive types of knowledge.

With these types of distinction in mind, it appears that any method of validation will have drawbacks, whichever type or source of knowledge is concerned. Experience is subject to distortion and illusion. Rational processes are culture-bound and subject to systematic error. Intuitive insight, powerful though it is as a personal experience and as a guide for subsequent rational analysis, is difficult to formalise or to convey in any explicit way. It will therefore be liable to distortion and misinterpretation when used by others.

So, how are we to test our knowledge and beliefs? When it comes to science, Elizabeth Valentine proposes that objectivity is '... no more than inter-subjectivity'. This conclusion is perhaps a little surprising. Firstly, it seems to find the matter of experience, albeit shared experience, unproblematic. Experience can be subject to distortion and, even when not distorted, to misinterpretation. The fact that these distortions and misinterpretations are common to most observers doesn't alter the case. Secondly, the conclusion is challenged by examples she provides later to show that subjectivity is to a significant extent a matter of the cultural conditioning of raw experience. Therefore the inter-subjective agreement is not so much a guarantee of objectivity as a demonstration that human awareness may be rendered uniform by being passed through what Fromm called a 'cultural filter' of beliefs, assumptions and values.[1]

Even so, Western science does have powerful methods for systematic observation and hypothesis testing that have amply proven their worth in turning hypothetical insights into reliable knowledge. The technological expression of this knowledge surrounds us in the shape of the machines, structures and practices that provide the material basis of life in the developed countries. This is often pointed to by those, like Richard Dawkins and Lewis Wolpert, would defend science against the charge that its concepts and practices are culturally relative. Culturally relative ideas, they argue, do not translate so reliably into practical techniques that work wherever they are used.

Whether or not this quite disposes of the charge of cultural relativism, it is a powerful argument for the effectiveness of Western science. We might then use it as a framework for the issue of validation addressed in this chapter. Thus we may ask: are the resources of science, both methodological and theoretical, effective in turning hypotheses about the mind into effective techniques, for example, for controlling consciousness and helping with the mentally ill? The answer at first sight might appear to be 'yes'. After all, medical science and psychiatry have powerful techniques for intervening in cases of mental illness. On closer inspection, however, the case is less convincing. Intervention may be 'effective', as in the case of anti-depressant drugs, for example, but whose interests are served by this intervention? Once questions like this are asked it becomes clear that the effectiveness of an intervention may be quite a different thing from whether or not it helps in relieving mental suffering in the longer run.

This is where the postmodern turn is significant. In recognising that any system of cultural practices expresses value, it helps us to see that the methods and the concepts of science are not the absolutes that they might be taken to be, if we accept the rhetoric of scientism. We need a variety of discourses to understand any phenomenon. Such pluralism is not merely the acceptance that different points of view and different traditions exist. It is, as Vaclav Havel has pointed out, an active synthesis of new meaning by the combination of traditions distant in space and time.

It is in just this sense that this chapter compares Buddhism and Western scientific psychology. Elizabeth Valentine, like Rosch and others who are familiar with both systems of inquiry, suggests a number of areas where common ground is to be found.[2] This applies to both method and theory, in as much as Buddhism can be said to have a 'theory' of mental life. There may be more room for argument about how firm this common ground is. For example, both Valentine and Heywood find similarities between meditation and experimental methods but it is difficult to see much similarity beyond the fact that both are systematic. Moreover, this chapter suggests that meditation provides knowledge that 'Can be pointed to, experienced, but not described'.

Here is a clear qualitative difference between the objectives of Western psychology and Buddhism. Such differences are to be expected. Pluralism does not imply integration, but rather the holding within one view of a multiplicity of perspectives. The objective of postmodern psychology is not that of modernist science, namely, to create a unified theory of the mind. Rather it is to bring together the complementary resources of different traditions in order that new understanding may emerge from their interaction.

NOTES

1 Fromm, E. (1960) Psychoanalysis and Zen Buddhism. Souvenir Press, London.
2 Hayward, J. & Varela, F. (Eds.) (1992) *Gentle Bridges*. Shambala, Boston.

★　★　★

The Validation of Knowledge: Private and Public

Elizabeth Valentine

'If a philosophy and a practice for a sustainable future is to be created, the merging of the contrasting wisdoms of East and West will be essential.'[1]

In this chapter, the approaches of Buddhism and contemporary science to the problem of the validation of knowledge are compared and contrasted. There are many issues on which Buddhism and contemporary science agree, e.g. experience as the origin of all knowledge, the constructed nature of our mental life, and the importance of testability in the pursuit of knowledge. In some ways their contributions are complementary. Thus cognitive science provides a detailed analysis based on experimental data but Buddhism begins from a wider data base and importantly has a different aim: elucidation of the causes of human suffering and the means of its alleviation. Issues discussed include the contribution of sensory experience, rational thought processes and meditative insight to the acquisition of knowledge; and the problems of subjectivity, interpretation and consensual validation.

THE PRIMACY OF EXPERIENCE

Experience is the starting point of all our knowledge. This is as true of scientific knowledge as of any other. Though the resulting statements are public and generalisable, they are inferences from private and particular sensory experiences. As Schrödinger[2] remarked of physics: 'All this information goes back ultimately to the sense perceptions of some living person or persons, however many ingenious devices may have been used to facilitate the labour...The most careful record, when not inspected, tells us nothing.' Karl Pearson maintained that science was merely a set of formulae which enabled the prediction of future sense experiences on the basis of past ones. For him a scientific law was no more than 'a brief description in mental shorthand of as wide a range as possible of the sequences of our sense-impressions. The reality of a thing depends upon the possibility of its occurring in whole or part as a group of immediate sense-impressions.'[3] This might be seen as part of the general positivist programme of Comte and Mach to found science on sensory observation. Thus, all knowledge is essentially mental, psychological.

Here, as so often, Buddhism has penetrated to the truth; indeed no sharp distinction is drawn between sensations and thoughts. In Buddhism real existence is attributed only to dharmas – momentary elements of experience. In the early schools much effort was expended on the analysis of experience into dharmas (the abhidharma). These were categorised into 'aggregates' known as the five skandhas: form, feeling, perception, formation and consciousness. Form consists of eleven dharmas: the five senses (sight, hearing, smell, taste and touch), the five corresponding sense objects (colours and shapes, sounds, smells, tastes, and objects of touch), with the final class consisting of such phenomena as hallucinations. Feeling is the automatic affective response to form: positive, negative or neutral evaluation. Perception involves the detection and discernment of objects. Formation is conceptual – meaningful interpretation: object recognition, emotions, beliefs or attitudes. Consciousness integrates and contextualises all these. Buddhism and cognitive science are agreed that consciousness is 'a narrative ... that checks out the coherence and meaningfulness of the entire scene... Anything that does not fit in is finally excluded from the level of consciousness.'[4] Compare also Dennett's[5] multiple drafts model of consciousness according to which the self is a centre of narrative gravity rather than the audience in the Cartesian theatre: information entering the nervous system is under continuous editorial revision[6]. The Sanskrit word vijnana actually contains the meaning of 'divided', indicating the fact that at this stage separation between knower and known has crept in.

Later Buddhist schools in the Mahayana tradition recognised a residual dualism in the earlier Hinayana traditions between sense and sense object. They argued that not only the 'inner' self but also the 'outer' world must be deconstructed and that the craving for an ultimate ground or foundation of knowledge should be abandoned. Nothing is intrinsic in nature or has independent existence. Hence the doctrines of sunyata – emptiness or groundlessness, and co-dependent origination. The Madhyamika or middle way of Nagarjuna avoids the extremes of Hindu absolutism on the one hand and Theravadan nihilism on the other.

AUTHORITY AND TRUTH

In Western philosophy there have been two views on the validation of knowledge, two theories of truth: empiricism and rationalism. For the former the touchstone is sensory experience and the correspondence of ideas with observed 'facts'; the latter places credence on coherence between ideas and emphasises thought. In extreme form, each has been seen by its supporters as the source of self-evident truths. Both are necessary; neither are sufficient. Each has its contribution to make but both are subject to error – no method carries its own guarantee. Sense-experience provides evidence for particular existences but may be subject to illusion. Thought provides an important corrective but cognitive science has shown it to be subject to many heuristics and biases[7].

There are two notorious problems with experience: (1) privacy or subjectivity, and (2) interpretation. If experience is confined to the individual, there are the problems of replication by, and generalisation to, others. However, objectivity is no more than inter-subjectivity. As we saw above, generalised, public statements are inferences based on particular, private observations. The other side of the coin is that private experiences can be made public: public evidence can be provided for them, notably in the form of verbal reports but also behavioural and neurophysiological data. Thus the division between objective and subjective, or public and private, is not so clearly defined as is first apparent. Buddhism has attempted to go beyond this duality (see below).

With regard to the problem of interpretation, it is interesting to note that traditions as diverse as Structuralist psychology, phenomenology and mysticism have all attempted to remove the effect of interpretation in the effort to reach the holy grail of 'pure' sensory experience. Thus the Structuralists warned against committing the stimulus error, i.e. relying on known properties of the object resulting from prior experience; phenomenologists pursued 'bracketing', i.e. literally putting in brackets commonsense everyday assumptions of the 'naturalistic attitude', such as belief in the existence of physical objects, time and space; mystics have practised meditational techniques aimed at reducing or removing what psychologists would refer to as 'top down processes' with the aim of shifting attention to 'bottom up processes'. This has been one of the central teachings of Buddhism – to shift from conditioned to unconditioned processes. Indeed, one wonders whether this isn't the aim of almost all psychotherapeutic techniques from psychoanalysis to cognitive therapy – to dislodge maladaptive habits of thought, thus making room for alternative, more productive ones.

CONSTRUCTIVISM

One of the insights of postmodernist thought has been to reveal the theoretical embeddedness of observation. Theories are almost invariably underdetermined by the evidence: observations are theory-laden. There are no such things as pure facts. Facts do not speak for themselves; they are useless unless one takes the intellectual risk of thinking about them. As Darwin pointed out, one cannot simply observe without knowing what counts as an observation. Theories determine what counts as data. Popper[8] argued that the discovery of penicillin was dependent on the existence of prior expectations. Observations are inextricably dependent on the belief systems of the scientists who make them. Hence justified true belief may be no more than conformity to the norms of the day. Scientific hypotheses are generally embedded in a whole network of theoretical assumptions (the Quine-Duhem thesis) and thus cannot be tested in isolation. These assumptions vary in the degree to which they are dispensable; some may be 'protected'[9] and thus lead to revision of the observation base as a preferred way of resolving dilemmas (i.e. discrepancies between observations and predictions).

Buddhism too has stressed theoretical embeddedness and the role of presuppositions. Empiricism assumes the possibility of making pure observations unadulterated by the beliefs of the observer. Buddhism and cognitive science agree that perception and action depend on unconscious assumptions; they are affected by profound prejudices beyond our conscious control. Science has deconstructed the external world but (by and large) not the self[10]. According to Buddhism, both the external world and the self, the perceiver, are constructions, conceptual fabrications. The fundamental insight from meditation is that the projecting process knows itself, that is all, nothing else; there are no atomic minds and no unknowable things in themselves.

CRITERIA FOR SCIENTIFIC KNOWLEDGE

Scientific knowledge is supposed to be (1) objective, (2) the result of employing a specifiable method, and (3) revisable. With regard to objectivity, this means that such knowledge must be public and consensually validated. Hence the requirement of replication (and the need for a specifiable method). It must be universal, for example not specific to a particular culture (cf. Merton's imperatives[11]). This does not mean that one cannot study an individual case or a particular culture, but the knowledge must be publicly specifiable and available. How far this needs revision in the light of current postmodernist thinking is a moot point. Some would maintain that no absolute standards are now possible or conceivable, that all knowledge is socially constructed[12].

With regard to a specifiable method, Buddhism of course has this. There are clear instructions for what procedures to follow for what consequences: all that is asked of the practitioner is that s/he test these out for her/himself.

Hayward[13] asserts that the grounds for validating the method of meditation are not very different from those for the scientific method: the refusal to take anything for granted and the requirement to try it out for oneself. He claims that the intersubjective communal checking that takes place in mindfulness meditation is similar to that of the scientific community. Indeed, the practice of mindfulness can be regarded as a form of scientific method. Science is experiential, testable, public, replicable. The hallmark of science is that knowledge claims are open to experiential validation: verification or refutation. The contrast is not with religion per se but with dogma.

Postmodernists, e.g. Feyerabend[14], protest that there is no fixed method which will guarantee arriving at the truth. In particular, they will point out that frequently it is necessary to depart from the conventionally accepted method in order to progress. It is in the nature of creative solutions that they are unspecifiable in advance.

REVISABILITY

Popper[15] has popularised the view that the distinguishing criterion of science is falsifiability. (He was led to this by considering the application of the logical positivists' verification principle to scientific hypotheses and noting the asymmetry between confirmation and falsification in this context. He also observed that what was often considered to be the strength of theories such as psychoanalysis,

Marxism and evolution was in fact their weakness, namely their imperviousness to refutation.) He advocated that science should proceed by way of conjecture (the bolder and riskier the better) and refutation. On his view, knowledge is essentially conjectural and provisional. All that can be attained are approximations to doubtful truth. One may arrive at the truth but one can never know this.

The extent to which science is indeed revisable and subject to falsification is arguable. Wason's[16] experiments on reasoning (using a quasi-scientific task) forced him to reject Popper's falsificationist philosophy of science as a psychological model, in favour of Kuhnian paradigms. Intelligent subjects repeatedly failed to test their hypotheses adequately, typically indulging in 'confirmation bias', sometimes even to the extent of reformulating formally identical hypotheses; they seemed incapable of attempting to falsify their hypotheses. Mitroff[17] took the opportunity to interview NASA geoscientists during the period when lunar soil samples were being returned by Apollo space missions. Scientists characterised as hard-nosed were relatively responsive to the new data, whereas theoretical scientists were much more committed to their hypotheses and often refused to change their views in the face of strong contradictory evidence. As noted above, some assumptions are more easily dispensable than are others. The behaviour of any group of practitioners is subject to social rules and norms. Taylor et al.[18] show that this applies even in the 'hard' sciences: the values of physical constants have been known to shift substantially but gradually over time, explicable on the grounds that scientists are unable to tolerate too marked a deviation from the established value. The dramatic change in the fortune of previously accepted journal articles, re-submitted with only a change of authors' names and affiliations, demonstrates the power of the establishment[19]. Mahoney[20] found that reviewers were much more likely to recommend papers for publication when the evidence supported their own positions; when the data contradicted their opinion, they criticised the method and interpretation and recommended against publication. Religious groups may be particularly subject to the influence of gurus and ideologies but scientists are not utterly exempt. It may be a difference of degree rather than kind.

THE WAY OF BUDDHISM: MEDITATION

In the Sangarava sutta three groups of thinkers are contrasted: (1) traditionalists, (2) rationalists and metaphysicians, and (3) experientialists, who have personal experience of higher knowledge. The Buddha says he belongs to the third. Buddhism relies in particular on a different kind of experience from that of ordinary sense-experience, namely intuition or insight. This revelation or realisation is common to the spiritual traditions but alien to Western science. In Buddhism it takes the form, in particular, of reflection on one's mental states. According to the spiritual traditions, personal commitment and methodical cultivation of such practices can lead to the elimination of biases, the refinement of powers of extra-sensory perception and the development of higher knowledge. Two main kinds of meditation are practised in Buddhism: (1) samathi, mindfulness, bare and deliberate attention to the details of one's sensations, the resulting calm being an antidote to the evil of craving, and (2) vipassana, insight – attending to the arising, dwelling and ceasing of one's sensations, and to their interdependence, an antidote to the evil of ignorance. Sometimes described as direct seeing into the causal nature of thought, emotion, perception and environment, it aims to be free from the barrier of preconception and to recover nonduality, healing rather than promoting the split between mental content and knowing.

BEYOND SCIENCE?

To what extent are new methods required and possible? Hayward[21] claims that we need to go beyond dualistic science. Abstract mathematical time deletes the presence of the experiencer; science as currently practised excludes the observer, Eddington's[22] Mr. X: 'Physics is not at all anxious to pursue the question, What is Mr. X? It is not disposed to admit that its elaborate structure of a physical universe is 'The House that Mr. X built.' It looks upon Mr. X – and more particularly the part of Mr. X that knows – as a rather troublesome tenant who at a late stage of the world's history has come to inhabit a structure which inorganic Nature has by slow evolutionary progress contrived to build. And so it turns aside from the avenue leading to Mr. X – and beyond – and closes up its cycle leaving him out in the cold.'[23] Buddhism claims that dharmas arise within the gap in which there is no sense of self or of separateness from nonduality. These unconditioned dharmas, gaps in the percep-tual process, unique moments, are inaccessible to the methods of dualistic observation but accessible to direct experience – primordial, nondual, intelligent openness and insight. Hayward claims that the sacredness which opens up from the point of nowness cannot be examined or described with dualistic methods based on the linear concept of time as past, present and future. He offers two reasons why cognitive science remains unaware of unconditioned dharmas: first, it has not realised the need to train attention to fine time intervals and has not fully acknowledged the importance of the discontinuity of the process; (2) unconditioned dharmas can only be pointed to and not verbally described. Practitioners claim that, by properly guided investigation, one can verify and experience for oneself insights which can only be pointed to but not described. But then, in my view, they cannot form part of science.

On the other hand, I have some sympathy with Hayward's expressed view that it is important that science does not lose its authority (which seems unlikely in view of the value placed on science by society) and that the change in contextual beliefs that our science-created society so desperately needs – if we are to deal with what Crook[24] refers to as the 'aching void of ultimate meaninglessness' or to save life on our planet from extinction – should come about not by denouncing science (wherein lies the gateway to blind faith in the magical and occult) but by science showing the way its own context and therefore society might change. It should arise from within rather than in opposition to science.

Buddhism, like phenomenology, can provide data but its methods cannot replace the experimental and theoretical analysis of science. As Crook[25] observes: 'Ways of investigation and modes of modelling 'reality' each have their realms of meaningful applicability'.

THE PERSONAL AND THE SOCIAL

Many writers on the history and philosophy of science[26] (e.g. Boring, 1954; Kuhn, 1963) have recognised two opposing tendencies, each of which has strengths and weaknesses. The personal (Boring's 'egoism') is necessary to provide the motivation to initiate and sustain scientific enquiry. However, these creative forces need to be restrained and checked by the social (Boring's 'Zeitgeist') through the demand for replication. The latter alone would impede progress. Kuhn refers to the essential tension required between these two forces to maximise productive gains.

The 'social' spans the cultural and the universal. The cultural lies between the poles of the individual at one end and the universal at the other. The analysis of mystical experiences may be used to illustrate the contrast between cultural and universal features. Some features are likely to be universal, such as the enhancement of sensory aspects of the stimulus and the decline of interpretative top-down factors, distortions of space and time, and the loss of object perception and the distinction between self and other. However, the specific religious interpretation of these effects is likely to be the result of particular training (doctrine or dogma). For example, the loss of the distinction between self and other may be interpreted internally as the world being in one's head, or externally as the subject flowing out into the world[27]. Hood[28] distinguishes pure experience factors of ineffability, unity, timelessness and spacelessness from interpretative factors of knowledge, holiness and positive feeling, the latter being more context bound. As a result of careful examination, Brown[29] has similarly argued that the stages of perceptual change in meditation practices are very similar in different traditions but the way these changes are experienced depends on the philosophical training of each. In particular this applies to the discontinuity of awareness. All agree about the incessant nature of change but experience the nature of this change differently. The Theravadin Buddhist tradition sees discontinuity only at the deepest level of the ground of perception, seeing nothing between moments; on the other hand, the Hindu Yoga tradition sees the discontinuities as fluctuations of a permanent mind-stuff (because of its eternalistic, dualistic assumptions). Mental events unfold in a discontinuous manner for the Theravadins but a continuous manner for the Hindu yogis. Later tantric or Vajrayana schools recognised the continuity of awareness from moment to moment (one meaning of 'tantra' is continuity or thread) but for them it is one of process rather than stuff – a middle way between Hindu eternalism and Theravadan nihilism.

CONCLUSION

In this chapter we have considered the contribution of sensory experience, rational thought processes and meditative insight to the development of knowledge; and compared and contrasted their treatment in Buddhist and scientific epistemologies. Each has its role to play but each has its limitations and dangers. In particular, the problems of subjectivity, interpretation and consensual validation have been considered, and the necessity but difficulty of refutability stressed. Current thought inclines to the view that there is no fixed method or guarantor of absolute truth. Not only conclusions but the methods by which they are reached must be open to constant revision.

The Validation of Knowledge: Private and Public

This is as true for Buddhism as it is for science. As Heraclitus observed so long ago: All things flow; change is the only reality.

NOTES

1 Crook, J. (1990) East-West psychology: towards a meeting of minds. In J. Crook & D. Fontana (eds.) *Space in mind.* Shaftesbury: Element. p. 23.
2 Schrödinger, E. (1958) *Mind and matter.* Cambridge: Cambridge University Press.
3 Pearson, K. (1892) *The grammar of science.* London: Scott. p. 98.
4 Hayward, J.W. (1987) *Shifting worlds, changing minds.* London: Shambala. p. 151.
5 Dennett, D.C. (1991) *Consciousness explained.* Boston: Little Brown.
6 On the similarity of his 'pandemonium of homunculi' to the doctrine of anatta, see Valentine, E. (1989) Perception and action in East and West, in J. P. Forgas and M. J. Innes (eds.) *Social Psychology: An international perspective.* Amsterdam: Elsevier.
7 Tversky, A. & Kahneman, D. (1974) Judgment under uncertainty: heuristics and biases, *Science* 125, 1124–31.
8 Popper, K. (1963) *Conjectures and refutations.* London: Routledge & Kegan Paul.
9 Lakatos, I. (1970) Falsification and the methodology of scientific research programmes, in I. Lakatos & A. Musgrave (eds.) *Criticism and the growth of knowledge.* Cambridge: Cambridge University Press.
10 Though see Valentine, *op. cit.*
11 Merton, R.K. (1967) Science and democratic social structures, in R.K. Merton (ed.) *Social theory and social structure*, pp. 550–61. Free Press. Revised edition.
12 Gergen, K. (1992) Toward a postmodern psychology. In S. Kvale (ed.) *Psychology and postmodernism.* London: Sage.
13 Heyward, *op. cit.*
14 Feyerabend, P.K. (1975) *Against method.* London: NLB.
15 Popper, *op. cit.*
16 Wason, P.C. (1960) On the failure to eliminate hypotheses in a conceptual task. *Quarterly Journal of Experimental Psychology*, 38A, 5–33.
17 Cited in Mahoney, M.J. (1976) The truth seekers. *Psychology Today*, April, 60–65.
18 Taylor, B.N., Langenberg, D.N. & Parker, W.H. (1970) The fundamental physical constants, *Scientific American*, 223, October, 62–78.
19 Peters, D.P. & Ceci, S.J. (1982) Peer review practices of psychological journals: the fate of previously published articles submitted again, *The Behavioral & Brain Sciences*, 5, 187–225.
20 Mahoney, *op. cit.*
21 Hayward, *op. cit.*
22 Eddington, A. (1935) *The nature of the physical world.* London: Dent.
23 *Ibid*, p. 254–55.
24 Crook, *op. cit.*
25 *Ibid*, p20.

26 E.g. Boring, E.G. (1954) Psychological factors in scientific progress. *American Scientist*, 42, 639–45; Kuhn, T.S. (1963) The essential tension: tradition and innovation in scientific research, in C.W. Taylor & F. Barron (eds.) *Scientific creativity*. New York: Wiley.
27 I am grateful to John Valentine for this point.
28 Hood, R.W. (1975) The construction and preliminary validation of a measure of reported mystical experience. *Journal for the Scientific Study of Religion*, 14, 29–41.
29 Brown, D. (1986) In K. Wilber, J. Engler & D. Brown (eds) *Transformations of consciousness*, pp. 219–84. Boston: New Science Library.

Chapter 10

EDITOR'S PREFACE

John Crook's chapter is a sustained inquiry into authority and authenticity as related to personal discovery and practice. He shows that what a teacher or therapist offers will have a certain sort of authority if it arises directly from their own effort and experience. Buddhism is not a textual or scholastic resource alone, although it is both of these things. It is also, and perhaps more importantly, a systematic practice. From this practice knowledge of a particularly powerful and personal type arises. This, if communicated, can profoundly influence others not only by its content but also, and more importantly, by the way in which it is transmitted.

This means that teaching is far more closely tied to the personal qualities of a teacher than it is in other systems of knowledge such as science. Indeed, it is said to be one of the strengths of science that its methods and content can be formalised and hence depersonalised. It is this that makes it the democratised system of knowledge that it is. It may be learned by anyone who can understand its formal basis and taught by anyone who can also communicate clearly. This effort after a systematic methodology has been one of the enduring achievements of logical positivism. Despite the limitations revealed by later philosophers of science, it remains the strength of scientific thinking that to be convincing, a scientific idea or practice must be explicit and parsimonious. Of course, this can degenerate into sterile reductionism. As Einstein said, 'theories must be as simple as possible, but not simpler'.

Teachings based on insightful experience rather than formalised methods are rather different, both in how they are transmitted and how they are understood in the first place. They have far more to do with the powers of individuals and far less to do with grasping formalised methods. As such, the personal resources of the teacher and learner come far more strongly into play. Such personalisation of authority, both in teaching and in learning, has obvious dangers. As John Crook points out, the last decade or so of Western Buddhist development has been marred by corrupt teachers, scandals and sectarianism. These are things that the media have, quite rightly, been quick to expose.

John Crook

Here, some conventional atittudes towards religion and science are confirmed. Such scandals as may arise in science usually have to do with corrupt methods. However, because science has depersonalised, formalised practices which test claims against reality, fraud will ultimately come to light and can be repaired. The harm that the fraud and its repair cause will in general be felt by those who are guilty of it. However, in a system such as Buddhism, where teaching and knowledge itself are personalised, corrupt behaviour may be concealed by complicity and self-delusion. And if it is exposed, the suffering is caused to innocent as well as guilty parties.

This is simplified but not inaccurate. The authority of science lies more in its practice than in the people who conduct that practice. Buddhism, from its very begining, accepts the notion of the exceptional individual as authority. Hence, since mere charisma can confer bogus authority, especially when a system of practice moves into a new cultural setting, Buddhism is more vulnerable to distortion in this way than is science. John Crook provides a broad and honest survey of this problem that faces anyone wishing to practice science and Buddhism. His conclusion, based on his own informed engagement with both, is that '. . . it is never possible to know that the path taken is the right one.' Even so, a path must be chosen and, once chosen, honestly followed. This chapter helps us to do both.

★   ★   ★

Authenticity and the Practice of Zen
John Crook

THE NEED FOR AN EXAMINATION

The authority of experience depends upon authenticity. If we base our action or feeling in inauthentic experience it can only lead to play acting or pretence with potentially catastrophic consequences. Sadly, many of our justifications for action rest on the outcomes of past personal, familial and social tensions that have remained unresolved and which distort our perception of ourselves and other people. They lead to a biased repression of emotion and a ritualisation of personal behaviour into rigid moulds that may later produce an inability to recover the repressed experiences in understanding. Such 'stuckness' commonly leads to damaged lives inhabited by persons in permanent low level stress whose behaviour is often socially damaging. Such a condition is widely prevalent, almost a norm in human society[1] and some have argued that it amounts to a disease.

Buddhist thought has accepted this position for some 2500 years, arguing that the human mind is normally in a state of delusion from which it is difficult to recover.[2] The Buddha has often been called the great doctor and the task of Buddhism as soteriology is to replace illusion by clarity and this process is what is meant by 'enlightenment'.[3] Yet so normal is the state of illusion that Buddhist institutions and teachers are by no means immune from it and there are those who would argue for the necessity of a constant and watchful cultivation.[4] Such a viewpoint is often ignored especially in heady periods of Buddhist history when the Dharma is expanding rapidly into new cultural settings. Since Buddhism, and especially Zen, claims to restore authenticity to consciousness we need to ask how successful it is or whether the teachings and teaching personalities hold us in some illusory thrall.

Today there are strong reasons for pressing such an enquiry. The behaviour of teachers, both Oriental and Western, participating in the dramatic spread of Zen and Tibetan institutions in America has often fallen severely short of the ethical ideal. Stuart Lachs[5] has recently reviewed developments that reveal widespread lapses in conventional morality. The causes for this are not solely due to an irresponsibility attributable to teachers, their followers have also been severely at fault. The context of such problems lies in the almost desperate Western need for personal meaning in a world which lacks the old certainties of Christianity and Humanism. The post-modern context is ruled by a relativity of values at all levels. Out of the plethora of religious and ethical possibilities, Celtic traditions, the nostrums of Merlin, orthodox faiths, unorthodox creeds or North American native practices, which one gives a meaning to me?

In spite of the democratic tradition in the West, a prime problem in the arrival of Buddhism in the USA has been that the authoritarian attitudes natural to traditional Eastern cultures have been passed from Eastern teachers to those they appointed as first generation Western 'masters'. Their conferred infallibility as an 'enlightened' person was often uncritically accepted by naive westerners desperate to believe in a human representation of the sublime but who, in the course of time, only discovered the ridiculous. Some such teachers came to dominate the institutions they led establishing neither democratic means for self criticism nor advisory boards to provide feedback. In many sad cases the result has been the sexual exploitation of naive young followers of both genders and severe financial irregularity. Furthermore, some Oriental teachers themselves, succumbing to the permissiveness of the West they failed to properly understand, also revealed comparable faults. Clearly when such behaviour is discovered not only is the validity of the transmission to teach called into question but the whole system and the texts that sustain it become suspect. Finally, not only have many men and women become disoriented and distressed by the deceits practised upon them but authentic teachers truly worthy of their titles are smeared by gossip, suspicion and doubts.

WHAT IS AUTHENTICITY?

'Authenticity' has a range of overlapping meanings. The Oxford English Dictionary gives:

- real, actual or genuine as opposed to pretended;
- original as opposed to copied;
- proceeding from it's reputed source or author;
- of established credit and genuineness;
- in accordance with or as stating fact;
- having legal validity, authoritative.

There is also a usage in music meaning a sound or note belonging appropriately to a scale, mode or melody. This meaning may be extended to appropriateness of a verbal expression within a form of discourse. An authentic statement is one that comes from the 'heart' expressing a genuinely held, unambivalent belief or undistorted feeling.

Experiences that lack such characteristics are questionable, one may doubt their validity and suspect that they stand in for something else, a hidden agenda, motivation or bias. Yet how can one be sure that an experience is genuine? Most experiences are representations of internal and external circumstances in complex relations that may easily be mistaken or incorrectly perceived. How can we know that we know? Furthermore, how can we know when others, especially teachers and guides of all kinds, are authentic in their accounts of their experiences and practices? In what can we trust? In attempting to define ways of life appropriate to the problems of these millennial years an understanding of what is and what is not authentic is critical.

In the practice of psychotherapy the importance of the 'unconscious' and the power of repressed experience to modify thought, behaviour and action has been well attested since Freud's original work. Studies by Winnicot, Guntrip, Miller and many others of the 'object relations' school[6] have shown how negative experiences in childhood create buried scenarios that fester in repression creating attitudes, failures in self knowledge and behaviour severely debilitating to the practitioner and harmful to his or her relationships in adult life.

The humanistic orientation in psychology emphasises the existential realities of personal lives, in particular the need to develop awareness, expression of feeling, capacities for choice and relating all of which are seen as essential for effective self development in the expression of human potential. 'A person is authentic in that degree to which his being in the world is unqualifiedly in accord with the givenness of his own nature and of the world. Authenticity is the primary good or value of the existential viewpoint.'[7] This perspective argues that authenticity entails a way of being in the world in which the person is in harmony with himself, others and the world. Inauthenticity means conflict within self, with others and the world. Yet here the idealisation of the term in language may become a danger. Authenticity is no mere adaptation or some mystical transcendence. Rather, we are concerned with a direct facing of the immediate realities of life with a willed affirmation of difficulties, an acceptance of them and their past origins and a letting go into a pro-active acceptance of change. It is not inauthentic to be faced with problems of ambivalence and paradox, indeed these are the very food of life. Modern therapy is essentially any effective interpersonal process that aids this process of comprehension and personal change.

The living circumstances into which human beings are thrown have been described in terms of four main issues; finiteness, potential to act, capacity to choose, and the realisation of existential aloneness.[8] We only have finite, limited understanding of ourselves and the world and such understanding as we do have is contingent upon circumstance, the availability of others, health and well being, none of which can be taken for granted and none of which are permanently available. We are subject to the 'fate' into which we are born and realise ourselves only briefly before death. Yet we have a capacity for action and gradually realise our responsibility for action in the world. No action can be perfect so we are faced by the risk of condemnation and anxiety generated by guilt or shame. We can only act within that context. So we have to choose a path and in such choice we experience autonomy. Yet within that very autonomy we experience our finite limitations and may thus be faced by a sense of meaninglessness. Seeking a meaning beyond our finite worlds we may get lost and experience such emptiness as a great fear. Yet, even while we experience our loneliness we discover we are not alone. We are 'alone with others', as Steven Batchelor puts it.[9] In this, however, there remains the threat of the disappearance of the other or withdrawal from us leaving us in total isolation. Such anxiety is terrifying and the terror genuine.

INAUTHENTICITY, EMOTIONAL DEPENDENCY AND THE DISINTEGRATED SELF

The life task of every human individual is inevitably to confront the uncomfortable truths of existence and to find the way through the givens of personal limitation in a manner that evades pretence, avoidance of difficulty and uncomplimentary truth to create an authenticity of being and expression that is both accepting and open. Perhaps that is what creativity is. The same task faces all those would-be carers in the helping professions and to this we must pay particular attention.

Therapeutic models and processes have struggled to find ways to alleviate the difficulties individuals face in coming to terms with these irreducible facts of life. Many have become caught in behaviourist, cognitivist or other reductionist fallacies that fail to meet the existential realities of human being.[10] Some therapies of dubious or partial validity impose years of expensive time consuming work often with little deep consequence. The burgeoning market place of therapy has encouraged careerists who, in inventing new glosses on old Freudian insights, often benefit their pockets more than their clients. The creation of ever new therapeutic and counselling methods all in competition with one another has created a commercial world in which the selling of new dependencies flourishes.

In spite of the genuine concern, expertise and courageous dedication of many therapists there is also emerging a puzzling inauthenticity within the whole 'business' that only occasionally receives a degree of exposure. A skilled therapist may have a good idea, start to promote it in a small way only to find that his/her clients begin to develop wants to become therapists themselves. In such contexts the cryptic power of the therapist's role and the issues of transference may not have been adequately addressed. There thus develops the temptation to start a school for therapists who may well have been the sponsors' own clients. Such developments cannot but be viewed with suspicion. What has been going on here?

There has been a search for more direct methods less dependent on long term therapist-client relationships and centred on self-help often in group contexts. In this area work on chemical dependency (alcohol and drug addiction) has begun to turn up valuable insights of wide social application.

In working with addicts and their families it became apparent that family members who look after, treat, placate or otherwise manage the addicted person commonly show psychological symptoms of excessive caring for others, reduced independence, fixated referencing to family issues, depression and evasive, if not dishonest, behaviour, lying about the family etc., which do not necessarily improve when the alcoholic improves. The syndrome has become known as co-dependence – the individual being dependent on the addiction indirectly by way of a fixation on the addicted. There is often a mutual or co-dependence between them.

It is now suspected that such a syndrome occurs widely in society and not only in relation to chemical dependency. Anne Wilson Schaef[11] considers it to be an aspect of a hydra-headed personality disorder produced by addictive processes widespread in society. Co-dependents have been defined as *all* persons in close emotional relationships with alcoholics or who have alcoholic parents or grandparents or who grow up in emotionally repressive families.[12] Co-dependency has also been described as an emotional, psychological and behavioural condition developing from prolonged exposure to a set of oppressive rules determined by social situations or family members which prevent the expression of natural feelings as well as the discussion of personal family or group problems.[13] It arises, therefore, as a set of coping skills under an enforced restriction of emotional expression.

Others have argued that co-dependence operates not only in families but in communities, businesses and institutions. Alcoholism thus begins to look like a response to this condition, as an especially negative coping skill in relation to forbidden or unexpressed distress, rather than as an essential determinant of co-dependence. If co-dependence is prior and as widespread as Whitfield[14] and Schaef believe then I prefer to refer to it as *emotional dependence*, a personality disorder that produces distortions in social perception, behaviour and feeling in others as well as the prime sufferer. It is socially infectious and socially tolerated. Its presence in a group commonly remains unidentified. The problem begins to emerge as truly vast.

Such distortions preclude an open awareness of personal problems because these are filtered through a wide range of unconscious pretences developed to prevent pain and distress. The individual becomes addicted to these responses and the object relations within which they occur due to the temporary and illusory relief they provide. The repeated performance of these patterns provides an illusory security as when someone who has lived for years with an anxious mother comes to placate and attempt to relieve the tension of significant others in life. With the mother such behaviour may have been essential for the child to have survived at all but, in adult life, the addiction to such a habit of security creation becomes destructive of straightforward relationship.

Schaef's list of personal traits achieving such ends is formidable. Emotional dependants are so focused on the activities of others (which may include their health, their approval, their withdrawal of control or punishment etc.) that they feel their own being to have little or no meaning. The meaning of their lives comes from outside and their intentionality is entirely determined by this. Relationships tend to conform to a pattern in which the clinging cannot be free from the clung. Personal boundaries are then so weak that psychological invasion is inevitable, the emotionally dependent quickly taking on the moods and responses of others. To sustain their dependent relationships they are forever trying to manage the impressions they make on others and are excessively and cleverly sensitive to another's moods and adapt to meet them. The insecurity and low self esteem associated with such responses leads to depression and the consequent induction of further dependence in others who respond as carers. Caring for others is in this context not a valuable and helpful trait, rather it is a protective obsession designed to control the very one cared for and on whom meaning has become dependent. Self martyrdom and seeming indispensability are actively cultivated to obsessive and overworked degrees. To sustain this picture, dishonesty of self expression including active lying may become habitual – it becoming quite impossible for such persons to say how it is for them. The actual state of their distressed feelings is no longer available for expression in any direct way and referencing all activities on others becomes a form of endless self concern.

These symptoms may appear in mild to severe forms of neuroticism. In particular the widespread distribution of the milder versions suggests that most carers may be suspected of being to a degree emotionally dependent and caught in the very addictive process they attempt to cure in others. Therapists, counsellors, ministers, therapeutic colleagues may all be affected unknowingly thereby basing their views of themselves on entirely inauthentic grounds. Whitfield indeed argues that the 'untreated professional' virtually characterises the staff of caring institutions and may be sustaining the malfunctioning of those they treat. Recent dramatic examples may include the problems of responsibility in some cases of False Memory Syndrome where the recall by adult children of sexual abuse by parents has sometimes been shown to be due to an induction of such belief by involvement with the therapist. Much further research on this topic is essential.

We have reached a point where we are suggesting a condition of society whereby individual and social malfunctioning is widespread.

While emotional repression and the disguising of motivation may have had some functional value in the social environment of human origins[15] we must suspect that in the developed societies of modern civilisations it can constitute a maladaptation through informational distortion of a serious kind. We may therefore be facing a 'design fault' in our mode of social being that has been present for millennia and to which we have yet to construct an adequate remedy.[16] Certainly this appears to have been the view of the Buddha 2500 years ago and to this we must now turn.

AUTHENTICITY AND BUDDHIST DISCOURSE

The Buddha was a man with vast experience of the yogic psychologies and philosophies of his time which were both rich in content and in debate. His personal search culminated in experiences which, as in an experiment, confirmed the views he was developing. In his very first sermon he argued that life was characterised by suffering, that suffering was due to craving, wanting or, in other words, addiction, and that it was possible to go beyond addiction by following a careful path. This looks very relevant to our discussion above.

His model of mind was essentially dynamic in spite of the rather static way in which the *abhidharma* expresses it. Sensation, perception and cognition build up the roots of conscious experience and inference about the world. In addition however, and crucially important, ongoing experience produces attempted solutions to problems that become relatively fixed patterns of response. These *samskara* are thus both the root of personal idiosyncrasy and also the source of change. In that they are essentially volitional they are both the repository of past *karma* and again the process wherein *karma* projecting into the future can change.

We can see here a close similarity to the discussion of social dependency above. *Karma* distorts the appreciation of the present through inducing habitual, biased prejudicial or destructive modes of being that may have been valuable once as a response to a situation but which, at a present moment, may be distorting, unrelated to what is and thus illusory. The task therefore is to establish the mind in the present actuality and penetrate the snares of karma so as to go beyond them.

The discourses of the Buddha and subsequent Mahayana literature and commentaries are all essentially discussions of this endeavour. Sometimes leading into abstract phenomenological and metaphysical philosophies the core remains a practice. Buddhist thought is soteriological, designed to save; the take-home message is to penetrate illusion wherever it arises for illusion is considered widespread.

The main task advocated by the Buddha was to live 'rightly' according to the Eightfold Way and the means to doing this was through the cultivation of awareness. The Maha Satipatthana Sutta[17] gives very precise instructions which focus on meditative attentiveness to the body, to the environment and eventually to the way of life itself. It is clearly proposed that attentive awareness is a tool with which to penetrate illusion.[18] It is essential first to calm the mind and then to gain insight into its process so as to distinguish the prejudiced from the authentic. From Satipatthana to Mahamudra, to the Silent Illumination of Ch'an and the Koan practice of the Japanese the essential quest is the same.

In Ch'an it is pointed out that attachment to quiet sitting, however agreeable it may be, is a 'cave of demons', an addiction to tranquillity that must be broken up. The essential task of awareness is not trance or samadhic states but the perception of actuality directly. This means that in meditation one faces in various ways the actuality of existence. Contemplating the koans is one way of doing this.

The koans are paradoxical questions which cannot be answered but which can be resolved. The most basic are the Who questions. 'Who am I?' Of course at one level one knows exactly who one is but, at another, one realises much is hidden from one. There are several contrasting ways of using Koans but the modern method developed by Charles Berner and known as the 'communication exercise' is especially valuable for beginning Westerners and I use it as an introduction to Ch'an (Zen) in Western Zen Retreats at my centre in Wales.[19] It leads through a vigorous examination of personal illusions to an exhaustion of opinion and language in an immediate apprehension of 'just being.' Finding this essential base line of existence throws all other concerns into a realm of mere relativity and the grip they have on one's life relaxes. Recalibration of a practitioner's attitudes and action in life then becomes possible from a phenomenological base that lies outside opinion. Since it cannot come from another it is also a rediscovery of an essential self and the basis for renewed autonomy.

The communication exercise is done in groups that divide into couples, dyads, who sit together. Over a 30–40 minute period a bell is rung every five minutes. In each five minute period one of the partners asks the other his or her question which may be ; 'Tell me who you

are?'; 'Tell me what life is?'; 'Tell me what love is?' ;Tell me what
another is?; "Who is dragging this old corpse along?'; 'What was your
face like before your parents were born?' etc. Most beginners and
many others use the Who am I? formulation. It is basic. The
practitioner works with his or her question throughout the retreat
unless a resolution appears. After each period the partners change
over. The rules are that the one who is questioning never says anything
other than the question, only asks it a few times and maintains an
open, interested demeanour without expressions of encouragement or
scepticism. The one who answers is encouraged to respond in
whatever way most truly expresses his or her state of mind, which
need not be by words alone. They are however asked to sustain
contact with the partner through frequent eye contact. The five
minute alternation imposes emotional discipline as each partner
occupies in turn the complimentary role to the other. The exercise is
repeated over a period of at least three days which, in the case of the
Western Zen Retreat (5 days) also includes exercise, meditative sitting
(zazen), meals, walks and periods in which the group process is
reviewed.

Individuals usually spend many hours describing their various roles
in life and their experiences in these roles. They then begin to express
their feelings under a range of remembered conditions until some
feeling is actually engendered in the present moment. To express that
feeling, sadness, tears, joy, anguish, self doubt directly is to give one
self unreservedly to the other in trust. This is especially difficult when
feelings of guilt or shame are around and a practitioner may spend
many hours fearfully and cunningly editing his responses to the
question. Finally, unless the practitioner is severely blocked, he trusts
enough to share. Such sharing rapidly becomes mutual and personal
secrets of a lifetimes duration may be shared for the very first time
with accompanying emotion.

It is a fact that the rehearsal of the past within the session does not
have to be repeated once full expression has been given to it. It is as if
the latent energy locked up in an issue has been released. The
consequence is a sensation of increasing freedom and openness both
of which probably relate to the rising levels of trust in the group.
Often, however, the flow of expression finally dries up and there is a
silence but no feeling of having resolved the question. This is called
'crossing the desert'. It requires sensitive reappraisal of all that has
been said and maybe just silent musing and waiting. The role of the
retreat director or 'master' is to interview practitioners and to interact

with them in such a way as to facilitate their process. Naturally this requires considerable skill and imagination. The role cannot be undertaken by an untrained or an inappropriately trained person.

When the practitioner is fortunate, has managed to focus the question well and penetrated blockages the result is a gradual or sudden awareness that he or she is everything that has been said and, since the negative energies associated with the themes of life have been expressed, there is a glowing sense that what one is is indeed alright after all. There is a moment of relief and acceptance in which the question drops away. One 'knows' who one is in the same way that one 'knows' water only when she tastes it. Such a person may be very joyful and experience a number of states of consciousness that may be entirely new – a spacious clarity, bliss, love, emptiness; words which in truth have meaning only for those who have been to the same spaces.

Most of these experiences are moments of personal integration around a sense of total oneness with what one is. In Zen this is called the 'one man.'[20] Such work facilitates but cannot in itself produce the experience known as *satori* or *kensho* in which self reference itself disappears so that, 'empty headed', one simply regards the world as it is, unfiltered, all personal bias gone. Such an experience, usually felt to be of inestimable value, may be said to arise through 'grace' since any egoistic quest for it is bound to fail.

The ego cannot lose itself, it sometimes just gets lost. The practitioner is overcome by emptiness in much the way one may suppose that a blackbird is overcome by its song. Such rare moments are known as 'enlightenment experiences'. Because the texts consider these events desirable, practitioners naturally but mistakenly make a great effort to attain them: with the result that many such claims may be invalid. Most such experiences are probably of the 'one man 'type.

I believe this is also true of the results of the other meditation methods in Zen. Master Sheng Yen doubts, for example, whether the so called satori in Japanese Rinzai Zen retreats is really such. In discussing the effects of the 'Enlightenment Intensive' of Charles Berner, which uses the Communication Exercise exclusively, Roshi Kennet felt that most of them would have been' satori orgasms' – that is to say emotionally induced experiences. In both cases it seems likely that most such outcomes are likely to be experiences of the 'one man 'type induced by the stresses of such retreats. Some masters may collude in passing responses to koans as successes.

In fact all notion of success or failure in relation to *kensho* is illusory. Such events may occur spontaneously as the natural mysticism described in the writings of Walt Whitman, Richard Jefferies and Krishnamurti attest. Indeed many people may have had such an experience without being able to perceive its nature or its value. This is perhaps likely to be particularly true of those whose work in the country involves manual labour of skills requiring high present attention- rustic sages as it were.[21] Training is thus significant after all and Master Sheng Yen argues that for an experience to merit the label '*kensho*' it needs to occur with reference to a Zen perspective, otherwise the conceptual frame of the event is insufficient.[22]

The process of Zen training appears to involve a number of steps:

1 Direct acknowledgement of how one is, however negative that may be. One simply says 'Yes' to the negativity and holds it in the frame of meditative focus.
2 When the matter is sufficiently explored, the negative emotional energies tend to resolve themselves and die down as the practitioner penetrates their meaning in an acceptance of personal inadequacy. This of course does not mean approval of oneself.
3 Once this acceptance is total then, in a natural humility, the practitioner simply knows who and what he is. In such acceptance, energy (*chi* or *prana*) flows free and a positive yet curiously apophatic self affirmation arises. In time one can then face another question, 'How is life fulfilled?'

Needless to say the habits of a lifetime are unlikely to be totally removed in one go and repeated training and the development of day to day mindfulness are also required. Those who think an experience of the type described is sufficient to break their habitual illusions are deluding themselves. To realise that Zen means long term cultivation is for practitioners in a hurry an unwelcome surprise. Furthermore, the very texts and ritualistic imagery of traditional Buddhism may need challenging in the way the ancient masters have always told practitioners to do.

It looks nonetheless as if the practise of Buddhist meditation when skilfully taught and directed[23] may have a considerable effect in breaking up the social addictions that are the cause of so much misery. The stages of acknowledgement, acceptance, realisation in humility and self affirmation have much in common with the Twelve Steps recommended as training in recovery from co-dependency.[24] These include: admitting that life has become unmanageable; making a fearless inventory of oneself, acceptance of one's negativities and awareness of their powerfully addictive nature; continual cultivation of such awareness, direct attempts to make amends in life and the placing of the whole endeavour within a spiritual context believing in the possibility of higher power and its influence for good. Here the Christian would refer to God, the Buddhist to the Three Refuges. These parallels suggest an important convergence between contemporary psychotherapeutic insight into the social processes of our time and the ancient wisdom of Buddhism. On this basis much could be built.

AUTHENTICITY IN ZEN PRACTICE

The pervasiveness of emotional dependency is no new thing. It invades the practice of spirituality at all levels. As Christians might say – the devil is cunning indeed. The sensationalism of the modern media and the gossipy desire for the exposure of fault at all levels in society – so characteristic of the mediocre attempting to justify themselves – lead to endless accounts of inauthenticity in church and state. A reading of Chaucer shows such faults to be no new thing but the modern addiction to journalistic social pornography has produced a debilitating and depressive process in which the potential for good in anything is undermined by its inevitable lack of perfection. Yet the press performs a valuable function. We cannot pretend to ourselves for long and the appearance of iniquities among Buddhist lamas and masters who should be the exemplars of their tradition has been a shock to many. We need to examine it critically.

The Master

In the Mahayana tradition the lama or master, the guru, was to be treated with total devotion as an infallible teacher. This was conceivable because such a one had attained enlightenment through his or her practice and received a transmission to teach from his own teacher, a person of the same quality. That which was to be transmitted was nothing less than the enlightenment of Buddha himself coming down through the ages. From this notion came the significance of lineage and the vital importance of ensuring the purity of transmission.

We have here at least the scriptural tradition. Individual teachers were often much more reticent, being aware of their faults and showing a genuine humility. Indeed it was this humility and personal discipline through loyalty to the terms of practice inherent in transmission that preserved the idea as valid in the training of others.

Clearly the validity of this viewpoint could only be maintained if the behaviour of lamas and masters was indeed inspiring and irreproachable. The Rinpoche, precious jewel, really had to be above the common herd if he was to function as the tradition demanded. Doubtless falls from grace were commonly observed but the institutional framework of peer supervision among monastics usually corrected or managed these faults and the regard with which common people treated their teachers suggests this was usually both successful and authentic.

The arrival of such teachers in the West gave rise to problems. The fantasy world of the hippy generation, courageous and searching as it was, needed holy teachers to represent the sublime. There was a need for such a person to combat the horrors of our time and the post-modern shift in the Euro-American scene with its rampant scepticism and subscription to ethical relativity. There was need for spiritual dependency.

Such teachers came from a monastic world, highly disciplined, authoritarian, with supervision from peers and teachers alike and little opportunity to know the world outside the walls. The monasteries were supported by the local population and by land owners or nobility through social subscription, gifts of land, service to monks of many kinds and unquestioning faith.[25] In the West such teachers found a questioning faith, multiple ethical and religious positions, no authority apart from self yet great dependency need. They themselves were usually cut off from both their own teachers and from their peers and the walls were paper thin. Furthermore, the most usual centres in which they worked were not monasteries. For the most part they were centres offering meditation instruction to lay people of varying ability, understanding and degrees of social neuroticism sustained by fluctuating and uncertain sources of finance much subject to shifts in fashion.

James Low and I once interviewed Zhabdrung Rinpoche in his north Indian home. Unlike many of the traditional Tibetans with whom we had been working, this Bhutanese lama, the reincarnation of former religious rulers of Bhutan, had led a troubled life of political exile for many years under risk of assassination. He was fluent in English and knew the West well. He was extremely critical of his fellow lamas who taught in the West. He argued that the tendency to create large organisations with a high profile lama as guru was typically Western and detrimental to true understanding. Such lamas become figures of fame, spiritual celebrities who jet set around the world from one idolising centre to another, spending little time in each and knowing their many followers only in occasional brief encounters.

'The true guru-pupil relationship is between two people who get to know one another intimately. The disciple can then be of value to the guru through reflecting the latter's faults. It is important that the disciple should be free to be critical from his side within his devotion and to share his feelings with his teacher. In this way a teacher keeps in touch with his own defects. Where a teacher retains a footing in his tradition his fellow monks will keep him in order. Where teachers in the West have cut this connection and gone flying off on their own they can substitute fluency in Western culture for an in depth understanding of their own original practice. Although a lama may have received initiation for personal practices unless he maintains them he can lose contact with their meaning. Such a person's spiritual growth has become superficial and lacking in comprehension of some of the difficulties involved in transmission. Initiations he gives may then have little power and may open their recipient to delusion.'[26]

Much the same can be said of Zen masters coming from Japan. It is significant that so far Western Theravada monks have been immune from these criticisms. This is because they have established genuine disciplined monasteries in the West with tough old abbots well able to keep order and respect so that a deviant simply opts to disrobe. From this comparison there is perhaps much to be learnt.

From 1975 a series of scandals has erupted in both Zen and Tibetan institutions in America and to a lesser extent (there are fewer of them) in this country (UK).The details of these are mostly well known now and need not be reviewed except in outline here. The Western teachers had all received transmission from Japanese or Tibetan masters and therefore held the lineages they represented. Their followers, imbued with devotion, allowed these men to become authoritarian rulers, real bosses, of the institutions they ran. They received little feedback or criticism and were treated as beyond reproach. Soon covert sexual lessons with students were revealed, relationships, literally cases of spiritual incest, commonly deeply disturbing and damaging to the young people involved. The sexual predation of some of these teachers was extraordinary. Such activities became associated with lying and the misuse of funds. Once the scandal broke their institutions became divided by factionalism concerning the best course of action to take. Some individuals whose faith had been broken in this way became severely distressed not knowing where to turn. Sometimes elaborate cover ups were engaged upon, the teachers not being reprimanded or corrected by their own teachers or monastic order. Some Oriental teachers themselves also committed similar misdemeanours causing comparable anguish.[27]

A major puzzle revolves around the question how can it be that a person who has received from a master a recognition of his or her 'enlightenment' and transmission to teach within a lineage behave in this way? There seems to be no reason to doubt the original insight of such a person nor the fact that this was recognised by an Eastern teacher in eye to eye contact. The error lies in the supposition that past karma is wiped out by such an event. Zen scriptures are sometimes unclear on this issue but early Buddhism makes a clear distinction. Enlightenment is indeed a breakthrough beyond the self but afterwards the karmic traces reassert themselves and need constant attention. It is said that even the Buddha spent his life following enlightenment working through the traces of his former *karma*. A person who has had deep experience in Buddhism may remain problematic in his or her ethical dimension. Eastern masters have perhaps paid insufficient attention to the vital importance of precepts, personal values and vows in transmitting Zen in America. A brilliant insightful pupil may be ethically unsound in everyday life especially when subject to the stress of becoming a master without local supervision.

Master Sheng Yen distinguishes clearly between the recognition of *kensho* and the transmission to teach. The former confers no authority – it is simply a mutual understanding between master and disciple. The giving of transmission does not depend on this alone but also upon the moral character of the practitioner, his/her continued training, capacity to teach and opportunity to do so in terms of pupils being available and willing and the existence of material circumstances within which teaching may occur.[28]

The answer to these problems clearly lies in a radical overhaul of the structure of Western institutions led by teaching masters. Democratic criticism, the formation of advisory boards, open discussion of personal matters and careful auditing of finance are all obvious remedies. As important, however, as Lachs has pointed out, is a critical appraisal of key themes in Mahayana Buddhism. What exactly does Master or Lama mean? What is a monk? Should the rules for monks and nuns be the same or different? What is transmission? What indeed is enlightenment?

Current Western scholarship, developing biblical criticism in the Buddhist context and in detailed study of history through ancient textual material, is revealing how the meaning of such terms has varied through the long Buddhist history thus raising questions as to the best way to interpret and use them today. Such scholarship is to be welcomed although the danger of developing an arid understanding without a life of devotion has to be avoided. Reducing bibles to 'texts' can take the life out of them.

I cannot finish this section without an appreciation of those many outstanding teachers, Eastern and Western, men and women, who in their authenticity have brought and continue to bring the wisdom of Buddhism to our shores. This very critique of developments that many of them could not have suspected is a tribute to their success.

Renunciation and the monkhood

Although the Buddha left teachings for the laity, he clearly focused primarily on the training of the Sangha, the body of monks or 'left-home-ones.' To become a monk one forsakes all the activities and relationships of lay life- celibacy, no companionship with the opposite sex, no drinks, perfumes, high beds, dancing etc. and etc. into a great list of restrictions. From a lay perspective the precepts of a monk appear to be highly onerous yet their intention is to give the practitioner an especial freedom – freedom from the addictions of lay life.

Yet joining the Sangha could never be the path for everyone because somebody had to provide support for it, this had to come from the donations of laity. Somebody had to procreate, have babies, run businesses, rule the country, provide food. None of this was the business of the Sangha. Yet the relationship was not intended to be one sided. The Sangha in its turn benefited the laity through providing them with opportunities for earning merit through supplying monks and monasteries with the wherewithal of daily life, through giving sons to monasteries as novices, through financing long liturgies. Merit was a means whereby individuals could ensure a higher rebirth – and that usually meant birth into a higher caste. The old Indian system was still very much alive although the Buddha was clearly not one of its supporters and the Sangha was, in principle at least, open to all castes.

Was there a deeper meaning to 'merit'. Did the selfless behaviour and psychological wisdom of the monks provide insight, peace of mind and education to the laity. Plausibly yes, although the scriptures do not emphasise this point. In traditional Ladakh, monks often function as shaman in ceremonies to control weather, benefit crops, effect cures. The wisdom of Rinpoches is sought in the selection of *lha-bas,* the healer oracles who operate in trance, and many matters of local ethics and social valuation are settled in conference with monks. They are ethical arbiters within the society.

Yet, in contemporary Ladakhi villages monks are also judged for their goodness. False monks who sell monastery property, defraud their clients or behave excessively in any way are treated with scorn and disrespected. Maintenance of an authentic role is essential.

In Zen, monks work their own lands and do their own labour. It was this that allowed the Ch'an sects to survive various holocausts in China when other orders dependent on the receipt of gifts went under. Zen scriptures use labour as a motif in teaching. Dogen, who brought Soto Zen to Japan, learnt much from cooks whom he met in China. The way a monk worked illustrated his capacity for mindfulness.

Mindfulness is the means whereby monks sustain their discipline. As in the corrective training of the army 'glasshouse', attention to detail is the focus of the disciplinary regime. Why should anyone find the monkish life attractive? It seems to be fact that many young monks coming from lowly families, as indeed did the Dalai Lama, suffer no harm from being reared after infancy by men alone. They often turn out to be remarkable meditators, scholars, teachers, friends with a surety of self possession that most would admire. It is the motherliness of these mindful monks free from the daily anxieties of village mothers that perhaps plays a key role in achieving this.

The practice of meditative mindfulness within the freedom of sustained discipline takes a monk through the stages we have discussed above. He thus comes to know blissful states of conscious awareness that are rare among the laity. The disciplined freedom from social addiction allows a relative 'enlightenment' that gives them an unique charisma and beneficial social influence in a strife torn world.

Modern Western Buddhists rarely contemplate becoming monks nor as yet are there many suitable institutions to receive them. Only the Theravada goes quite vigorously down this path. Western practitioners of Tibetan Buddhism and Zen are predominantly members of the laity.

What is Lay Zen?[29] For a lay practitioner who has not given up the pursuit of material delights and continues to 'keep up with the Jones', social competitiveness may creep into his Dharma expression. Yet he or she pretends to follow scriptures and practises clearly designed for 'left-home-ones'. It is little wonder that they may find the practices unrewarding or difficult when the rest of life is devoted to work, play arguing with the wife or worrying about the children. Such practitioners may become 'hobbyist' Buddhists[30] who may soon depart to investigate some more promising path enhancing in some subtle way their spiritual egoism.

The dependency of the Western laity on their teachers is understandable since they give themselves so little opportunity to actually experience Dharma practice. For a lay person the only way to approximate to monastic training and hence gain some of the insights available to monastics is through intensive retreat, not once but many times. They then find that change becomes apparent. Not only do they begin to 'taste the chocolate', as Lama Thubten Yeshe used to say, that is benefit from conscious states of joy and peace, but they begin to recalibrate their lives quite naturally around actions beneficial to themselves and, crucially, also to others. Life gets happier whatever falling aside may also from time to time occur. The vows begin to take on meaning as progressive change becomes apparent. The illusion of chasing enlightenment experiences or expecting spiritual rewards and the favours of charismatic masters subsides in a realisation that the grind of cultivation is essential. In such authentic practice monk and layman become indistinguishable in the perspective of Zen.

Understanding Dharma

Many of those who attend meditation classes at Buddhist centres are coming to benefit themselves through improving their self image. To assume an identity as a Buddhist makes one feel better as a member of a positive group in the swim of the current 'turn on'. Unaware of Buddhist teaching they do not see this as merely another form of the addiction to self interest.

Others come for their health or to reduce mental stress. Certainly meditation is relaxing, may save one from a heart attack, gives one a new perspective on life. And none of this lacks merit. These are sound things to do – but they are not Buddhism – and in particular they are not Zen.

Even those who practice intensively and come on difficult retreats requiring will power and disciplined determination may not yet have any insight into the teachings. It is thus vital that anyone

239

training in Zen quickly attempts to gain some insight into the message of the Buddhas. Basic Buddhism is fortunately expressed in a number of relatively simple and memorable formulae- the Four Noble Truths, the Eightfold Way, the Four Vows, the Ten Precepts, the Principle of Interdependent Causation. These need digestion and contemplation. From here topics such as Impermanence, Emptiness, and the meaning of meditative practice may be entered from a firm base.

The Dharma never constitutes dogma in the way that the Bible or the Koran is often used. Buddhist teachings are suggestions, signposts for those who wish to test them out. The Buddha's last injunction was not to follow his teachings mindlessly but to 'work out your own salvation with diligence'. The practice gradually becomes more meaningful and one can test it out in day to day living. Although reading books and scholarship can be helpful, we are in the West today beyond the book addiction phase of development. Opportunities for real practice and receiving sound teaching are now available in most cities of the realm and there are a range of teachers to evaluate. Hobbyism does not express authentic interest for it is merely playing games with spiritual ambitions.

Personal practice

At a weekly meeting someone comes up to me and says something like – 'I'm sorry John I have not been able to do my evening half hour all week !' Others may only attend retreats when a famous or charismatic Eastern master is running it. Needless to say such persons find retreat more difficult than they need. Someone else may object – 'People have troublesome enough lives as it is – why make retreats so difficult for them. We could get up at 6 am rather than 4. You could attract more participants that way!'

All such attitudes miss the point of Zen. The ego craves self esteem. We want to do things that make us feel well regarded. When one friend found that he was not going to become a Zen rabbi quickly on retreat he gave it all up. The toughness of Zen is deliberate for it provides in microcosm those confrontations to self that are always with us – but gives us them in a context where they demand recognition and reflective management through insight. Little things like worrying about the place one will get at the meal table: Did I have enough to eat? Am I going to have time for a shower? Do I have time for a banana before Shi fu closes the meal?

Can I have a pee within the next half hour? Can I stand this aching knee for another ten minutes? Oh Oh When will the bell go? Poor me, I am such a noble sitter. Such questions are not nonsensical, but the way they invade the mind shames one into a recognition of their socially addictive nature. The training is to 'let through, let be, let go'. Negativity arises, it is comprehended, it is released. Meditation continues. Not at all easy. The mill wheel of the addicted mind spins on taking its time to come to rest. One begins to learn patience- with oneself.

Such training in self recognition not only reveals gradually the benefits of intensive practice but can also be transferred into everyday circumstances – shopping, washing up, going to work, whatever it may be. And it is for this reason that on retreat one is told to be 'present' not only on one's cushion but when cutting carrots or filling oil lamps. I was once reminded that in washing up the enormous pots and pans in Throssel Hole Priory kitchen that I should do it as if I was arranging an altar. The mind should never be somewhere else. When no-one is cutting carrots yet carrot cutting is happening in clarity and with precision one is making progress. The rest is idle self concerned chatter. If one does these things insights sometimes come quite suddenly, surprising one with joy.

In the result

Success is not success. Failure is not failure. Someone who has experiences on retreat that are deeply rewarding is often at great risk. Self congratulation sets in, followed perhaps by comparison with those others struggling away not knowing who they are and then by subtle pride that immediately denies itself. Master Sheng Yen says that pride and low self esteem are the opposite ends of the same road – the road of ego involvement. To get off that road altogether is often difficult for the successful practitioner. Perhaps fortunately, good experiences are commonly followed by bad ones. A wonderful insight-yielding retreat may be followed by a gloomy depressive one. The practitioner simply has to learn, often painfully, that that's the way things are – not only in Buddhism but in everyday life. As is said Zen is no different from everyday life. It is the attitude that counts.

There was once an individual who had a profound experience which he decided was enlightenment. He therefore proclaimed himself a Zen master and began to run workshops. These were powerful events for he indeed had talents as a group facilitator. I was phoned by one of his adherents asking did I want to meet a *real* Zen Master. I found this man to have experienced no training under a qualified Zen master, to have never attended retreat, to have no respect for lineage or tradition and to be touchy when faced with searching questions. Such a person is like someone who awards himself a cap after playing a practice game.

Another individual who had trained well with the Tibetans and who had undoubted attainments both in meditative skill and teaching ability suddenly began to promote himself through various assumed titles right up to Rinpoche. Since he actually had some wisdom – why these games? Here an addiction to personal image would seem to be rampantly in play. The inauthenticity is damaging to the lineage in which he works.

A fine Tibetan teacher, trained in Lhasa, has reputedly taken to having himself described as a Buddha. Need I say more. When such affectations can overcome even the great and good it behoves us lesser mortals to take care. Self-deluding teachers, self-deluding helpers, self-deluding pupils are all caught up in a linked set of difficulties.

Authentic self acceptance has nothing to do with either pride or self reproach. It is the straightforward recognition of how things are. The practitioner simply moves along as best he or she can with whatever presents itself. Occupying the present with such presence is authentic being.

HONESTY AND 'ONE GREAT MISTAKE AFTER ANOTHER'

Buddhist practice begins and ends with honesty, but this honesty is not easy to achieve. There is ordinary honesty and insightful honesty. The latter arises when through some form of training the illusions that bedevil one's life have at least to a degree been recognised and some progress in relieving them achieved. We have argued that much of human behaviour is inauthentic in the sense that insightful honesty is not available. In Buddhism this is the state of 'not seeing' or ignorance. In both Buddhism and within the modern concern at the state of society, individuals are seen to be often addicted to patterns of thought, feeling and behaviour that have arisen in some familial or social circumstance in the past, patterns the Buddhists refer to as *karma*. The pain involved in coming to self recognition often seems extraordinary and working with it may remain problematic.

The attempt to reach the 'enlightenment' of a straightforward relationship with the world involves practice on a hard path full of illusory successes and failures. Sometimes, whatever a practitioner does, it seems to fail or to have no effect. Sometimes success leads to another experience of failure. The mind is extremely tricky – a maddened monkey as some have said. Whether one is attempting to work with oneself or with others it is never possible to be sure that the path taken is the right one. One time, walking in those wonderful hills above Green Gulch Farm north of San Francisco, I was discussing how to teach Zen with the Abbot of the monastery there, Tenshiñ Reb Anderson. He remarked that he had found that if you say one thing it is bound to be wrong and if you say its opposite you will find that is wrong too. Whatever you say is likely to be wrong. To be silent may be no help either. One simply goes ahead in trust as best one may. Here is the fundamental honesty of the Zen position. You try it and see – in a trust that knows you may be wrong. Only the authentic self can do that in the faith that has lasted two thousand five hundred years. As some master said in defining Zen – 'One great mistake after another'.

NOTES

1 Scheaf, A. W. 1985. *Co-dependence: -Misunderstood -Mistreated. Understanding and healing the addictive process.* Harper. San Francisco.
2 See Low J, 1990. Buddhist developmental psychology. In: Crook, J. H. and D. Fontana (eds) *Space in Mind: East-West psychology and Contemporary Buddhism.* Element Books. Warminster. (Distributed by Penguin. London)
3 See discussions in Crook, J. H. and J, Low. 1997. *The Yogins of Ladakh.* Motilal Banarsidass. Delhi.
4 See discussion in Buswell, R. E. 1983. *The Korean Approach to Zen: The collected works of Chinul.* University of Hawai Press. Honolulu.
5 Lachs, S. 1994. *A slice of Zen in America.* New Ch'an Forum Issue 10. 1994.
6 Winnicot, D. W. 1988. *Human Nature.* Free Association Books. London. Winnicot. D. W. 1990. *The Maturational Processes and the Facilitating Environment.* Karnac books. London. Guntrip, H. 1983. *Schizoid phenomena , object relations and the self.* Hogarth Press. London. Miller, Alice. 1990. *The Untouched key. Tracing childhood trauma in creativity and destructiveness.* Virago. London. For a wider ranging anthropologically oriented discussion on the nature of the self see Carrithers, M. Collins, S. and S. Lukes. *The Category of the Person.* Cambridge. U. P. Cambridge.
7 Bugenthal, J.F.T.1965. *The search for Authenticity: An existential-analytic approach to Psychotherapy.* Holt, Rinehart and Winston. New York. p. 32.
8 Bugenthal, see note 7 above.
9 Batchelor, S. 1983. *Alone with Others: An existential approach to Buddhism.* Grove. New York.
10 Harré, R and G. Gillett. 1994. *The Discursive Mind.* Sage. London.

11 Schaef. A. W. *loc cit.*
12 Wegscheider Cruse, S. 1984. Co-dependency-the therapeutic void. In: *Co-dependency – an emerging issue.* Health Communications. Pompano Beach. Florida.
13 See discussions by R. Subby and others in *Co-dependency – an emerging issue.* Health Communications. Pompano Beach. Florida.
14 Whitfield, C.1984. Co-dependency – an emerging issue among professionals. In: *Co-dependency-an emerging issue.* Health Communications. Pompano beach. Florida.
15 See for discussion: Trivers, R. 1971. The Evolution of Reciprocal Altruism. *Q. Rev. Biol.* **46**, 35–57. Trivers ,R. 1985. *Social evolution.* Benjamin/Cummings. Menlo Park Ca. Byrne, R. W and A. Whiten. 1988. *Machiavellian Intelligence. Social expertise and the evolution of intellect in Monkeys, Apes and Humans.* Clarendon. Oxford.
16 Crook, J. H. 1995. Psychological Processes in Cultural and Genetic Coevolution. In: Jones, E and V. Reynolds. (Eds) *Survival and Religion: Biological Evolution and Cultural Change.* Wiley. London. For a wide ranging discussion see Berman, M. 1989 *Coming to our senses; body and spirit in the hidden history of the West.* Unwin. London.
17 See Ling, T. 1981. *The Buddha's Philosophy of Man Early Indian Buddhist Dialogues.* Dent.London pp. 71–85. (translation)
18 For a contemporary exploration of this viewpoint see Blackmore, S. 1995. *Paying attention.* New Ch'an Forum. Issue 12.
19 Berner created this approach through comparing the practice of zen interview with a master with co-counselling. He invented a group workshop called the 'Enlightenment Intensive' which uses this method exclusively. I was taught this method and to run intensives by Jeff Love in the 1970s. Berner has made some revisions to it since and such events are still offered from time to time. Berner has provided a manual for those directing such events.
20 The 'True man of the Way.' See Schloegl. I. 1975. *The Zen Teaching of Rinzai.* Shambala. Berkeley.
21 Crowden, J. 1996. *Mind in Agriculture.* New Ch'an Forum .Issue 12. The term 'rustic sages' I owe to John Clark's 1983 *A Map of Mental States.* Routledge and Kegan Paul.
22 Master Sheng Yen is the director of the Institute of Chung Hwa Buddhist Culture in New York and Taipei. He leads retreats in New York and has done so threee times at my centre in Wales. I have participated in ten of his training retreats and continue to work with him. He has published many books on Ch'an.
23 This caveat requires close examination as the next section of this article will make clear.
24 Schaef, A. W. *loc cit* p. 30.
25 For examples and review see the chapters on monastic life in Crook, J. H. and H. Osmaston (Eds). 1994. *Himalayan Buddhist Villages.* Bristol University and Motilal Banarsidass. Delhi.
26 Crook, J.H. and J. Low. 1997. *The Yogins of Ladakh.* Motilal Banarsidass. Delhi. p. 248.
27 See Lachs, S. 1994. *loc cit.*

28 See Sheng Yen, Master.1994. *Transmitting the Lamp*. New Ch'an Forum. Issue 9.

29 Over the last year the Bristol Ch'an Group has been asking this question and members are attempting tentative answers. Some American masters and their followers have also addresed this issue. See New Ch'an Forum, Issues 10, 11, 12. Also: Abe, M. 1985. *Zen and Western thought*. MacMillian. London Kraft, K. 1988. *Zen: tradition and transition – an overview of Zen in the modern world*. Rider London. Tworkov, H. 1989. *Zen in America; profiles of five teachers*. North Point Press. San Francisco.

30 A term used by Simon Child in an article in press. *New Ch'an Forum*, Issue 13.

Note: *New Ch'an Forum* is the journal of the newly created Western Chan Fellowhsip. Copies available: Peter Howard, 22, Butts Rd, Chisieldon, Swindon SN4 0NW (01793 740659).

ACKNOWLEDGEMENTS

I am grateful to all those who have helped me realise the extent of my own emotional dependencies and led me to sustain continuing work on such vexation. Carol Evans introduced me to the current literature on co-dependence and additionally Ken Jones, Peter Reason and John Pickering have commented helpfully on the text. My understanding of Zen , such as it is , owes much to Master Sheng Yen whose exemplary personal stance and masterly teachings are an inspiration in these troubled times. An especial debt is owed to all those hard working practitioners who attend the demanding retreats at the Maenllwyd and whose resiliance and authenticity command my respect and appreciation. To work with you all is an inspiration in an often difficult task.

Afterword

Scientific inquiry into the mind is gathering pace. Our mental life and the workings of the brain are the object of a powerful research programme. These essays on the resemblances and contrasts between Buddhism and Western psychology have been written to contribute to this programme. However, they are written bearing in mind that the postmodern turn has brought scientific inquiry under sharp critical scrutiny.

Science may have arisen as a seach for wisdom but its significance now is that it produces techniques for intervening in nature. There is growing concern that a more inclusive and realistic worldview is needed to avoid their misuse. Implicit in science is a belief that mechanistic reduction is possible and that technological domination of nature is of value. When the nature in question is human nature such implicit beliefs and values need to be fully recognised. If they are not, scientific investigation of the mind may prove as destructive of human integrity as technology is of environmental integrity. Unless we enrich our view of the mind and its place in nature, psychology may simply yield effective but insensitive techniques.

However, the postmodern turn towards pluralism helps to contextualise scientific discoveries within a richer framework of other traditions. Even though the brain is a physical system, no complete or balanced view of human mental life will come merely from knowledge of its workings. Instead, such knowledge will need to be placed alongside the wisdom gained from other traditions of inquiry.

These essays have proposed Buddhism as one such tradition, where the authority of experience is paramount. Despite the vast body of scholarly and intellectual work they represent, all Buddhist traditions emphasise that mere intellectual engagement with the teachings is not enough. These must be balanced by experiential practices. Of course,

Afterword

Western psychology also values experience, but only once it has been harnessed to the methods of science. However, these methods are powerful and have revealed structure and function at levels that may not be available for phenomenological inquiry.

Thus the two systems will complement each other, though in taking psychology forward in this way, there is a danger that eclecticism could lapse into mere relativism. However, so long as a critical attitude is taken towards both traditions and towards their interaction, objective investigation of the mind can be combined with techniques for investigating experience itself.

But will this enlarged agenda be at all coherent or productive? After all, it might be objected that Buddhism, like any religion, will deal in beliefs and values while science deals in hypotheses and facts. But this again is to muddy the situation with Western divisions and oppositions. Buddhism is not a religion in the Western sense and its foundations lie in practice rather than belief. Moreover, belief is more intimately involved in science than it may at first appear. To frame a hypothesis and to choose a method for testing it, is to express a belief about what a phenomenon might be and how it will disclose itself. The beliefs implicit in science in turn reflect values which change as culture changes.

For example, at the beginning of the nineteenth century, Goethe proposed that science, especially biology, should aim for an intuitive perception of nature and of organisms.[1] Now, at the close of the twentieth century, the goal of biology is primarily to manipulate organisms for human ends. This illustrates the tendency of Western science to become a search for means. This search has been highly sucessful, but doubts are now felt on all sides about the use made of these means. Instead of Goethe's search for a sensitive understanding we have mere deep technology. This misuse is reducing the natural diversity from which human life has emerged. Detached from a broader world view and a more inclusive set of purposes, science is in danger of becoming merely instrumental. It has drifted away from values that naturally promote moral and ethical restraint and has come to express a belief in mechanism and the value of unlimited control.

Therefore, scientific inquiry into the mind needs to be treated with caution. If psychology is to be for well-being rather than merely for control, then change is needed. And there is change, since it is a great virtue of science that it is intrinsically open to fundamental revision. There are moves towards organicism in science in general. In psychology, there are also moves towards a more even balance between quantitative and qualitative methods. This will help to provide a richer framework of value within which psychological research can be carried out. This in turn opens the way to a more humane science and to closer contact with other traditions for investigating the mind.

Buddhism is one such tradition. To engage more deeply with Buddhism is to blend experience and experiment. But there are obvious difficulties here, since what epistemological function might a direct inquiry into experience have and how might it be compared with experimental data? In psychology, since it models itself on natural science, the experience of the psychologist is merely an adjunct to accumulating data. After all, experience appears to be incorrigibly subjective while progress in science is based in a public discourse of theoretical conjecture and empirical refutation. Moreover, it is the theory that changes, not the theorist. Buddhism, however, encourages individuals to change by becoming more aware of their own mental processes. Thus the criteria for progress here are experiential, based in an essentially private discourse of insight and reflection.

However, such contrasts do not mean that Buddhism and scientific psychology are incompatible. The struggles that psychologists have had to make in order to be accepted as a scientists can make them defensively rigid in their commitment to its methods. But nothing of the clarity and power of science will be lost if psychology engages with other traditions. Buddhism does not oppose or undermine scientific psychology, but rather complements it. Pluralism in theory and methods encourages us to explore the interaction between traditions previously regarded as incommensurable.

What is taking shape is a new discipline in which the direct exploration of experience complements the scientific investigation of its vehicle. This is an opportunity to rebalance the investigation of mental life. It opposes the identification of psychology as the latest manifestation of destructive technocracy. If psychology addresses experience and selfhood more directly it will become more reflexive and will also have to address feelings and meaning. This will help repair the separation of fact and value that Weber detected at the heart of modernist disenchantment. As David Bohm has proposed: *postmodern science should not separate matter and consciousness, and should not, therefore, separate facts, meaning and value.*[2]

Personal experience is a powerful means by which to investigate the mind, despite being vunerable to cultural distortion. However, we can proceed despite this vunerability. Indeed, postmodernism helps us to recognise more fully how our worldviews and our experiences are culturally constructed. But rather than a collapse into relativistic paralysis, this recognition is the prelude to action. For psychology this action means the broadening and diversification of our theories and methods. The essays in this book have been assembled in just this spirit. In bringing Buddhism and scientific psychology closer together the authors hope to enrich our view of the mind and to promote more sensitive techniques for investigating it.

NOTES

1 Goethe, W. (1917) 'Die Absicht eingeleitet.' Translated as 'The purpose is set forth' in D. Miller's *Goethe: Scientific Studies*, New York, Surkamp, 1988. Pages 63–64. See also *Goethe On Science*, Naydler, J., Floris Books, Edinburgh, 1996 and *The Wholeness of Nature: Goethe's Way of Science*, Bortoft, H., Floris Books, Edinburgh, 1996.
2 Bohm, B. (1988) Postmodern Science and a Postmodern World. In *The Reenchantment of Science: Postmodern Proposals*, edited by Griffin, D. R., State University of New York Press, Albany. Reprinted in *The Postmodern Reader*, edited by Jencks, C., Academy Editions, London, 1992, where this quotation appears on page 385.

Index

Abhidhamma 52, 57, 171, 228
Anatta 4, 56, 173–179
Anicca 56, 169
Arahant 57, 61, 134
Armstrong, D. 35, 40

Baudrillard, J. 164
Becker, E. viii
Behaviour modification 64
Behaviourism xi, 225
Bergson, H. 72, 75, 76
Bhavana 87
Body and mind 17
Bohm, D. 149, 196, 249
Bohr, N. 41
Bruner, J. 162

Capra, F 33
Citta 74
Cognitive Science xi, 8, 29, 155, 185, 193
Cognitive therapy 43, 65
Computational metaphor xi, 29, 155, 170
Comte, A. 35, 209

Derrida, J. 164
Dilthey, W. 88
Discursive psychology 194
Disenchantment viii
Dukkha 55, 104, 160

Empiricism 205

Feyerabend, P 212
Folk psychology xii, 7, 10, 15
Freud, S. 10, 58, 84, 125–129, 173, 187

Gnosticism 195
Goethe, J. W. 248

Havel, V. 171
Heidegger, M. 73, 76, 84, 87
Helmholtz, H. 35
Hillman, J. 196
Hobbes, T. vii
Husserl, E. xii, xiv, 73, 91, 153

Information processing 8
Introspective methods 3, 5

James, W. 13, 22
Jantsch, E. 74
Jaspers, K. 76
Jencks, C. x
Jewish mysticism 195
Jung, C-G. 78, 79, 137

Karma, Kamma 32, 192, 228, 242
Keluké, F. 41
Koans 104
Krishnamurti, J. 31, 232

Lacan, J. 84, 163
Lankavatara sutra 37
Leibnitz, G. W. 4
Lewis, C. S. 3

Index

Mach, E. 35, 209
Maslow, A. 62, 108, 129
Meditation 7, 11, 15, 110
Mendeleev, D. 41
Merleau-Ponty, M. 73
Mindfulness 11, 139–42
Misplaced concreteness xiii, 160

Nagarjuna 190, 196, 210
Nagel, T. 143
Neoplatonism 158, 195
Nirvana, Nibbána 38, 56

Object relations 223

Pali canon 51
Papanca 53, 60
Paticca Samupadda 4
Patriachy 10
Phenomenology xi
Plato 85
Popper, K. 211, 212
Postmodernism x, 154, 161, 166, 206, 247
Prajnaparamita 31
Psychoanalysis 10, 99, 100, 107, 111–115, 124, 143

Rational emotive therapy 43, 65
Rationalism 205
Reductionism xii, 35, 225
Rogers, C. 62, 103, 106
Rorty, R. x, 72

Samadhi 67
Samatha meditation 63, 214
Samsara 7, 10, 38
Sati 67, 130, 136, 158
Satori 29, 38, 41, 231
Schopenhauer, A. 138
Schrödinger, E. 208
Scientific method viii
Secularisation 10
Self, selfhood 13
Skandhas 36
Soto Zen 32
Spinoza, B. 72
Sunyatta 33, 87
Suzuki, D. T. 36, 57

Tanha 58
Taoism 19
Time perception 134–135

Varela, F. 5, 189
Vipassana meditation 63, 214

Weber, M. viii, 249
Whitehead, A. N. xiii, xiv, 72, 89, 149, 152–155
Witness consciousness 16
Wittgenstein, L. 31
Wundt, W. 11

Zukav, G. 33